BCL - 3rd ed.

The Behavior
of Industrial Prices

NATIONAL BUREAU
OF ECONOMIC RESEARCH

NUMBER
90
GENERAL SERIES

The Behavior
of Industrial
Prices

GEORGE J. STIGLER
University of Chicago

&

JAMES K. KINDAHL
University of Massachusetts

NATIONAL BUREAU OF ECONOMIC RESEARCH
New York 1970

Distributed by
Columbia University Press
New York and London

National Bureau of Economic Research

Relation of the Directors to the Work and Publications
of the National Bureau of Economic Research

This report is one of a series
emerging from an investigation
of prices, productivity,
and economic growth
made possible by a grant from
the Alfred P. Sloan Foundation.
The Charles R. Walgreen Foundation
also supported this report.

Contents

Tables

Figures

Acknowledgments

We wish only to acknowledge our vast debts.

Our first large debt is to the large number of companies, hospitals, and public departments which have cooperated in supplying the data on which this study is based. Although we have promised not to enumerate these organizations and individuals, we must express our gratitude for the generosity with which we were treated.

Our second large debt is to Claire Friedland, whose industry and intelligence have preserved us from innumerable errors and interminable delay.

We benefited from the careful reading of the manuscript by Robert Lipsey, Melvin Reder, Yoel Haitovsky, Eli Goldston, Charles Berry, Saul Nelson, and Arnold Chase.

Substantial assistance was given by Ruth Westheimer, William Poppei, Charles Clough, and Hemchandra P. Kalle. Maxine Offill persevered through the preparation of successive drafts.

Gnomi Schrift Gouldin edited the manuscript and H. Irving Forman drew the charts.

George J. Stigler
James K. Kindahl

The Behavior
of Industrial Prices

1

Introduction
and Summary

THE SETTING

"When you cannot measure", Lord Kelvin tells us, "your knowledge is meager and unsatisfactory", to which Jacob Viner proposed the addition that even with measurement our knowledge would usually remain meager and unsatisfactory. The central task of this study is to determine what measurement has done for our knowledge of the behavior of industrial prices.

Our measurement problem is posed by the wholesale price index of the Bureau of Labor Statistics. This index of "wholesale" prices began publication in 1902 (extending retroactively back through 1890),[1] and has been maintained ever since on a continuous monthly basis, with frequent expansions of coverage. The primary purpose of the index was to measure changes in "the purchasing power of money", a function which gradually has been yielded up to the Consumer Price Index and the Implicit Price Deflator of the Gross National Product (although the latter index is of course based heavily upon the wholesale prices).

Other questions were later addressed to the wholesale price data, and of these one of the most interesting was: how do industrial prices respond to major fluctuations in business and price levels? The inquirer was Dr. Gardiner Means, and his famous answer was that large numbers of industrial prices were wholly unresponsive to cyclical fluctuations

[1] "The Course of Wholesale Prices, 1890 to 1901", Bulletin of the Department of Labor, No. 39, March 1902.

of markets. These prices were "administered" by large industrial enterprises and bore little resemblance to the volatile prices which are tossed about by supply and demand in traditional competitive markets such as the wheat pit. The contemporary interest in Means' findings, published in 1934, was much reinforced by his association of sticky price behavior with the economic malaise of the Great Depression.

The present study is primarily an independent examination of the behavior of industrial price indexes—the first moderately comprehensive "test" of the official wholesale price statistics since they were initiated two-thirds of a century ago. The word "test" is at least partially misleading because when the indexes of the Bureau of Labor Statistics and of our study (labelled NBER or NB) differ, it remains to be determined which is more correct. "Test" is also misleading when it implies that we employ the same procedures and sources of data as the BLS.

THE NATURE OF PRICES

The physical variety of products produced by most industries is substantial and for some industries it is essentially unlimited. Consider hot rolled carbon steel sheets, which are arbitrarily defined to be .23 inches or less in thickness if 12 to 48 inches wide, and .18 inches or less in thickness if over 48 inches wide. (Other dimensions are called bar, strip, or plate.) The buyer may choose among

1. Seven gauges of thickness
2. Ten classes of width
3. Four classes of length, if cut
4. Two classes of flatness
5. Two classes of squaring of ends
6. Six lot sizes
7. Three classes of oil treatment
8. Ten classes of carbon maximum
9. Seven classes of manganese maximum
10. Five classes of sulfur maximum
11. Three classes of silicon maximum
12. Seven classes of packaging

And a dozen other dimensions of product variety! Many of the 135 million varieties implied by the twelve attributes have never been produced, one may reasonably conjecture, but the varieties produced in one year must be immense. Each class has its own price. This is one product category in steel.

Tier after tier of further differences may be piled upon the physical varieties. There are terms of credit, transportation charges, guarantees of performance, facilities for replacement, techniques of arbitration of conflicts, promptness of delivery in normal times and in crisis. To be told that the base price of hot rolled carbon steel sheets was $5.30 per 100 pounds on May 15, 1963, is rather an oversimplification of the price structure.

Faced by this indescribably numerous body of prices and terms, the Bureau of Labor Statistics chose to price a few well-defined, "typical" products and transactions. Necessarily these prices must usually be collected from sellers: every major steel producer will offer a typical product, but not one buyer of steel sheet in a hundred will continuously buy that typical product. One may certainly quarrel with the procedure of selecting typical products because it lacks a defensible basis in sampling theory, but that is not a quarrel we pursue (less out of magnanimity than due to our equal vulnerability to the charge!).

We proceed differently: we ask the cooperative buyer to tell us the price he has been paying for a particular kind of sheet he has bought over some period. Seldom will two buyers purchase identical physical products, to say nothing of the other terms of the transaction. We combine movements of these diverse prices into one index, whereas the BLS lets the well-defined product represent the class of product.

Two other details. First, the BLS will use an average of about three reporters per commodity, but with many based upon one or two reporters. We have a maximum of nearly 1,300 price reporters (many less in earlier years) for the seventy commodities, or an average of about seventeen reporters per price series at the time of best coverage. This heavier coverage reflects our distrust of the belief that there is only one price in a market at a given time (more on this topic later).

Second, we chose commodities (really classes of commodities as we have just said) which have figured prominently in the discussion of "administered prices". They include steel, nonferrous metals, basic chemicals, paper, petroleum products, and ethical drugs. By a universal consensus that rests upon intuition much more than upon evidence, everyone believes that it is easier to price over time a pound of steel than a typewriter or other more elaborate product—if for no other reason than that the more elaborate product changes more frequently and substantially. Our study is thus heavily biased toward widely used staple industrial materials, where quoted seller prices are widely believed to be most accurate. The commodities are listed in Table 3-2, pp. 24–25.

As a final element of this orientation, let us look at the transactions whose prices we seek. The buyer of copper ingots is usually a continuous buyer—he needs copper every month or quarter, and for many years. We have shifted our example from steel to copper because the price of copper changes often (although the BLS reports unbelievably few price changes—eleven in the seventy-two months of 1961–66). A buyer *could* go out each day and shop for the cheapest seller of copper, but he would be a profligate buyer—profligate in his expenditures on search, negotiation, testing of products, and all the other costs of creating and maintaining a trading relationship. So he commonly buys on contract, often at a fixed price which is his estimate of the average price over the contract period. (The contracts often allow for a renegotiation if the market "spot" price moves outside the range of expected fluctuation.) This is more economical than buying *de novo* each time, exactly as it is cheaper to rent an apartment for a year rather than by the week. We are not the first economists to be surprised at the economic sophistication of the market: we must record our regret that we did not make a systematic study of the use and duration of contracts.

The BLS collects "spot" prices (whether those actually paid or not); we collect the contract prices. A large part of the short-run (within the year) differences between the two sets of price indexes come from the difference in type of prices sought.

We, as others, wish to turn necessities into virtues: the contract prices seem to us more appropriate to the measurement of the effects of prices upon both costs of buyers and receipts of sellers.

THE MAIN FINDINGS

Trend

Our price history covers ten years, and we begin with the obvious question: do the BLS and NB indexes differ in the broad sweep of their movement over the decade? This was originally a mechanical question—one normally seeks to separate the trend of time series— to which we received an unexpected answer. The trend of prices was essentially the same in the two groups of indexes during the first five years (through 1961), and this was exactly what we expected. But the BLS rose about .7 per cent a year relative to the NB index in the second period, and the literature of price indexes had not prepared us for this. The difference was too strong and general to admit the possibility that it was merely a sampling fluctuation.

The only plausible explanation we have produced for the tendency of quoted selling prices to lag in the downward movements that dominated the period is that there is an asymmetrical inertia in industrial price movements. Price quotations are not revised immediately when market conditions, and transaction prices, change: both the costs of changing prices and the desire to confirm the persistence of the price change dictate some delay. This delay operates more strongly against reductions in price quotations than against increases: inflation has made for a general upward drift of prices (so, on average, price increases are more likely to persist than price decreases). In addition, the policy of price "guidelines" and the possibility of more formal price controls in an age of international violence make it prudent for a businessman to be slow in authenticating price reductions and prompt in authenticating price increases. The data bear this view out: there is no systematic trend difference between BLS and NB price indexes when NB prices are stable or rising, but a most pronounced difference when NB prices are falling.

Cyclical Behavior

The main thrust of the doctrine of administered prices is that contractions in business lead to no systematic reduction of industrial prices, and, much more equivocally, expansions in business may only tardily lead to price increases. Whether because of a simple desire for stability, or more subtly because perhaps profits are better protected by stable prices, it has been argued that prices have at best only one-way flexibility, and that upward. The finding of Gardiner Means in his original study that numerous prices changed not at all, once, twice or a few times in a decade including the Great Depression was *the* sensational part of his study.

A great majority of economists have accepted this finding even though no explanation for this behavior of oligopolists commands general assent. Prices of concentrated industries—and most of our products are produced by industries that are so viewed—do not respond to reductions in demand, or so it is believed. We raise grave doubts of the validity of this belief.

Our period contains two short contractions, July 1957 to April 1958 and May 1960 to February 1961, according to the National Bureau chronology. It also contains one ordinary expansion, April 1958 to May 1960, and one of extraordinary length, February 1961 to the end of our period. This latter expansion is so long that it partakes of a trend, and so we distinguish the short, sharp expansion at the end of the period (say, November 1964 to November 1966—months dictated by our use of three-month averages) as a second expansion. Our decade clearly does not test the flexibility of prices in major depressions or major inflations, but we could not repair (or rather, damage) this characteristic of recent economic history.

Even the BLS price indexes are not especially cordial to this view of cyclical rigidity, and our price indexes are emphatic in their contradiction of it. We may tabulate the directions of price change including and excluding steel products (which are numerous in our sample and atypical in their price behavior) in the two contractions:

Price Changes	All Prices		Excluding Steel Products	
	BLS	NB	BLS	NB
Decreases	23	40	23	40
No change (−.05 to +.05% per month)	19	10	16	7
Increases	26	18	18	10

Similarly in the two expansions, we tabulate the results including and excluding steel products:

Price Changes	All Prices		Excluding Steel Products	
	BLS	NB	BLS	NB
Increases	36	37	36	36
No change (−.05 to +.05% per month)	20	14	18	13
Decreases	14	19	5	10

It is difficult to generalize these results because our collection of commodities is in no sense random; indeed it is purposely concentrated in the areas where "administered" prices are most often said to exist. Even with this bias, if such it be, toward price rigidity, we find a predominant tendency of prices to move in response to the movement of general business. As a summary figure, in the four cycles we find prices moving in the same direction as business 56 per cent of the time; remaining constant 17 per cent of the time; and moving perversely 27 per cent of the time.[2] Since there is no reason on earth or in space why all prices should move in the same direction, especially during relatively mild expansions and contractions, we find no evidence here to suggest that price rigidity or "administration" is a significant phenomenon.

Short-Run Fluctuations

The short-run movements of the BLS and NB indexes differ systematically in one respect: the NB index changes much more smoothly. The BLS indexes usually alternate between periods of little or no change and periods of large and fitful movement. We consider this difference to be favorable to our index. We share with Alfred Marshall the view that *natura non facit saltum*.

The correlation of changes in the two indexes is not very high (for example, $r = .32$ for simultaneous monthly movements), and neither series systematically leads the other. Yet the BLS prices should lead; spot prices should lead an average of contract prices of varying months of termination.

---

[2] If we first remove the trend, the corresponding percentages are 54 per cent of prices change with business, 34 per cent are constant, and 12 per cent move perversely.

Other Studies

Lest the readers stop with this introductory chapter, we shall only mention three other topics:

1. We compare private and governmental prices for a small sample of products (Chapter 4).
2. We compare weighted and unweighted price indexes (Chapter 4).
3. The dispersion of movements of prices paid by individual buyers is analyzed in the light of the economics of information (Chapter 7).

2

The Emergence
of "the" Problem of
Industrial Prices

Prices "at wholesale" began to be published on a continuous basis by the Department of Labor in 1902.[1] The index began with approximately 250 commodities, largely concentrated in food and clothing. The prices were collected from trade journals, produce exchanges, and leading manufacturers. Thus began the statistical history of American industrial prices. This history has continued unbroken for almost 800 months and has expanded to where it now includes more than 2,000 commodities.

Certain of the wholesale prices published by the Bureau of Labor Statistics were observed to display a remarkable stability, if not rigidity. The price of steel rails was quoted at $28 per gross ton beginning in 1902, and continued at this level without change until the spring of 1916. Contemporary students attributed the price stability to the United States Steel Corporation, without explaining satisfactorily why this company should wish an unchanging price.[2] Surely such an explanation

[1] See *Bulletin of the Department of Labor,* No. 39 (Washington, D.C., March 1902). The data were collected back to 1890. The famous Aldrich Report of the U.S. Senate Finance Committee had compiled price information from 1840 through 1891.

[2] Abraham Berglund, *The United States Steel Corporation,* New York, 1907, pp. 143, 168, 171–72; Eliot Jones, *The Trust Problem in the United States,* New York, 1924, p. 230. Berglund suggested that the failure of the price to rise in booms discouraged entry of new rivals, which in turn made it easier to avoid cutthroat competition in depressions. The effect of the practice, one would think, would be only to encourage entry in depression rather than in prosperity.

seemed called for: both the generally accepted theory of monopoly price and the theory of competitive price state that market prices will change when demand and cost conditions change—and, of course, over long periods it is inconceivable that demand and cost remain rigid or dance together.

The flow of casual comments on price rigidity continued, but not until 1927 was the first comprehensive examination of the flexibility of industrial prices made, in Frederick Mills' *The Behavior of Prices*.[3] He plotted the frequency distribution of changes in all monthly wholesale prices by seven-year periods from 1890 and found a concentration of prices at the two extremes of frequent and infrequent change, a U-shaped distribution, that persisted throughout the entire period.[4] The "curious concentrations" at the two ends of the distribution were not explicitly associated with the operation of the price system, however, and this aspect of Mills' study received scant attention from contemporary readers.

The behavior of industrial prices entered a new era of study and opinion in 1935 when Gardiner Means' celebrated monograph, *Industrial Prices and Their Relative Inflexibility,* was published.[5] Means tabulated the frequency of change of some 677 monthly prices and found that a large number changed very infrequently. Indeed, in the eight-year period, 1926 through 1933, fourteen prices did not change a single time and seventy-seven prices changed only one to four times. He coined the phrase "administered prices" to describe the rigid prices and offered a definition:

[An administered price] is a price set by administrative action and held constant for a period of time. We have an administered price when a company maintains a posted price at which it will make sales or simply has its own prices at which buyers may purchase or not as they wish. Thus, when the General Motors management sets its wholesale price for six months or a year, the price is an administered price.[6]

[3] New York, NBER, 1927.
[4] *Ibid.,* pp. 56 ff. Mills also measured the magnitude of the within-year fluctuation of prices by the mean absolute deviation from the yearly average, pp. 39 ff, 489 ff. A corresponding measure of year-to-year variability calculated from link relatives was also presented, pp. 49 ff, 497 ff.
[5] Senate Document 13 (January 17, 1935), 74th Cong., 1st Sess.
[6] *Ibid.,* p. 1.

Such prices were distinguished by Means from a market-determined price, "which is made in the market as the result of the interaction of buyers and sellers".

The administered prices, Means believed, were destroying "the effective functioning of the American economy". In particular, the commodities whose prices were rigid in the Great Depression often experienced great falls in output, whereas those commodities whose prices had fallen greatly (farm products, in particular) experienced only small decreases in output.

These startling statistics of price rigidity—for which neoclassical price theory had no explanation—and the sweeping inferences that were drawn about the role of price rigidity in the economic malaise of the 1930's promptly commanded wide attention. In fact, Means was guilty of understatement when, two years later, he said that discussion of inflexible prices had been "somewhat stimulated by [his] previous articles". He had in fact created a new subject. In the forty-nine years from 1886 to 1935 the *Index of Economic Journals* lists three articles on rigid prices; in the next four years it lists fourteen. If we continue to use the *Index of Economic Journals* as our measure, interest in inflexible prices flagged from 1940 to 1954 (only seven articles) but then revived (twenty-five articles in 1954–65) after administered prices were charged with some of the responsibility for inflation. Although the *Index* crudely measures current writing, it does not measure cumulative effects, and the doctrine of administered prices had achieved an important place in professional thinking on industrial prices after World War II.

The proposition that in many important industrial markets prices do not respond quickly or fully to changing supply and demand conditions in the way a competitive market would had become generally accepted by the late 1930's. It was accepted first by the economists and then increasingly by the general public. Public acceptance is illustrated by the Congressional hearings to which changes in the price of steel products have been subjected since 1948.[7]

[7] For example, "Increases in Steel Prices", Hearings before the Joint Committee on the Economic Report, 80th Cong., 2nd Sess. (March 2, 1948); "December 1949 Steel Price Increases", Report of the Joint Committee on the Economic Report, 81st Cong., 2nd Sess., Report No. 1373 (March 27, 1950); and "1958

This attitude toward the industrial markets—at least those marked by a fair degree of concentration of output in a few large firms—was strengthened in the 1950's. A number of influential economists attributed inflationary price changes in periods of less than full employment precisely to the behavior of "administered prices." Again Gardiner Means was a leader of professional, and public, opinion. In widely publicized testimony before the Senate Subcommittee on Antitrust and Monopoly (the Kefauver Committee) in 1957, Means said,

As far as I can discover this recent price increase has not been the result of excessive buying power or demand but, at least to a very considerable extent, has been a result of action within the area of discretion in which prices and wage rates are made. This is suggested by the rise of administered prices while market prices were stable or falling. This is a new phenomenon. I do not find it anywhere in our history of prices.[8]

This view was endorsed in substantial measure by economists as eminent as Abba Lerner and J. K. Galbraith, and it led to influential statistical studies such as the monograph by Otto Eckstein and Gary Fromm which attributed a large share of the rise of wholesale prices in the 1950's to the price policy of the steel industry.[9] From this background there was a natural evolution to the "guidelines" of price and wage policy announced by the Council of Economic Advisers in 1962 and applied to steel, copper, aluminum and other products in a series of highly dramatic confrontations of the Presidential office and the industries in question.

We have not and shall not examine in detail these views of the various roles of "administered" prices in depression and inflation. The basic purpose in this sketchy outline is simply to emphasize that generally accepted views on the nature of the functioning of the industrial price system have emerged in the last generation. They have not

---

Steel Price Increase", Hearings of the Senate Subcommittee on Antitrust and Monopoly, Part VIII (1959).

[8] "Administered Prices," Hearings before the Senate Subcommittee on Antitrust and Monopoly, 85th Cong., 2nd Sess., 1958, Part I, p. 88; see also Part IX.

[9] "Steel and the Postwar Inflation", Joint Economic Committee, 86th Cong., 1st Sess., Nov. 6, 1959. The analysis was reviewed and seriously challenged by Martin Bailey, "Steel and the Postwar Rise in the Wholesale Price Index", *Journal of Business,* April 1962.

emerged in response to the development of a coherent, widely accepted theory that industrial prices will display downward rigidity in any meaningful sense; on the contrary, no theoretical explanation for price inflexibility has commanded wide and continued acceptance. The existence of inflexible industrial prices is accepted because it is believed to be an implacable empirical fact. One large purpose of our study is to determine whether it is indeed a fact.

THE QUALITY OF THE PRICE INFORMATION

Even if the wholesale price data had not become involved in controversy over the workings of the price system, one would expect the quality of the data to be subjected to periodic review and improvement. Many of the prices are used in the escalation of contract prices, so there are impressive financial stakes upon the movements of prices. The improvements in the quality of retail price data—influenced to a significant degree by controversies over the validity of the Consumer Price Index—would be expected to lead to contagious improvements in wholesale prices.

At the level of literal detail the wholesale prices have no doubt improved substantially since 1902, but the improvements have had two basic limitations. First, all improvements came from within the price collecting agency—there has never been a comprehensive outside review of the data. Second, the improvements have concentrated largely upon increasing precision in the specification of the commodities to be priced, to the neglect of other and possibly more basic questions. We now document this neglect.

When the continuous reporting of prices began in 1902, monthly prices were reported retroactively for twelve complete years. It was therefore possible for a price change to occur eleven times in January (January 1890 began the series and December 1901 terminated it) and twelve times in each other month. For most of the nonfood commodities initially included in the Wholesale Price Index, one would expect price changes to occur equally often in each month—or, perhaps better put, price changes should come when market conditions change, and these changes come throughout the year even for seasonal goods. Yet when the frequency of price changes of 19 commodities reported by companies in "metals and implements" is analyzed, it is found that 32 of 190 price changes (or 16.8 per cent) came in January, although only 7.6 per cent of price changes were expected in that month.[10]

Such a concentration in January could not arise by chance (the odds against it are a million to one). (For the 20 metals whose prices were reported by trade publications or governmental bureaus, January price changes were only 7.7 per cent of 2,081 price changes.) An even more striking result holds for cloth and clothing, where 272 of 1,839 price changes, or 14.8 per cent, occurred in January. The conclusion is statistically irresistible that many manufacturers reported prices on a calendar-year basis so the within-year price rigidity was due only to the method of reporting prices. Although this kind of test could have been made in 1902, it was not made then or afterward.

It should perhaps occasion little surprise that the quality of the wholesale prices was not examined with any care in the long period preceding Means' celebrated monograph.[11] It is more surprising that the importance of Means' findings attracted little attention to the question of validity after 1935. Means himself wrote as follows:

Do the Bureau of Labor Statistics figures accurately reflect actual prices? It has been held that the Bureau's price series have to do with list price, not with actual price. However, the Bureau of Labor Statistics asks for and usually gets net prices. Where there are list prices this means the list prices less all regular discounts. Presumably the resulting price quotations do not reflect unusual special discounts. In some cases, errors undoubtedly creep in. In examining a number of the Bureau's price series involving inflexible prices, I have become convinced the bulk of their quotations represented net prices. The exceptions seemed unlikely to falsify seriously the picture which I presented. Consultation with the technical staff of the Bureau of Labor Statistics supports this view. So far as this question is concerned, I am confident that the statistical picture is not seriously faulty.[12]

[10] That is, 11 out of 143 possible changes for each series (adjusted for the incompleteness of 4 of the 19 series).

[11] Even Wesley Clair Mitchell's justly famous monograph, *The Making and Using of Index Numbers*, Bulletin No. 173, Bureau of Labor Statistics, Washington, 1915, gives only passing attention to the quality of the price data.

[12] "Notes on Inflexible Prices", *American Economic Review*, March 1936, p. 28.

But this passage does not present the evidence which would lead the reader to share Means' confidence in the data.

In 1939 Saul Nelson made the first substantial study of the accuracy of the wholesale price data.[13] The variety of discounts, terms of trade, and secret concessions used by secretive price cutters was described by Nelson, and the failure of the BLS to capture all price movements was illustrated by fertilizer and salt. Receipts per unit of output, calculated from Census of Manufactures data, were also compared with prices for twenty-eight commodities. The sample was not felicitous: it contained three agricultural implements, and uninteresting commodities such as canned peaches and dried peaches. The agreement between Census unit values and BLS prices was good in perhaps half the cases and in the remainder varied from fair to very bad (men's shirts, sulfuric acid, bone black, asphalt). Nelson drew the conclusion:

These observations make the use of caution in dealing with individual price series imperative. However, they do not preclude the use of Bureau of Labor Statistics wholesale price data as statistical bases for broad economic investigations. In analyses of price rigidity and amplitude of price movement, it becomes necessary to place emphasis upon broad and consistent relationships and to avoid relying upon small differences in absolute figures. Yet, after all due allowance is made for the factors demanding caution, very marked and significant differences still remain between the behavior of rigid and flexible prices. For the statement and interpretation of such different types of price behavior, Bureau of Labor Statistics series can be regarded as furnishing an acceptable basis.[14]

This conclusion appears to go well beyond the assurance provided by Nelson's tests.

The second large test of quoted prices was made in 1943 by the Bureau of Labor Statistics under a contract with the Office of Price Administration.[15] The BLS collected more than 2,200 price series from 629 firms which bought steel products directly from steel mills in carload lots. Prices paid were compared with quoted prices (after adjust-

[13] "A Consideration of the Validity of the Bureau of Labor Statistics Price Indexes", Appendix 1 in the National Resources Committee report (of which Gardiner Means was the director), *The Structure of the American Economy*, Washington, 1939.

[14] *Ibid.*, p. 185.

[15] "Labor Dept. Examines Consumers' Prices of Steel Products", *Iron Age*, April 25, 1946, pp. 118 ff.

TABLE 2-1

Purchases at Invoice and Quoted Prices of Hot Rolled Sheets

		Percentage of Purchases at Invoice Price		
Period	Number of Purchases	Below Published Price	At Published Price	Above Published Price
2nd Qtr., 1939	137	79	9	12
3rd Qtr., 1939	178	96	4	0
2nd Qtr., 1940	210	78	22	0
2nd Qtr., 1941	253	15	85	Less than 1
4th Qtr., 1941	259	7	90	3
2nd Qtr., 1942	251	2	96	2

SOURCE: "Labor Department Examines Consumers' Prices of Steel Products", *Iron Age,* April 25, 1946, p. 134.

ing for charges for "extras" and transportation) in six quarters falling in the period 1939 to 1942. In 1939 and 1940, before industry operations reached high rates relative to capacity and before price ceilings were imposed, price cutting was extensive (a sample summary is given in Table 2-1).[16] This study certainly served to reduce confidence in the reliability of quoted prices in the period before World War II. The elaborate test (which cost several hundred thousand dollars) was never repeated.

The Price Statistics Review Committee, of which one of the present writers was chairman, devoted more attention to the problem of wholesale prices. One staff paper in particular, that of Professor Harry Mc-Allister, subjected the price reports of the Bureau of Labor Statistics to intensive analysis, to reach disquieting results. The Bureau's prices are based upon one, two, three, or more reporters (companies, in our context) and McAllister tabulated the frequency of price change by the number of reporters, on the basis of a sample of one-third of the BLS prices. His analysis (see Table 2-2) demonstrated that the number of

[16] The average ratio of invoice to quoted price for hot rolled sheets was 92 per cent in the second quarter of 1939 and 85 per cent in the third quarter, 94 per cent in the second quarter of 1940, and essentially 100 per cent thereafter (*ibid.,* p. 134).

TABLE 2-2

Frequency of Price Changes per Month, December 1953 to December 1956
(average number of price changes per item)

Commodity Class and Type of Reporter	Number of Price Reporters				
	1	2	3	4	5 or More
Company Data					
Crude Materials	.474	.470	.526	.500	.480
Intermediate Materials	.096	.143	.212	.207	.392
Finished Materials	.106	.112	.196	.215	.276
Nonfood Materials					
Company Data	.103	.143	.206	.207	.392
Publications Data	.239			.444	
Consumer-Goods Other than Food					
Company Data	.056	.101	.170	.200	.287
Publications Data	.258			.444	

SOURCE: "Government Price Statistics", Hearings before the Subcommittee on Economic Statistics of the Joint Economic Committee, 87th Cong., 1st Sess., 1961, pp. 388, 390.

reporters was a major determinant of the number of reported price changes. In fact, for certain classes of commodities the data permit one to assert that the probability that any one company will change its prices for a given commodity in a given month is independent of such change by other companies in the same industry in that month. To an economist such an implication seems absolutely unacceptable and casts grave doubts on the underlying data.

A possible explanation for this peculiar price behavior is that the industries with only one price reporter differ substantially from those with two or more reporters—in fact, the former industries are more concentrated. This explanation, however, was shown by McAllister to be insufficient.[17] No other plausible explanation is at hand.

[17] He took random samples of the prices reported by one, two, three, etc., sellers of commodities for which there were numerous reporters to obtain again the patterns of price change by number of reporters already observed. See "Government Price Statistics", Hearings before the Subcommittee on Economic Statistics of the Joint Economic Committee, 87th Cong., 1st Sess., 1961, p. 391.

Means once described his work as applying "a new kind of analysis to the best available supply of wholesale price data"—the new approach consisting of "taking a series of price data for an individual commodity and counting the number of price changes in a given time period".[18] So far as his original work is concerned, this description was largely true. The McAllister analysis effectively destroys the entire body of work resting upon frequency of price change. But even if Means' original work rested heavily upon frequency of price change, and made so dramatic an impact because of the startling findings on frequency, the importance of administered prices never rested upon this negligible basis. Its essential thrust was with respect to *amplitude* of price changes: few economists would have taken so seriously the infrequency of price changes if the prices had changed by large amounts.[19] Our own work, to which we now turn, confirms the view that frequency of changes in monthly prices is of little economic importance.

[18] "Notes on Inflexible Prices", *American Economic Review Supplement,* March 1936, p. 23.

[19] Indeed T. Scitovsky had shown that the U-shaped distribution of prices by frequency of price change arose because all prices which changed once or more per month were grouped together, and if price changes per day or hour were allowed, there would be no modal group of commodities with frequently changing prices. See "Prices under Monopoly and Competition", *Journal of Political Economy,* October 1941.

3

The Price Data:
Procedures, Characteristics,
and Limitations

It was necessary to collect a new body of price data for the various purposes of this study. The field work began in the fall of 1965, was the primary occupation of the authors in 1966 and continued on a part-time basis in the first half of 1967. The data collection methods are recounted in some detail because our procedures and decisions have certain important biases, which are not identical to those in the BLS price data.

THE PERIOD COVERED

Price data were collected back to 1957 when possible but reporters who preserved records for so long a period were in the minority. The price series were carried forward usually to the time of the interview, and a considerable number of reporters subsequently sent us prices to the end of 1966 on a second-round request.

The number of price series on which our work is based is not an unequivocal number. A substantial number of reporters supplied from two to twenty price series for closely related products: window glass of different sizes; gasoline purchases in various cities in a state, etc. Unweighted index numbers must be used in much of the work, for reasons discussed later, so including multiple series would implicitly

TABLE 3-1

Number of Price Series Collected by the National Bureau of
Economic Research

Year	Number of Price Series Reported in Both June and July	Year	Number of Price Series Reported in Both June and July
1957	601	1962	1,097
1958	663	1963	1,155
1959	731	1964	1,233
1960	842	1965	1,240
1961	1,022	1966	957

involve multiple weighting of the respondents who provided multiple series. The multiple series were therefore combined into a single series, by the same procedures as the prices of various reporters were combined into a single commodity index (however, using weights of the individual series where available). Each consolidated price series is counted as only one series. The number of price series reporting in both June and July of each year are tabulated in Table 3-1. The peak number of price series was 1,240 in 1965; the minimum number was 601 in 1957.

THE COMMODITIES COVERED

The commodities which are currently included in the wholesale price reporting of the Bureau of Labor Statistics are chosen, partly explicitly and partly implicitly, on the basis of

1. Importance, measured by value;
2. Availability of price data;
3. Representativeness—a commodity is preferred if its price history probably represents that of other commodities;
4. Persistent specifiability—a commodity which cannot be described or for which the description will not remain essentially unchanged for a time, is not included. There are exceptions, such as various types of machinery;

5. Historical inertia—a price series, once included, is generally kept until prices become difficult to collect.

It will be observed that there is no sampling of a formal statistical variety in the selection of commodities. The universe of which BLS wholesale prices is a sample cannot be described in economic terms; it is the product of criteria such as those just listed.

The present study, with its primary purpose of determining the actual transaction prices of industrial goods, necessarily follows the BLS, for these prices are the object of validation. Nevertheless, the present selection differs in important respects from that of the BLS.

1. We naturally pay special attention to the areas in which the charge of inflexible prices has been heard most frequently: ferrous and nonferrous metals, chemicals, and drugs. Accordingly, we omit certain areas in which no such charge seems important (foods generally and certain textiles) or where price behavior reflects different forces (charges by public utilities).

2. The BLS commodity list is compelled by the nonstandardization and rapid change in product characteristics to omit or under-represent most machinery, construction, electronic goods, and custom work. We go even further in excluding almost all such commodities because the problem of measuring change in the quality of products is *the* major unsolved task of all price collection. Any attempt to deal with it would completely swallow up the basic purpose of this study, the collection of genuine transaction prices. This is a grave limitation on the present study, whose effect, we suspect, is to lead to a substantial understatement of the average flexibility of industrial prices.

A list of the commodities is presented in Table 3-2, together with the December 1961 relative weights which the BLS assigned to these categories. Our index covers 14.3 per cent of the BLS weights, or 18.9 per cent of the BLS universe excluding farm and processed food prices.

THE PRICE SOURCES

The price data were obtained from both buyers and sellers. The sellers were negligible in number. Industrial companies are generally reticent to report selling prices other than list prices. (It should be observed that

TABLE 3-2

Commodities Included in the NBER Study, with Their Weights in the
Wholesale Price Index, December 1961

Commodity Name	BLS Codes	Relative Weight
Steel		
Sheet and strip, cold-rolled	1014–47, 51	.497
Sheet and strip, hot-rolled	1014–45, 46, 53	.304
Tinplate	1014–68, 69, 70, 73	.321
Plates	1014–26, 27	.246
Bars and rods, hot-rolled	1014–39	.206
Carbon steel pipe	1014–56	.097
Tubing	1014–63	.085
Oil well casing	1014–59	.062
Steel wire	1014–76	.156
Stainless steel sheet and strip	1014–49, 52	.124
Alloy steel bars, cold- and hot-rolled	1014–37	.068
Nonferrous Metals		
Aluminum		
Ingot and shot	1022–01, 1024–01	.270
Sheet and strip	1025–01, 07, 08, 09	.340
Wire and cable	1026–41	.038
Copper		
Ingot	1022–06, 1024–21	.279
Pipe and tubing	1025–51, 52, 53	.139
Wire and cable, bare	1026–01	.065
Insulated wire	1026–06, 11, 17, 21	.237
Magnet wire	1026–46, 47	.058
Zinc products	1022–31, 33	.069
Brass		
Bars and rods	1025–13	.074
Fuels and Related Products		
Petroleum Products		
Gasoline, regular	0571–00	2.378
Diesel and distillate oil No. 2	0573–00	.713
Residual fuel oil No. 6	0574–00	.399
Coal	0512–05	.064
Rubber and Allied Products		
Passenger car tires	0721–01	.287
Truck and bus tires	0721–11	.184
SBR, hot and cold	0712–11, 12	.096

TABLE 3-2 (Continued)

Commodity Name	BLS Codes	Relative Weight
Rubber and Allied Products (Cont.)		
Neoprene	0712–03	.033
Belting	0733–11	.004
Paper		
Book, magazine, etc.	0931–11, 21, 22	.409
Newsprint	0932–01	.340
Kraft papers (coarse paper and bags)	0931–51, 61 and 0952–01	.361
Paper board, unfabricated	0941–00 0942–00 0943–00	.412
Paper boxes and shipping containers, fabricated	0953–00	1.406
Bond	0931–31, 41	.280
Chemicals		
Sulfuric acid, bulk	0611–09	.101
Caustic soda, liquid	0611–69	.073
Titanium dioxide	0622–21	.091
Chlorine, bulk	0611–35	.074
Oxygen, pipeline, tonnage	0611–49	.036
Ammonia, bulk	0611–13	.036
Acetone	0612–01	.031
Acetylene	0612–03	.046
Benzene	0612–25	.028
Styrene monomer	0612–89	.038
Ethyl alcohol, tech.	0612–14, 15	.025
Methyl alcohol	0612–17	.047
Glycerine, natural and synthetic	0622–62	.015
Phthalic anhydride	0622–71	.048
Phenol	0612–83	.027
Polyethylene	[a]	[a]
Polystyrene	0673–31	.109
Polyvinyl chloride	0673–01	.109
Phenolics, i.e., phenolic resins	0673–11	.039
Drugs		
Antibiotics	0635–1	.148
Tranquilizers	0635–4	.057

(Continued)

TABLE 3-2 (Concluded)

Commodity Name	BLS Codes	Relative Weight
Drugs (Cont.)		
Cardiac glycosides	0635–6	.020 [b]
Miscellaneous		
Paint	0621–00	.311
Cement		
Portland cement	1322–30	.375
Glass Products		
Plate glass	$\left\{\begin{array}{l}1311\text{–}01\\1313\text{–}01\end{array}\right\}$	.136
Safety and flat (window) glass	$\left\{\begin{array}{l}1312\text{–}01\\1313\text{–}02\end{array}\right\}$	.104
Electrical Machinery and Equipment		
Electric motors, excluding DC	1173–13, 14, 32, 34	.360
Batteries	1178–15.	.007
Wood		
Plywood (softwood)	0831–00	.213
Flooring	0812–01	.006

[a] Not included among BLS products.
[b] Maximum.

seldom did a firm assert that its sales were predominantly and continuously at the quoted prices.) The reticence no doubt stemmed partly from reasons of commercial interest, despite our promise of complete confidentiality, but potential legal complications also discouraged the reporting of selling prices. The Robinson-Patman Act places a substantial burden upon any seller to justify differences in price (by cost differences, meeting competition in good faith, etc.) where the effect may be to reduce competition, and it was often cited to us as a reason for noncooperation.

Buyers, on the other hand, had fewer legal or commercial doubts and cooperation was much greater. Our data sources include:

1. Some thirty-three governments and governmental agencies: federal, state, and local. A half dozen others refused to cooperate because of the press of duties, inaccessibility of records, and other factors.

2. Some 137 industrial, utility, and transportation companies. Without important exception the respondents were large companies, and include many of the nation's largest enterprises. In addition some 100 companies did not cooperate, sometimes rejecting our request categorically and sometimes after a discussion deciding that they did not buy appreciable amounts of any commodity on our list or did not keep appropriate records. Another fifty companies sent unusable data, usually rejected because the period covered was short.

3. Some nine hospitals provided data on drug prices. A dozen more did not supply data, usually because their records were inadequate.

Given the fact that at least half of the inquiries for data were simple formal requests to corporate heads to whom the authors had no introduction, the response appears very good. Nevertheless it poses the question: how did nonresponse affect our results?

One type of nonresponse (even from cooperating companies) worked to overstate price levels and probably to understate price flexibility. This was the refusal to give information on commodities for which an extraordinarily favorable deal had been consummated: we were emphatically told by a retail chain, for example, that it would not give us the price of an automobile accessory whose price was remarkably low. There was no conceivable reason for suppressing information when prices were the published list prices, on the other hand, so a very pronounced bias could be introduced by this self-selection.

A second, but infrequent, source of nonresponse could on balance have worked toward omission of list-price buyers. In several cases, purchasing agents in effect refused to cooperate even though their company heads had instructed them to do so. Unnecessary fear of the detection of chicanery or incompetence (unnecessary because a few instances of demonstrable incompetence which we encountered were left undisturbed), as well as indolence, are possible explanations—no attempt was made to pursue these sources.

The sizes of the companies and other respondents who cooperated with our study are given in Tables 3-3 and 3-4. The overwhelming reliance of our study on large companies and institutions is obvious, although often these reporters bought only small quantities of the commodities for which prices were reported. A corresponding description

TABLE 3-3

Sizes of Companies Supplying
Price Data

Company Size ($ millions) [a]	Number of Respondents [b]
Over 1,000	25
500–1,000	28
100–500	44
10–100	33
Under 10	6
Not Available	1
Total	137

[a] 1962 assets.
[b] Including seventeen railroads of which six are in the over $1,000 million class, nine are in the $500 million to $1,000 million class, and two are in the $100 million to $500 million class.

TABLE 3-4

Noncompany Sources
of Price Data

Type of Reporter	Number of Respondents
Federal agencies	9
State governments	9
Local governments	12
1960 population under 1,000,000	7
1960 population over 1,000,000	5
Local government agencies	3
Hospitals	9

of nonrespondents cannot be given because nonresponse proved extremely difficult to identify. The lack of data might be due to great costs of exhuming records, or to lack of records, or the lack of purchases of items on our list, or to frequent changes in specifications—or the refusal may simply have been cloaked with such explanations. The nonrespondents were also consistently large.

The effect upon our price indexes of our reliance upon large buyers is discussed in Chapter 4.

OTHER PRICE SOURCES

Our analysis of the BLS price indexes will be based exclusively upon the price quotations which were collected for the present study. There exist other important sources of information which could contribute to the appraisal of the validity of the BLS prices. They will be briefly described and illustrated, and the reasons for excluding them from the present study will be given.

(1) The internal structure of prices published by the BLS is a

neglected source of information. Two related examples may be given; both are concerned with the "guideline" price ceilings which were imposed upon copper ingot prices in November 1965 (if not earlier). The price of copper ingots traditionally had a fairly close relationship to the price of moderately fabricated copper products such as bare copper wire. With the imposition of the price ceiling the series moved apart (see Figure 3-1) and we may infer that copper ingot was severely rationed to unintegrated pipe and tubing manufacturers buying at posted prices. As a second example, consider the price of prime copper scrap and copper ingots (Figure 3-2). The cost of refining the scrap is roughly one cent per pound, yet scrap prices reached a level 63 per cent above ingot prices. The existence of rationing on a nonprice basis, and hence the inaccuracy of the posted price of ingots, is again evident.

Figure 3-1

BLS Price of Copper Ingots and Copper Wire, Monthly, 1957–66

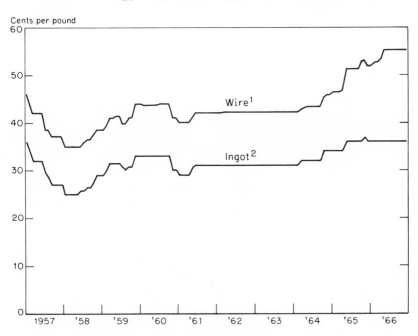

[1] Bare, solid, #8AWG, hard drawn, 30,000 lb. carlots.
[2] Electrolytic, producer's price, delivered f.o.b. cars, destination in U.S.A.

Figure 3-2

BLS Price of Copper Ingots and Market Price of Copper Scrap, Monthly,
1957–66

[1] Copper ingot, electrolytic, producer's price, delivered f.o.b. cars, destination in U.S.A.
[2] Dealer's buying prices at New York for No. 1 heavy copper scrap.

(2) Several intensive studies have been made of particular prices in connection with antitrust and other legal proceedings. An example is provided by the study of prices of electrical generating and distributing equipment by Charles R. Dean and Horace J. De Podwin.[1] The quoted and realized sales prices for large circuit breakers for the years 1954–59 are reproduced from their study (Figure 3-3).

(3) An essentially unlimited supply of more or less informed commentary on market prices is presented in published trade sources. Scarcely a trade journal fails to remark on deviations from list prices from time to time. One use of our data, indeed, could be to investigate

[1] "Product Variation and Price Indexes", a paper presented to the American Statistical Association, December 29, 1961.

Figure 3-3

Price Indexes of 23 KV Large Outdoor Circuit Breakers (Specified in BLS Code 11.75-32.03); as Reported in BLS-WPI and
Electrical Equipment Price Study

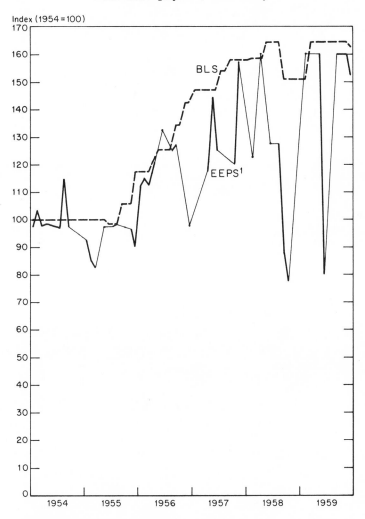

SOURCE: Charles R. Dean and Horace De Podwin, *Product Variation and
Price Indexes: A Case Study in Electrical Apparatus,* General Electric Company; data supplied by Mr. De Podwin.
1 Thin line indicates no orders for this circuit breaker.

TABLE 3-5

Tinplate for Beer Cans [a]

Date [b]	Price per Ton [c] (dollars)	Cans per Ton	Price per 1,000 Cans (dollars)
April 1957	208	16,000	13.00
Jan. 1958	224	17,067	13.12
Jan. 11, 1959	212	17,067	12.42
Jan. 1960	221	17,067	12.95
Jan. 1961	224	21,333	10.50
Jan. 1962	238	23,273	10.23
Jan. 1963	238	23,273	10.23
Jan. 1964	238	23,273	10.23
Jan. 1965	238	23,273	10.23
April 1966	248	23,273	10.66

[a] Data supplied by a steel producer.
[b] As of the first of the month, unless noted.
[c] Delivered, Los Angeles.

this source of information: does the trade press comment upon any substantial price reductions that are reported by us but not by the BLS?

(4) We have encountered numerous examples of price reduction by the route of quality improvement. One example will suffice: the number of beer cans (including ends) which can be made from a ton of tinplate has risen sufficiently to reverse the direction of cost of tinplate per can (see Table 3-5).

These types of evidence of price flexibility are all potentially as important as the kind of price data we have collected for this study. Nevertheless they are unreliable for a test of the validity of price quotations for two reasons. The first, and lesser, reason is that some of the information is nonquantitative; not only the trade press commentary but much of the quality change information is of this sort.

The second reason for exclusion is that two of these information sources are biased. The trade press will not comment continuously on strict adherence to quoted prices, and conversely price studies inspired by antitrust actions are likely to pertain to periods of collusive pricing. Formally, at least, there is no such bias in analyses of the internal structure of prices, nor need the quality changes in products all be improvements, although as an empirical matter economists are generally agreed that they are preponderantly so.

Although we shall henceforth ignore these other sources of price information in our discussion, the full appraisal of the published prices should of course take them into consideration.

4

The Nature of
the Price Indexes

THE UNIQUE PRICE

There is a pervasive belief that each standardized industrial commodity normally has one price at a given time. This belief may stem from the well-known proposition of economic theory that under competition (of buyers *or* sellers) only one price can survive in a market, although in a fuller and more accurate version one must add, *for an identical transaction*. The belief is certainly fostered by the statistics of prices; the Bureau of Labor Statistics does not report and does not discuss the dispersion of industrial prices at a point in time or the diversity of movements of prices over time. The Bureau reports that the price of an oil storage tank of 55,000 barrel capacity was $37,026.75 in February of 1967, when the index stood at 111.4 (January 1961 = 100). In fact, the practice of basing prices upon one, two, or three reporters, and almost *900* wholesale prices are so based,[1] must represent a pledge to

---

[1] The distribution of company reporters at an unspecified date in the late 1950's was:

1 reporter	243
2 reporters	216
3 reporters	432
4 reporters	216
5 or more reporters	243
	1,350

Source: *Frequency of Change in Wholesale Prices*, BLS Report No. 142 (1958). In January of 1965 prices of 1,152 commodities were based only upon company reports, and they had an average of 3.6 reporters per commodity; see *BLS Handbook of Methods*, Bulletin No. 1458 (1966), pp. 94–95.

the same doctrine of Unique Price, for these are hardly reassuring sample sizes.

Of course, prices are known to vary with quality of commodity and size of order, so these characteristics are specified more or less precisely by the BLS, and most prices vary with location of seller or buyer, so origin or destination is also usually specified. These qualifications of the Unique Price merely redirect our questions: are the price differentials for variation in quality, lot size, and location stable over time—and stable in absolute or in relative terms? Yet surely these three dimensions do not describe the full complexity of the pricing process. Transactions differ, to cite a few varieties of influences, with

—credit-worthiness of the buyer
—engineering services supplied to the user of the product
—"trade relations", the euphemism for reciprocity in dealings
—tie-in sales, the purchase of related goods
—introductory offers, which compensate the buyer for the additional costs of changing sources or techniques
—speed of delivery
—guarantees of supplies in times of "shortage" (rationing).

These factors may be common to many customers, or they may be quantitatively of small importance, but neither of these reasons for believing in the Unique Price has been demonstrated empirically for ordinary industrial goods.

The *duration* of a price is a variable which deserves special comment. Suppose that the price for individual orders (that is, the "spot" price) has a systematic seasonal pattern (which we illustrate in Figure 4-1). A contract for deliveries over a year will usually be based upon an annual price equivalent to the average of the expected spot prices, minus a saving because of the reduction in costs of negotiation, testing of quality, devising of methods to settle controversies, etc., which is permitted by repetitive dealings. Even if the spot price fluctuates irregularly, a corresponding equivalent annual price will often be contracted (as in Figure 4-2). In this latter case, the contract price will be revised if prices move substantially outside the expected range: many contracts, we found, could be reopened or cancelled by either party with appropriate notice. Thus the contract will be reopened in the situation illustrated in Figure 4-2 and a price of R agreed upon. About half of the

Figure 4-1

Uniform Seasonal Pattern in Price

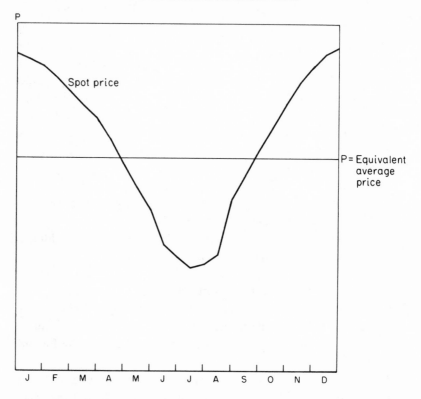

commodities in our sample for both industrial firms and governmental bodies are purchased on the basis of explicit contracts, and approximately half of these contracts are occasionally renegotiated within the contract year. Therefore a price index based upon a number of contract prices will fluctuate frequently only if the contracts are numerous and the contract periods vary among contracts.

Buyers' Prices

When prices are collected from buyers there is less temptation to adhere to the Unique Price. The greater dispersion of price one encounters is, to be sure, partly due to differences in transportation costs and particular technical specifications of goods. Even here, however, we should note that buyers' prices have some advantages. If one wishes to measure costs of production, buyers' delivered prices are the correct ones: it is what steel (of the types actually purchased) costs the automobile manufacturer that influences his costs, not what the steel mill receives for the steel. Moreover the distinction between delivered prices and prices f.o.b. the production center is becoming progressively more ambiguous (or irrelevant) when much shipping is done in carriers be-

Figure 4-2

Irregular Fluctuations in Price

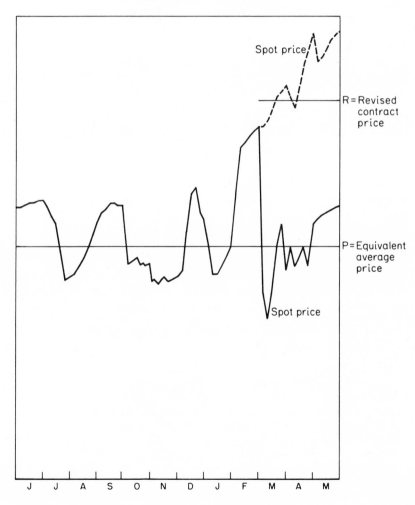

longing to buyers or sellers; and we frequently encountered the comment that sellers shaded prices by negotiating on freight.

A second source of differences in movements of buyers' prices and sellers' prices is the fact that each buyer is not permanently assigned to a given seller. From time to time a buyer will shift to a new supplier, presumably in response to a better price or other advantages which we would hope to represent by a price difference. Then the index of buyers' prices could decline while every seller's price remained constant. Of course an index of sellers' prices with current weights would reflect the shift of buyers, but no price index is constructed with current weights.

A third source of difference in buyers' and sellers' prices is the different ways in which commodities are chosen. Each seller's price will be that for a particular commodity—e.g., "hot-rolled carbon steel sheets, 10 ga. x 48″ wide x 120″ long, sheared edge, cut length, base chemistry, commercial quality, base packaging, base quantity, mill to user, f.o.b. mill" (so the BLS)—and this price will be collected whether or not any steel of this precise description is sold. Each buyer, on the other hand, will be asked to report the price of that type of hot-rolled carbon steel sheet which he has purchased continuously for some period of time, and it is not only possible but highly probable that no two of a small number of buyers will purchase to precisely the same specifications. Hence a sellers' price index is based upon a more or less precisely defined commodity, which it is hoped reflects the movements of similar commodities, and the buyers' price index is based upon a broader range of commodities.[2]

No matter how precisely the conditions of a transaction are specified,

---

[2] The range of products included in one of our commodity classes may be illustrated by cold-rolled carbon steel sheet and strip. The physical dimensions include:
.062″ x 36″ x 96″
20 gauge x 36″ x 120″ (USS drawing, oiled)
.125″ x 22″ x 96″
.032″(±.0025) x 7.50″ (AISI 1010, hard temper, RB-90 min.)
AISI, C1213, ½″ diameter
.036″ x 72″ x 142″ (drawing quality AISI 1010, manganese .60 max.)
.030″ x 1⅜″ x coil (SAE 1010, 6,000 lb. skids, No. 4 temper)
.0225″ x 36″ x coil
16 gauge x 36″ x 96″ (C.Q. oiled)
.040″ x 7½″ x 48″
.020″ x 36″ x 48″

the buyers' prices display a dispersion of level and variation in time of change which represent fundamentally the incompleteness of the buyer's, and possibly seller's, information. One must resist the common practice of immediately labeling this incompleteness an "imperfection" of the market; it is a rational adjustment to the costliness of collecting information on prices. If there are numerous sellers, a buyer will find it prohibitively expensive to canvass each seller, or be canvassed by the seller's representative, each day or hour. In a world of change there will not be a Unique Price. We pursue this matter in Chapter 7.

Of course every price paid by some buyer in a given time interval is received by some seller, so in principle the same information can be obtained from a seller. The seller's price *quotations,* however, will not display the multiplicity of prices and the frequency of revision that the transaction prices actually display. Quite aside from legal questions of price discrimination, it would be too costly to revise price quotations continuously.

THE DESCRIPTION OF PRICE MOVEMENTS

A collection of prices collected from buyers will display dispersion in level and timing of changes. Our interest is in the timing and size of price changes and, in any event, differences in level of prices due to lot size and delivery point are uninteresting as sources of dispersion, so we adjust all price series to the same level. Sample price series for ammonia are shown in Figure 4-3. They were chosen to display the varieties of price data reported: unchanging prices, irregularly changing prices, broken price series, and frequently changing prices.

From these and other prices we calculate an equally weighted index, which is presented in Figure 4-4 along with the BLS index for ammonia. The comparison of our price index with that of the BLS is made later, here the main interest is the method of presentation of price indexes.

An index of prices has more to report than *the* price, once the myth of the Unique Price is abandoned. Some measure of the statistical reliability of the index is essential. Unfortunately in the absence of random sampling it is impossible to assign an unambiguous statistical measure of reliability to an index. Nevertheless two descriptive statistics are helpful in appraising an index: (1) The number of reporters on which the index is based. (2) The standard deviation of the movements of individ-

Figure 4-3

Ammonia: Selected Individual Price Series

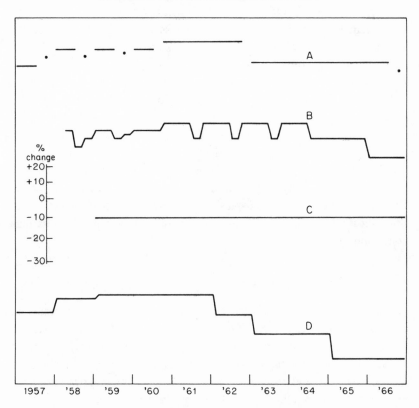

ual prices about the movement of the index (= mean of individual price movements). The latter measure is also included in Figure 4-4 as an annual average.[3] The average number of reporters during each year is reported with the basic tables.[4]

[3] The formula for the annual average standard deviation is as follows:

$$\frac{1}{T}\sum_{i=1}^{T}\sqrt{\sum_{j=1}^{N_i}\frac{(P_{i,j}/P_{i-1,j} - I_i/I_{i-1})^2}{N_i - 1}}$$

where $P_{i,j}$ is price j in month i, I_i is the index number in month i, N_i is the number of series reporting both in month i and $i - 1$ and T is the number of months for which $N_i \geq 2$.

[4] More precisely, the count of series is based upon number of series entering the monthly rates of change of prices, and the number for a year is the average of the monthly numbers.

Figure 4-4

Ammonia: Comparison of BLS and NBER Price Indexes and Annual
Average Standard Deviation of NBER Index

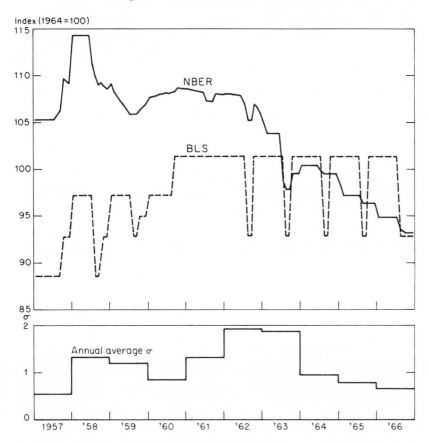

METHODS OF COMPARISON OF PRICE INDEXES

We shall compare the BLS and NB indexes in the next chapter; subsequently in this chapter we shall compare the movements of price
indexes of different classes of buyers. What comparisons shall we make?
Two price indexes, each covering 120 months, permit a vast number
of comparisons—and all within one minute by a computer! Our selection of criteria of concordance is governed by the leading uses of indexes
of industrial prices.

Trend

The simplest test of the concordance of movement of two price indexes is a comparison of their secular trends. The average annual percentage change of price is of course a widely used number; it is requisite to the measurement of secular inflation and essential to the deflation of dollar product in the calculation of labor productivity. A constant percentage change equation, $\log_e P = a + bt$, is fitted to each price index.[5] The monthly relative change in price is

$$\frac{P_{t+1} - P_t}{P_t} = e^a \frac{(e^{b(t+1)} - e^{bt})}{e^a e^{bt}} = e^b - 1,$$

which is approximately equal to b, and we use b as the measure of price change. For small changes it is also satisfactory to take $(12 \times b)$ as the annual relative change in price. In order to form some estimate of the goodness of the fit of the trend line to the indexes, graphs of the indexes have been examined and the correlation coefficients of the indexes with time computed. The constant-percentage-growth trend fits tolerably well in the great majority of series but there are a small number for which this is not true. In these exceptional cases there is usually a reversal of trend within the period. The exceptional cases are given special treatment in the trend analyses.[6] In addition trends have been calculated for the first and second five-year periods.

The indexes for the price of ammonia will illustrate the comparison of trends. The regression coefficients of the logarithms of the monthly indexes on time (b in the above notation) are, in percentage terms:

BLS: .068
NB: −.134

Hence the BLS index rose an average of $12 \times .068 = .82$ per cent a year and the NB index fell by $12 \times .134 = 1.61$ per cent a year.

Cyclical Behavior

The good fortune of the American economy not to have experienced large short-run fluctuations in the level of economic activity in our

[5] In which $(dP/dt)(1/P) = b$.
[6] These series are identified in Appendix C.

TABLE 4-1

Reference Cycles and Selected General Measures of Economic Activity

Date	Phase of Cycle	BLS WPI [a]	Rate of Unemployment (per cent)	Production Index of FRB [a]	GNP ($ billions) [b]
July 1957	Peak	100.8	4.3	96.2	447.8
April 1958	Trough	101.9	7.5	89.8	434.5
May 1960	Peak	100.8	4.9	109.9	505.0
Feb. 1961	Trough	101.1	8.1	103.7	501.4
Nov. 1964	Trough [c]	100.7	4.5	135.9	634.6
Nov. 1966	Peak [c]	105.9	3.4	160.2	762.1

[a] 1957–59 = 100.

[b] Closest quarter, seasonally adjusted at annual rates.

[c] The period November 1964 to November 1966 is treated as an expansion for reasons discussed in the text. The date of the peak, November 1966, is arbitrarily chosen.

period means that there were no cyclical pressures upon prices comparable to those experienced before 1941. Therefore we are not able to judge the amount of price cutting that would emerge if general business entered a severe depression. The National Bureau reference cycles within our period are listed in Table 4-1, together with a few select numbers to indicate the modest extent of general business declines in this decade. We shall employ as one measure of cyclical price behavior the average monthly rates of price change in the two reference cycle contractions and in the first reference cycle expansion (1958–60), together with the expansion in the last two years (November 1964 to November 1966) because this sharp expansion strongly resembles a reference expansion even though it was not preceded by a contraction. The long reference cycle expansion which began in 1961 is omitted. Its duration was such that large expansions of capacity were possible. Therefore the growth of demand was not likely to have a substantial impact upon prices of the type associated with short-run demand fluctuations.

The illustrative measures for the monthly rate of change of the price of ammonia are as follows:

	BLS	NB
Trough to Peak	−.1806%	−.2504%
April 1958–May 1960	0	−.2270
Nov. 1964–Nov. 1966	−.3687	−.2747
Peak to Trough	.7545	.4742
July 1957–April 1958	1.0287	.8996
May 1960–Feb. 1961	.4802	.0489

The price of ammonia thus moved opposite to the movements of general business: the National Bureau Index rose less in business contractions but fell more in the combined business expansions than the Bureau of Labor Statistics Index. We conclude that for ammonia the NB Index conformed less well in expansions and better in contractions than the BLS Index.

When there are strong trends in the price indexes, the cyclical responsiveness of price may be swamped or exaggerated by the trend component. The constant percentage trends just described then allow us to subtract out the trend changes to get a better measure of cyclical responsiveness. Since a single type of trend line is fitted to all seventy commodity price indexes, trend corrections are only rough, and the trend-corrected price changes are clearly better only when the trend is strong.[7]

In addition, specific cycles (rather different from those usually employed in National Bureau studies) were analyzed for the commodities for which data are available. A specific cycle is determined by the movements in the physical volume of the specific commodity, and the responsiveness of prices to movements of industry output is determined. This relatively unsuccessful investigation is reported in Chapter 5 and Appendix D.

[7] In the case of ammonia, where the trend is *not* strong (the NB Index, which has the larger trend, fell 1.6 per cent a year), cyclical changes become:

	BLS	NB
Trough to Peak	−.2730%	−.1243%
April 1958–May 1960	−.2309	−.2203
Nov. 1964–Nov. 1966	−.3168	−.0243
Peak to Trough	.5236	.4809
July 1957–April 1958	.7978	.9063
May 1960–Feb. 1961	.2493	.0556

Now the NB Index conforms better in expansions, but the two indexes are similar in contractions.

Short-Run Fluctuations

The final set of comparisons involve movements independent of trend and shorter than periods of general business expansion or contraction. We shall employ three measures to this end.

The first measure of short-run movements pertains to the amplitude of fluctuations. For this purpose we calculate the first differences in the natural logarithms of the indexes to be compared; so, say,

$$x_t = \log_e I_t - \log_e I_{t-1}$$

and calculate

$$\sigma^2 = \frac{\Sigma(x_t - \bar{x})^2}{119}.$$

This variance is .00077772 for the BLS index for ammonia, for example, and the standard deviation is $\sqrt{.00077772} = .0279$, so if the monthly percentage changes in the BLS were normally distributed, two-thirds would fall within 2.79 per cent of the mean (which is virtually zero).[8] The corresponding variance for the NB price index for ammonia is .00007992 and the standard deviation is .008940, or .89 per cent. Hence the BLS index is much more volatile than the NB index.

Our second set of measures describes the degree of simultaneity of movements in the monthly price indexes. Simultaneous monthly movements of the two price indexes are compared by the correlation between the first differences of the logarithms of the two indexes; the coefficient is .4310 for ammonia.

Because the monthly price series are often volatile, the comparison of monthly changes is supplemented by comparisons for longer periods. The correlation coefficients of first differences of the logarithms of the price indexes of ammonia will again illustrate our results:

Time Interval	Correlation Coefficient
Quarterly	.6347
Semiannual	.5476
Annual	.5016

In this instance the correlations of monthly changes are very similar to those for longer periods, but often the correlations rise greatly or fall slowly with the lengthening of the time interval.

[8] Actually the distribution of BLS monthly percentage changes is far from normal: 101 of the monthly percentage changes for ammonia are zero. The NBER percentage changes are much closer to a normal distribution (see pp. 66, 67).

Leads or lags in the movement of one price index relative to the other are examined by the corresponding correlations: illustrative calculations for ammonia are given in Table 4-2. Where a nonsimultaneous correlation is largest, the corresponding time difference is taken as the measure of lead or lag.

Some attention has been devoted also to the large price changes in each series. A "large" change is arbitrarily defined as one of 5 per cent or more in any quarter. The large changes in the price of ammonia are listed in Table 4-3. We encounter here a seasonal pattern in the BLS quotations, with absolutely identical reductions of price in August and September in the last five years of the period. Our series has no such seasonal pattern, presumably because of our dependence upon annual contract prices. These "large" change comparisons could, in principle, serve either of two purposes: to measure responsiveness in the indexes to large changes in market conditions; or to identify erratic and implausible movements of either index.

TABLE 4-2

Correlation Coefficients of Monthly Relative Changes, NB and
BLS Price Indexes for Ammonia
(measured by first differences in logarithms)

Lead or Lag		Correlation Coefficient
NB	BLS	
Jan.–Feb., Year 2	July–Aug., Year 2	.0226
	June–July, Year 2	−.0002
	May–June, Year 2	.0084
	April–May, Year 2	−.1906
	March–April, Year 2	−.1079
	Feb.–March, Year 2	.2751
	Jan.–Feb., Year 2	.4071
	Dec., Year 1–Jan., Year 2	.0113
	Nov.–Dec., Year 1	−.1399
	Oct.–Nov., Year 1	.0176
	Sept.–Oct., Year 1	−.0521
	Aug.–Sept., Year 1	.0577
	July–Aug., Year 1	.0174

TABLE 4-3

"Large" Quarterly Changes [a] in the Price of Ammonia
(per cent)

Period	BLS	NB	Period	BLS	NB
1958			1964		
2nd–3rd Qtr.	−5.8953		2nd–3rd Qtr.	−5.6459	
1962			3rd–4th Qtr.	5.9838	
2nd–3rd Qtr.	−5.6459		1965		
3rd–4th Qtr.	5.9838		2nd–3rd Qtr.	−5.6459	
1963			3rd–4th Qtr.	5.9838	
2nd–3rd Qtr.	−5.6459	−5.4919	1966		
3rd–4th Qtr.	5.9838		2nd–3rd Qtr.	−5.6459	

[a] A "large" change is defined as one of 5 per cent or more in any quarter.

Choosing between these interpretations requires having outside information on whether market conditions have actually changed. We have not been able to collect sufficient data on output, inventories, and orders to make an effective investigation of this subject, but a few scraps of analysis are presented in Chapter 5 and Appendix D.

PRICE MOVEMENTS BY TYPE OF BUYER

In the process of developing new price indexes, we collected information which allows the construction of indexes for classes of buyers. These class-of-buyer prices are not only interesting in their own right but also add to the understanding of general price movements. Two classifications of buyers are examined: governmental vs. nongovernmental buyers; and (related to size of purchase) weighted vs. unweighted indexes.

Governmental vs. Private Buyers

We requested from buyers the prices of commodities which they bought frequently and in substantial quantities. The buyers' responses led to a sort of self-selection of commodities; governmental units seldom bought most chemicals or semifabricated metals, industrial concerns did not buy drugs. In fact only eight commodities were reported by a sufficiently large number of both public and private buyers to permit the construction of useful indexes. These commodities are:

Commodity	Maximum Number of Price Series	
	Public	Private
Book and magazine paper	9	19
Chlorine, in bulk	5	21
Paper boxes and shipping containers	9	25
Passenger automobile tires	17	15
Portland cement	8	26
Regular gasoline	38	22
Residual fuel oil	24	34
Truck tires	15	15

These commodities are heavily clustered (two each of paper, petroleum, and rubber products) so our comparison will have small claims to generality. We follow the basic scheme of comparison which has just been described.

Trend. The monthly percentage change in prices over the ten year period is given for each series in Table 4-4. The trends of only two commodities differed substantially (chlorine and boxes)—in both cases

TABLE 4-4

Monthly Percentage Trends of Prices of Public and Private Buyers, 1957–66

	Monthly Percentage Change		
Commodity	Public	Private	Public Minus Private
Book and magazine paper	.084	.034	.050
Chlorine, in bulk	−.323	−.098	−.225
Paper boxes and shipping containers [a]	−.116	.006	−.122
Passenger automobile tires	−.098	−.146	.048
Portland cement	.036	.082	−.046
Regular gasoline	−.090	−.064	−.026
Residual fuel oil	−.172	−.144	−.028
Truck tires	−.108	−.119	.011

[a] July 1960 to July 1966.

TABLE 4-5

Variances of First Differences of Logarithms of Price Indexes of
Public and Private Buyers, 1957–66

Commodity	Private Buyers	Public Buyers
Book and magazine paper	.15	1.62
Chlorine, in bulk	.12	.99
Paper boxes and shipping containers [a]	.15	1.28
Passenger automobile tires	.72	.35
Portland cement	.15	.16
Regular gasoline	.36	.21
Residual fuel oil	1.17	1.44
Truck tires	.44	.70

[a] July 1960 to July 1966.

public prices fell more rapidly—and the difference was statistically significant only in the case of chlorine. We have no reason to expect the trends to differ for the two sets of prices, and the trends are in fact similar.

Cyclical Analysis.   One may correctly say that there was no difference on average and hardly any in detail in the degree of conformity of price movements for public and private buyers during the reference cycles (not presented here). It would be disingenuous, however, not to add that the prices of most of these commodities were insensitive to general business fluctuations, so their agreement was to disagree with general business movements.

Short-Run Movements.   The amplitude of short-run fluctuations of the price indexes, as measured by the variance of the first difference of logarithms, is the same for public and private buyers of five of the commodities (Table 4-5). The exceptions all run in one direction: the public price movements are much larger and jerkier in the two paper products and chlorine.

There is little correspondence between the short-run movements in prices of public and private buyers; only the annual price indexes show high correlations (Table 4-6). If one permits leads or lags of one period, most of the quarterly correlation coefficients (not reproduced here) are at least .3.

The buying practices of public bodies may be the source of these low correlations. Both public and private buyers usually use contracts in purchasing the commodities in our sample. The governmental contracts, however, do not have the provision for renegotiation of price within the year which is often found in private contracts—indeed, if

TABLE 4-6

Correlation Coefficients of First Differences of Logarithms of Price Indexes of Public and Private Buyers

Commodity	Time Unit of Price Change	Correlation Coefficient
Book and magazine paper	Monthly	.01
	Quarterly	.13
	Annually	.51
Chlorine, in bulk	Monthly	.20
	Quarterly	.10
	Annually	.27
Paper boxes and shipping containers [a]	Monthly	−.23
	Quarterly	−.25
	Annually	−.94
Passenger automobile tires	Monthly	.03
	Quarterly	.21
	Annually	.26
Portland cement	Monthly	.45
	Quarterly	.48
	Annually	.22
Regular gasoline	Monthly	.13
	Quarterly	.46
	Annually	.84
Residual fuel oil	Monthly	−.13
	Quarterly	−.13
	Annually	.84
Truck tires	Monthly	.03
	Quarterly	−.01
	Annually	.44

[a] July 1960 to July 1966.

public contracts were renegotiable in a month or two, competitive bidding would be purposeless. Hence public prices will be revised less often and by larger amounts.

Conclusion. Our sample is much too small to allow a confident conclusion, but tentatively we may say: public and private buyers pay prices with similar trends and sustained movements but their short-run movements are often different in magnitude and usually in timing.

Weighted vs. Unweighted Price Indexes

Although the BLS price indexes are unweighted averages of prices reported by individual sellers, there can be no doubt that indexes using quantity weights would be preferable. Whether one wishes to use the price index to adjust sales of sellers to stable prices or to adjust costs of buyers to stable prices, there simply exists no valid reason for using unweighted indexes. This is not to say that the difference between weighted and unweighted indexes will be large; that is an empirical question we investigate here. Primary attention is devoted to unweighted indexes in this study to maintain comparability with the BLS indexes.

The data on annual rates of purchase in, or near, 1961 were sought from every company reporting prices to us, but often no quantity information could be obtained. For seventeen commodities there are a sufficiently large number of reporters who gave adequate quantity information to allow us to compile satisfactory weighted price indexes, and our comparisons are based upon these seventeen commodities. The unweighted indexes will pertain only to those reporters who reported quantities, but in general, the unweighted indexes of quantity reporters were similar to those of all reporters. The seventeen commodities are listed in Table 4-7.

Trend. For eleven of the seventeen commodities the trend of the weighted index was downward relative to that of the corresponding unweighted index.[9] The eleven relative declines of the weighted indexes were in general larger in absolute value than the six relative increases: the mean difference in trends was $-.045$ per month or about $-.5$ per

---

[9] For only one commodity, electric motors, did the trend of the unweighted index differ substantially between all price reporters and the reporters also giving quantities: the respective slopes were $-.262$ and $-.048$. Our comparisons are nevertheless between weighted and unweighted indexes for identical reporters.

TABLE 4-7

Monthly Percentage Rates of Change of Weighted and Unweighted
Price Indexes, 1957–66

| Commodity | Percentage Change | | Difference in Percentage Change |
	Weighted Index	Unweighted Index	
Aluminum sheet	−.246	−.199	−.047
Copper magnet wire	−.100	+.033	−.133
Zinc	+.242	+.225	+.017
Regular gasoline	−.095	−.082	−.013
Residual fuel oil	−.073	−.118	+.045
Passenger car tires	−.309	−.181	−.128
Paper, book and magazine	−.008	+.057	−.065
Paper boxes and shipping containers	−.153	−.034	−.119
Sulfuric acid	+.030	+.022	+.008
Caustic soda	−.170	−.121	−.049
Chlorine	−.109	−.100	−.009
Ammonia	−.066	−.091	+.025
Benzene	−.323	−.316	−.017
Phthalic anhydride	−.759	−.797	+.037
Polyvinyl chloride	−.559	−.532	−.027
Tetracycline	−.983	−.651	−.332
Electric motors	−.008	−.048	+.040

year; the corresponding figures are −.027 per month or about −.3 per year if the large difference for tetracycline is omitted.

This comparison deals with trends of prices, not their absolute levels, so the downward tendency of prices to large-quantity buyers has no direct connection with quantity discounts. We suspect that the same forces which, we shall see, lead to a secular fall of NB prices relative to BLS prices in general are operative here. Indeed, since our study is based upon large buyers generally, and BLS prices are probably those quoted to small buyers, the same issue arises in BLS-NB and weighted-unweighted index comparisons (see Chapter 5, p. 56).

Cyclical Behavior. The differences in cyclical behavior of the weighted and unweighted indexes of prices are of trifling magnitude during reference cycle expansions and contractions. Almost never (four times in sixty-five opportunities) is there a difference in direction of price movement, and the differences in magnitude are usually quite small. The conformity to business contractions is unaffected by the use of trend-corrected indexes, but conformity to expansions is measurably improved with trend-corrected prices—and generally conformity is excellent in both directions.

Short-Run Fluctuations. The amplitude of short-run movements in the weighted price indexes is on average quite substantially larger than in the corresponding unweighted price indexes (Table 4-8). In eleven of seventeen commodities the former variance is greater, and

TABLE 4-8

Variances of First Differences in Logarithms of Weighted and
Unweighted Price Indexes, 1957–66

Commodity	Weighted Index	Unweighted Index
Aluminum sheet	1.63	1.98
Copper magnet wire	5.15	2.17
Zinc	7.78	6.29
Regular gasoline	1.64	0.32
Residual fuel oil	3.88	0.99
Passenger car tires	4.08	5.60
Paper, book and magazine	0.26	0.21
Paper boxes and shipping containers	1.13	0.28
Sulfuric acid	0.16	0.22
Caustic soda	0.73	0.36
Chlorine	0.19	0.13
Ammonia	4.31	1.23
Benzene	3.73	4.38
Phthalic anhydride	7.24	9.51
Polyvinyl chloride	5.26	3.43
Tetracycline	2.95	4.87
Electric motors	0.29	0.46

TABLE 4-9

Correlation Coefficients of Weighted and Unweighted Price Indexes

Correlation Coefficient	Monthly Data	Quarterly Data
Price Indexes		
.95 or more	9	9
.90 to .95	3	3
.85 to .90	1	1
.80 to .85	1	1
.75 to .80	0	1
.70 to .75	1	0
.65 to .70	0	0
.60 to .65	1	1
Less than .60	1	1
Total	17	17
First Differences of Logarithms of Price Indexes		
.95 or more	1	2
.90 to .95	2	4
.85 to .90	5	3
.80 to .85	2	2
.75 to .80	1	3
.70 to .75	1	0
.65 to .70	0	1
.60 to .65	2	1
Less than .60	3	1
Total	17	17

often much greater, than the latter variance. The weighted indexes are dominated by a few large buyers, as a rule, so a part of the larger variance of weighted indexes is presumably due to smaller *effective* sample size.[10] Each of the underlying price series usually has many zero price changes between adjacent time periods, but the average index for a group of series tends to have fewer zero changes and to move more

[10] The number of buyers necessary to account for at least 80 per cent of total quantity weights, varied as follows:

Buyers	Commodities
1–3	8
4–6	5
7 or more	4

smoothly; hence in the small sample range the variance of first differences of logarithms of the indexes diminishes as sample size rises. Nevertheless the agreement between the weighted and unweighted indexes is fairly good. Not only do the indexes lie close together, but also their movements are well correlated: the mean correlation of the first differences of the logs of the monthly series is .77 (Table 4-9).

Conclusion. Subject to the limitation of a fairly small sample of commodities, we may conclude that the unweighted indexes agree well with the weighted indexes in their short-run and cyclical movements, but the weighted indexes fall relative to the unweighted indexes over the ten-year period. This latter finding anticipates and reinforces a major finding in our comparison of NB and BLS indexes, to which we now turn.

5

Comparison of Indexes for
Individual Commodities

We come now to the formidable task of proofing the pudding of price indexes we have prepared. Price indexes are available for sixty-four more or less "specific" commodities, reproduced in Appendix C, and seven other commodities which we do not present for obligation of confidentiality. The present chapter compares the BLS and NB price indexes with respect to trend, cyclical fluctuations, and short-run movements. Chapter 6 extends the comparisons to price indexes of groups of commodities.

TREND

The varieties of distrust of quoted prices are numerous, but perhaps no one has suggested that there ought to be a secular bias in the quoted prices. Compounding is so formidable a process that eventually grotesque and surely purposeless discrepancies would arise between list and transaction prices. In very long periods this argument must be valid; list prices that have lost all relationship to transaction prices simply would not be published.[1]

It is truly a surprising finding of our study, therefore, that the BLS indexes have a strong upward tendency relative to our indexes. The

---

[1] Sometimes only the structure of prices, and not the level, is conveyed by list prices: for example, various sizes of glass sell in proportion to list prices but at discounts sometimes exceeding 80 per cent.

unweighted average monthly rate of change of our indexes for the decade is −.107 per cent whereas that of the BLS is −.068 per cent— a difference of .039, or 1 per cent every two years (Table 5-1). The difference in trend, it should be observed, was essentially zero in the first five years and almost twice as large (.73 per cent a year) in the second five-year period. If we consider two trends equal if they differ by less than .025 per month (or ⅓ per cent per year), in the latter five years there are fourteen prices which have equal trends, eighteen series in which the BLS index rose less rapidly than the NB index, and thirty-eight series in which the BLS index rose more or fell less rapidly. We shall postpone to the next chapter a discussion of the industrial areas in which marked differences in trends of prices occurred; here it will suffice to say that in the chemical products the excess of BLS over NB trends was especially large.

TABLE 5-1

Difference Between the Monthly Rates of Change, BLS and NB Indexes

BLS Change *Minus* NB Change (per cent)	Number of Commodities		
	1957–66 [a]	1957–61 [a]	1962–66
−.20 or less	1	5	3
−.20 to −.15	0	0	2
−.15 to −.10	2	4	3
−.10 to −.05	8	7	3
−.05 to −.025	3	6	7
−.025 to 0	6	9	3
0 to .025	13	5	11
.025 to .05	8	10	2
.05 to .10	10	9	11
.10 to .15	6	7	6
.15 to .20	7	3	8
.20 to .25	3	1	2
.25 or more	1	2	9
Total	68	68	70
Average	.037 [b]	.002	.061

[a] Excludes two products for which 1957–61 data are not available.

[b] An average difference of .039 is obtained if we include 1962–66 rates of change for the two products referred to in the preceding footnote.

The upward trend of BLS prices relative to NB prices is for the most part independent of questions of statistical coverage: it is equally evident for commodities for which we have few and many reporters.[2]

Perhaps the simplest explanation for the difference in trend of BLS and NB prices would be that there is inertia in quoted prices relative to transaction prices. The possibility at each moment that soon there will be a reversal of movement and the existence of costs of making changes in quoted prices, together imply that there should be a lag of quoted behind changed transaction prices. This argument is on its face symmetrical for both price increases and price decreases, but two factors tend to make the lags longer for price reductions.

The first factor is the general experience of all industrial prices. This has been an age of inflation, and therefore, on average, price reductions are reversed more often than price increases. The second factor is the growing intervention of the federal government in the fixing of quoted prices in conspicuous industries (for example, in the "guideline" policies). A reduction in quoted prices will be more difficult to reverse than a price increase, and a price freeze as of a recent date cannot be wholly impossible in this age of war. We encountered many businessmen who were acutely aware of the growing threat of public intervention in pricing.

A partial statistical test of this argument is provided by Table 5-2. We should expect that when transaction prices (measured by NB indexes) are rising, BLS prices will also rise—the rise in price should be registered rather promptly for both customers and the public price collecting agency. When transaction prices are falling, however, the quoted prices should lag because of the factors just discussed. This pattern is

[2] The effect of number of NB reporters may be summarized:

Number of NB Reporters	Number of Commodities	Number with Higher BLS Trend	Mean Difference in Trend per Month (BLS–NB) (per cent)	Standard Deviation of Difference in Trend (per cent)
Under 5	20	11	.025	.170
5 to 10	15	7	.045	.080
10 to 20	18	9	.043	.107
20 or more	17	9	.046	.084

TABLE 5-2

Comparison of Differences in Trends of Prices, BLS Minus NB, with Trend
of NB Price Index

BLS Minus NB Average Monthly Trend	Average NB Monthly Rate of Change (per cent)		
	Falls More Than −.05	−.05 to +.05	Increases More Than .05
1957–66			
Positive	18	6	4
Negligible (±.05%)	13	8	9
Negative	7	1	4
Total	38	15	17
1962–66			
Positive	25	3	8
Negligible (±.05%)	4	7	12
Negative	4	2	5
Total	33	12	25

in fact found in the data: for the whole period, and particularly in the
last five years, there is a vast preponderance of positive differences
between BLS and NB monthly price trend slopes in the case of falling
prices, and no systematic difference in slopes when transaction prices
are rising.[3]

If this hypothesis on asymetrical lags is tentatively accepted, it raises
an important question: does the lag in registering price reductions
eventually stabilize? The main reason for delay in registering this year
the fall in transaction prices over the previous year or two—uncertainty
as to the persistence of the reduction—would lead one to reduce quoted
prices after the lower level was reliably established. A *steady* fall in
transaction prices should, on this line of argument, be registered more

[3] A X^2 test may be applied to the data underlying either panel of Table 5-2,
with the null hypothesis that there will be an equal number of positive and
negative differences in slope in periods of falling prices as in the periods of
stable or rising prices. For 1962–66, for example, X^2 is 29.92 with two degrees
of freedom, and the probability that the differences could arise by chance is much
less than .01.

promptly than an irregular fall. The determination of the secular bias in quoted prices is a new problem of price behavior.

CYCLICAL BEHAVIOR

The aspect of price behavior upon which the literature of administered and rigid prices has placed emphasis is cyclical behavior: how do prices respond to the alternating periods of expansion and contraction of aggregate economic activity? We have already observed that the decade covered by our price indexes fortunately does not contain any severe and extended contractions, and this must be kept in mind in the following discussion. We examine first the changes in the price indexes during the cyclical phases, then briefly discuss what little additional evidence we have on price flexibility.

Cyclical Patterns of Price Behavior

Classical theory leads one to expect prices to fall in competitive industries during a business contraction, because both demand and marginal production costs fell, and that reverse movements will occur in expan-

TABLE 5-3

Monthly Percentage Rates of Price Change During Two Business Contractions, 1957–58 and 1960–61 Combined, Sixty-Eight Commodities

Percentage Change in NB Index	Percentage Change in BLS Index							
	−.5 or Less	−.5 to −.2	−.2 to −.1	−.1 to −.05	−.05 to +.05	.05 to .1	.1 to .2	.2 or More
−.5 or less	13	2			2	1		
−.5 to −.2	1	3	2		2	1	1	2
−.2 to −.1					2	1		1
−.1 to −.05		1	1		3			1
−.05 to +.05					7	3		
+.05 to .1					1	3	2	
.1 to .2					2	1	2	2
.2 or more								5

sions. This expectation was not subjected to elaborate analysis perhaps because a similar pattern was expected under monopoly. Here too, marginal costs would fall and there was no strong reason to expect marginal revenues to rise, although a price reduction was no longer a *necessary* result of a leftward shift in demand and cost functions.[4] The great impact of Means' writings on administered prices is attributable to the contradiction of this expectation by the price statistics.

What is the verdict of the present price data? We tabulate average monthly rates of price change during the two reference cycle contractions in Table 5-3. In summarizing the data we treat the class −.05 to +.05 per cent as showing no change and also show a tabulation excluding prices of steel products because they provide so large a share of all nonconforming price indexes:

Price Changes	All Prices		Excluding Steel Products	
	BLS	NB	BLS	NB
Decreases	23	40	23	40
No change	19	10	16	7
Increases	26	18	18	10

There are two NB price movements in the expected direction for each perverse change; in the BLS indexes the expected and perverse movements are virtually equal. Contrary to a widely held view, there is substantial cyclical conformity in the nonsteel prices. Neither the number of price reporters nor the level of concentration in the industry whose prices are reported has a clear effect upon cyclical conformity.[5]

The results are qualified, but not reversed, if we measure price changes during contractions from trend-corrected data, using the constant per-

---

[4] For an illustrative discussion of these expectations, see J. Niehans, "Kartelle und Preisflexibilität", *Schweizerische Zeitschrift für Volkswirtschaft und Statistik*, Vol. 94, 1958, pp. 315–28.

[5] The data on concentration and price behavior during contractions may be tabulated:

NB Price	Concentration Ratio			
	Under 25	25 to 50	50 to 75	75 and Over
Decreases	5	15	12	8
No change (±.05%)	0	2	7	2
Increases	0	8	9	1

TABLE 5-4

Monthly Percentage Rates of Price Change During Two Business
Expansions, 1958–60 and 1964–66 Combined, Seventy Commodities

Percentage Change in NB Index	Percentage Change in BLS Index								
	−.5 or Less	−.5 to −.2	−.2 to −.1	−.1 to −.05	−.05 to +.05	.05 to .1	.1 to .2	.2 to .5	.5 or More
−.5 or less	2								
−.5 to −.2	1	2	1		1				
−.2 to −.1		1	2	1	4	1			
−.1 to −.05		0	0		1	2			
−.05 to +.05		1	1		7	2	1	2	
+.05 to .1		1	1		2	1	3	1	
.1 to .2					3	3	4	0	
.2 to .5					2		2	5	
.5 or more								3	6

centage trends for the period 1957–61. The tabulation of trend-corrected changes is:

Price Changes	All Prices		Excluding Steel Products	
	BLS	NB	BLS	NB
Decreases	25	32	23	31
No change	19	24	12	17
Increases	24	12	22	9

The main impact of trend correction, it will be observed, is to change numerous NB price index increases and decreases to no change. One may of course question the accuracy of the estimates of trend based upon a short period and a single constant-percentage rate of change equation. However, when we segregate those price indexes for which the constant percentage trend fits well (judged by the correlation with time), the trend correction of the prices has the same effect upon the cyclical price patterns as that reported above.

A comparable analysis may be made of the reference expansion of 1958 to 1960 and of the brief, strong upsurge of 1964 to 1966 (see Table 5-4). The cyclical pattern may be summarized:

Price Changes	Original Price Indexes		Trend-Corrected Indexes	
	BLS	NB	BLS	NB
Increases	36	37	36	43
No change	20	14	23	23
Decreases	14	19	11	4

The BLS and NB price indexes, uncorrected for trend are essentially identical in their behavior. This time the trend correction increases the conformity to expectations for the National Bureau indexes.[6] Although we do not report the two expansions separately, it is worth reporting that cyclical conformity was only fair in the 1958 to 1960 expansion but very good in the 1964 to 1966 expansion. Again neither the number of reporters nor level of concentration influenced cyclical conformity.[7] The 1961–66 expansion could be analyzed similarly, but the period is so long that we expect cyclical effects to be swamped by secular effects of technical progress so there is no longer a definite "expected" price behavior.[8]

Our general conclusion, then, is that the behavior of industrial prices in business cycles is not perverse. In fact, on balance we found slightly

[6] The prices of steel products fall primarily in the "no change" class. The trend-corrected tabulation excluding steel prices is:

	BLS	NB
Increases	34	40
No change	14	15
Decreases	11	4

[7] The tabulation of price changes, not corrected for trend, as related to concentration ratios is:

	Concentration Ratio			
NB Price	Under 25	25 to 50	50 to 75	75 and Over
Increases	4	15	13	5
No change	1	4	7	2
Decreases	0	6	8	5

[8] For what it is worth, the tabulation for 1961–66 is:

Price Changes	Original Data		Trend Corrected	
	BLS	NB	BLS	NB
Increases	29	21	22	28
No change	18	15	38	35
Decreases	23	34	8	15

In order to preserve some pretense that trend and cycle phase are distinct in this long period, the trends are based upon the ten-year period.

better conformity of prices and business changes in contractions than in expansions prior to trend corrections. The widely held belief in the "ratchet" behavior of industrial prices is contradicted by our study.[9]

Frequency of Price Change

We have already summarized evidence which essentially destroys the significance of the reported frequency of price changes in the BLS data (see p. 18). The NB price data are not easily brought to bear upon the matter. Since half our individual price reports are based upon contract data, and many of the remainder upon quarterly or other averages (which may also be based upon contracts), we cannot attach a simple meaning to a direct count of price changes.[10] Certain inferences on frequency of price change may nevertheless be made from our contract data:

(1) Certain prices change—if at all—always in one particular month, say September, because a firm price is contracted for twelve months. Then a price change or nonchange may occur each September covered by the price series, but of course only in that month. A price has missed an opportunity to change if it does not change between August and September.

(2) Other prices change sporadically and irregularly because the contract may be renegotiated when market conditions change appreciably. A change or nonchange may then occur in every month, but realistically not repeatedly in closely adjacent months simply because

---

[9] The reference cycles mark off a class of fluctuation in general business conditions; specific cycles is the name given by the National Bureau to the corresponding fluctuations in individual industries and markets. (See A. F. Burns and W. C. Mitchell, *Measuring Business Cycles,* New York, NBER, 1946, Ch. 2.) A variant of the specific cycles was defined for our study. It measured substantial movements (20 per cent or more) in seasonally corrected output series, persisting eight to ten months. Such cycles occur mostly in the first four years of our period. The behavior of BLS and NB price indexes during such "specific cycles" was examined (and is described more fully in Appendix D). Our results are essentially negative, neither price index generally moved in agreement with output changes. In the absence of a method of identifying demand and supply induced changes in output, and of reasonably full information on inventories, it did not seem useful to present this inquiry in the text.

[10] In fact, since interpolation is used to incorporate incomplete data, see Appendix B, our price indexes also contain price changes which are irrelevant to the question of frequency of price change.

TABLE 5-5

Frequency of Changes in Price Indexes and Number of Reporters,
December 1961 to December 1965

Number of Companies Reporting Prices	Average	Number of Products
Annual contracts with fixed terms: Actual price changes as percentage of possible changes		
1	58.3	12
2	67.7	7
3	50.2	5
4 or more	78.3	8
Annual contracts with variable term: Number of price changes		
1	3.7	15
2	5.0	9
3	8.8	6
4 or more	13.5	4
Monthly price series: Number of price changes		
1	6.2	27
2	12.9	15
3	15.7	9
4 or more	21.9	9

the purpose of the contract is to reduce negotiating costs. If the market price changes so frequently and substantially, either there will be no contracts or they will contain escalation factors.

In addition we have continuous monthly prices for some commodities. For each of these three classes of prices we may compare actual with possible changes in the index of prices.

We have then one class of price reporters, fixed contracts, from whose price indexes we calculate the ratio of actual to possible price changes, and two classes of price reporters, renegotiable contracts and monthly price series, where we present the actual number of changes in the price index. The averages of these measures by number of price reporters are given in Table 5-5.[11] We find that there is positive relationship between

[11] The indexes on which Table 5-5 were based were recomputed on the bases of the indicated types of price series. For example, the annual contract indexes

frequency of price change and number of price reporters, but one vastly weaker than McAllister found in the BLS data. Whereas the BLS pattern is baffling—how can one seller ignore changes in the price of the same commodity made by rivals?—our pattern is plausible. Irregular purchases and changes of supplier lead one to expect more price changes as the number of buyers rises.

SHORT-RUN MOVEMENTS

Amplitude of Short-Run Movements

We begin our comparison of short-run movements with a study of the magnitude of these fluctuations. The BLS indexes usually change less frequently than the NB indexes, in fact the *median* monthly change in the BLS indexes is often zero. But the movements of the BLS index are large and jerky, so the variance of these movements is usually larger than that of the NB. We may illustrate this sort of difference by the example of ammonia, our illustrative commodity in Chapter 4. We take the first differences in the logarithms of the price indexes as our measure of relative price change, and these differences are tabulated in Table 5-6. The NB distribution is intuitively much more plausible than the BLS distribution, which would reflect a world of alternating rigidity and fitful shifts in supply and demand conditions.

The variances of the first differences of the two price indexes of each commodity are compared in Table 5-7; the square roots of these variances are of course the standard deviations of the percentage changes in monthly indexes. In general the pattern of ammonia is reproduced:

BLS variance exceeds NB variance   38 commodities
Two variances are approximately equal
        (diagonal)   26 commodities
BLS variance less than NB variance   6 commodities

The main verdict of the comparison of variances is that the short-run movements of the BLS indexes are on average substantially more irregular, the respective means are 1.92 per cent for the NB index and 3.64 per cent for the BLS index.

---

are based only upon reporters giving annual contract prices for the four-year period.

TABLE 5-6

Distribution of First Differences in the Logarithms of the Monthly BLS
and NB Indexes: Ammonia
(number of months)

Percentage Change [a]	BLS	NB
5.0 to 10.0	4	—
2.5 to 5.0	5	2
1.5 to 2.5	2	2
1.0 to 1.5	—	0
0.5 to 1.0	—	7
Over 0.0 to 0.5	—	16
Zero	101	45
Under −0.0 to −0.5	—	28
−0.5 to −1.0	—	12
−1.0 to −1.5	—	3
−1.5 to −2.5	—	2
−2.5 to −5.0	1	1
−5.0 to −10.0	6	1
Total	119	119
Mean	.040	−.103
σ	2.789	.898

[a] Relative difference $(\times 10^2)$ = percentage change.

Timing of Short-Run Movements

A second characteristic of short-run movements is timing. Do the NB
price indexes move parallel to BLS price indexes and, if not, does one
index systematically lead or lag the other? We seek to answer these
questions by correlating the movements of the indexes (or, more precisely, the first differences in the logarithms of the indexes over periods
of one month and longer). We spare the reader the larger part of the
computer's verbosity since the results are disappointing.

There is no close agreement in the monthly movements of the two
indexes (see Table 5-8): the mean correlation coefficient is only .32
for the monthly comparisons and it is chiefly in the metals that there are
any considerable number of coefficients greater than .7. The coefficients
could arise because of small differences in the dating of price changes
in the two indexes, but the facts are exactly the opposite. When the
nonsimultaneous correlations are higher than simultaneous ones, both

TABLE 5-7

Variances (× 10⁴) of First Differences of Logarithms of Monthly Price Indexes

NB Variance	BLS Variance							
	Under .25	.25–1	1–2.25	2.25–4	4–6.25	6.25–9	9–16	16 and over
Under .25	7	9		3	1			
.25–1	1	11	3	2	1	2		1
1–2.25	1	1	3	3		1		
2.25–4		2	1	1	6	1		
4–6.25					3	1		
6.25–9						1	1	
9–16								
16 and over								3
σ = √Variance	Under .5%	.5–1	1–1.5	1.5–2	2 –2.5	2.5–3	3–4	4 and over

TABLE 5-8

Distribution of Coefficients of Correlation of First Differences in Logarithms
of BLS and NB Price Indexes, Monthly, Quarterly, Semiannual, and Annual
Changes

Correlation Coefficient	Monthly Changes	Quarterly Changes	Semiannual Changes	Annual Changes
Less than −.3	0	0	3	4
−.3 to −.2	0	1	0	1
−.2 to −.1	3	1	0	0
−.1 to 0	1	1	4	1
0 to .1	17	5	3	1
.1 to .2	10	8	1	0
.2 to .3	6	9	5	5
.3 to .4	8	9	5	4
.4 to .5	9	4	5	4
.5 to .6	4	5	9	11
.6 to .7	0	7	7	4
.7 to .8	5	9	6	7
.8 to .9	6	7	11	14
.9 to 1.0	1	4	11	14
Average	.32	.45	.54	.59

are usually small.[12] Conceivably, the poor agreement between the indexes is partly due to the existence of a considerable number of BLS price series in which there were very few price changes. We may separate out the BLS series in which the price changed at least thirty times, or once every four months, to obtain short-run movements of "active" BLS price indexes. The extent of agreement between the BLS and NB indexes is not changed by the exclusion of "inactive" BLS series: many of the largest and smallest correlation coefficients are eliminated.[13]

[12] We exclude nonsimultaneous correlation coefficients smaller than .18, which is approximately the 5 per cent significance level with $n = 119$.

[13] The distribution is as follows:

Correlation Coefficient	Number of Commodities	Correlation Coefficient	Number of Commodities
−.2 to −.1	2	.3 to .4	5
−.1 to 0	1	.4 to .5	4
0 to .1	3	.5 to .6	2
.1 to .2	3	.6 to .7	0
.2 to .3	1	.7 to .8	1

TABLE 5-9

Large Quarterly Price Changes (5 Per Cent or More) in BLS and
NB Indexes

	Changes in BLS Indexes		
Changes in NB Indexes	Increases of 5 Per Cent or More	Changes of Less than 5 Per Cent	Decreases of 5 Per Cent or More
Increases of 5 per cent or more	26	23	0
Changes of less than 5 per cent	40	2,473	56
Decrease of 5 per cent or more	0	27	49

Large Price Changes

The difference between the BLS and NB price indexes with respect to large price changes has already been remarked. If we define a large price change as one of 5 per cent or more in a *quarter,* the BLS price indexes had 171 such changes and the NB price index, 125—out of a possible number of some 2,700 quarterly price changes in each case. These larger changes in the two sources agreed only moderately well. There were no instances in which large changes occurred in opposite directions but many where only one index showed a large change (see Table 5-9).

Conclusion

Price indexes based upon buyers' prices should, but don't, lag behind price indexes based upon sellers' prices. We infer that the quoted prices lag behind the changes in transaction prices by an unknown but appreciable time interval. The NB and BLS indexes are not very closely related in timing, and the BLS index usually has many smaller and a few larger price changes than the NB index. Accordingly, the BLS short-run price movements are suspect, and the NB short-run movements are subject to the lags of contractual pricing. At present there is little hope of accurately measuring the short-run changes in transaction prices other than those for contractual purchasers.

6

Indexes for Commodity
Groups and for All
Commodities Included

The seventy price indexes that constitute the heart of our material have made anonymous appearances in the preceding chapter. We now regroup the prices in their traditional categories. These group price indexes, unlike the individual commodity price indexes, are weighted indexes, based upon the 1958 values of shipments of the commodities.[1] The same weights and the same commodity coverage are of course used for both BLS and NB indexes. The commodity groups are listed in Table 6-1. The extent of the NB coverage of the various BLS commodity groups is measured by the relative importance of the commodities included in the NB indexes. The coverage is reasonably good in basic industrial raw materials but almost negligible in machinery and fabricated goods. We discuss the first five broad commodity classes and then a more comprehensive price index. The tables and charts for the remaining three commodity classes for which we have only token representation are given at the end of the chapter.

METALS AND PRODUCTS

The BLS and NB price indexes for steel products and for nonferrous metals are presented in the two panels of Figure 6-1. They have little

[1] When a commodity first appears in a later year, it is brought in at its relative importance in that year. For example, if X and Y are combined with 1958 weights, and Z begins in 1961, Z is combined with X and Y on the basis of their

TABLE 6-1

Percentage of BLS Commodity Categories Covered by NB Indexes and Comparable BLS Indexes, Based upon December 1961 Relative Importance

Metals and Products	30
Finished steel products	66
Nonferrous metal products	60
Primary refinery shapes	58
Mill shapes	77
Wire and cable	64
Fuel and Related Products	46
Petroleum and products	86
Rubber and Products	43
Tires	93
Synthetic rubber	93
Paper, Pulp and Allied Products	67
Paper, converted paper and paperboard products	72
Chemicals and Allied Products	29
Industrial chemicals	28
Inorganic chemicals	43
Organic chemicals	19
Paints and paint materials	55
Plastic materials	82
Pharmaceutical preparations, ethical	42
Nonmetallic Mineral Products	21
Flat glass	100
Electrical Machinery and Equipment	8
Lumber and Wood Products	9
All Industrial Commodities	19

in common beside their metallic nature, and we therefore discuss them separately.

The BLS and NB prices of steel products move together so closely that a description of one is a description of the other (see Table 6-2). The upward trends in price are essentially the same: .05 per cent monthly (BLS) vs. .03 per cent monthly (NB). Neither index displays a noticeable cyclical movement in either expansion or contraction. Nor are the short-run fluctuations of appreciable size.

relative values in 1961. These 1961 relative values are 1958 value of shipments times the price relative for 1961 on 1958.

This finding, it must be confessed, comes as a surprise to us. The steel industry is now unconcentrated as compared with the first decade of the century, or indeed as compared with many other industries in

Figure 6-1

Metals and Products: Comparison of BLS and NBER Price Indexes of Product Groups

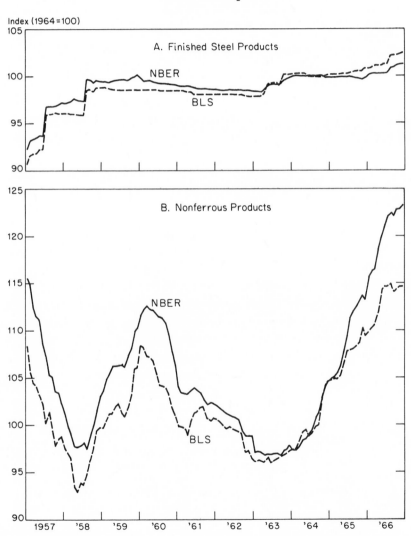

TABLE 6-2

Finished Steel: Comparison of BLS and NBER Price Indexes

	BLS	NBER
Trend		
Monthly Percentage Rate of Increase	.052	.032
Cycle		
Average Monthly Percentage Rates of Change		
Peak to Trough	.067	.077
Trough to Peak	.101	.066
Average Monthly Percentage Rates of Change		
Corrected for Trend		
Peak to Trough	−.024	.002
Trough to Peak	.020	.007
Short Run		
Correlation of First Differences of Logarithms		
Monthly	.946	
Quarterly	.944	
Semiannually	.932	
Variances of First Differences of Logarithms	.225	.156

our sample. Import competition was growing fairly steadily during the period. With the exception of three steel products, however, we were not able to learn of any important and continuous departures from quoted prices. The exceptions were reinforcing bars (where we saw, but could not obtain, records of extensive short-run price fluctuations), pipe, and stainless steel products. One encounters minor incidents of price cutting such as quantity discounts granted on small orders and the supply of qualities somewhat better than minimum specifications. Nevertheless the general picture was one of close adherence to quoted prices even for very large buyers of steel.[2]

In nonferrous metals the story is more complex (see Table 6-3). The large reversal of trend leads us to calculate trends for subperiods, and

[2] Allegations of wide-spread, informal price cutting in steel products were made in 1968, in the *Wall Street Journal* of October 7. For example, "A steel buyer for one large appliance plant says certain mills have agreed to forego until January a $5.50-a-ton increase in the price of cold-rolled sheet, the industry's biggest-volume product. What's more, he says the cold-rolled sheet currently is available at $15 to $20 a ton below the $150-a-ton list price".

TABLE 6-3

Nonferrous Metal Products: Comparison of BLS and NBER Price Indexes

	BLS	NBER
Trend		
Monthly Percentage Rate of Increase		
1957–63	−.038	−.102
1964–66	.516	.769
1957–66	.068	.045
Cycle		
Average Monthly Percentage Rates of Change		
Peak to Trough	−.760	−.917
Trough to Peak	.456	.628
Average Monthly Percentage Rates of Change		
Corrected for Trend		
Peak to Trough	−.805	−.919
Trough to Peak	.281	.430
Short Run		
Correlation of First Differences of Logarithms		
Monthly	.626	
Quarterly	.834	
Semiannually	.924	
Variances of First Differences of Logarithms	.949	.748

in each of them the NB index has a stronger trend. The greater rise in the NB index in 1964–66 reflects the more rapid rise in transaction prices than in quoted prices, which were under "guideline" control. The general agreement of cyclical and short-run movements is excellent.

FUEL AND RELATED PRODUCTS

The great preponderance of our fuel price data pertains to petroleum products (Figure 6-2 and Table 6-4). The great volatility of the BLS index, as compared with the NB index, is ascribable to the large role of contracts and quarterly average prices in the latter index, particularly for the large number of railroads reporting diesel oil purchases. Subject to this difference in type of price (the BLS has essentially a spot

Figure 6-2

Petroleum and Products: Comparison of BLS and NBER Price Indexes of
Product Groups

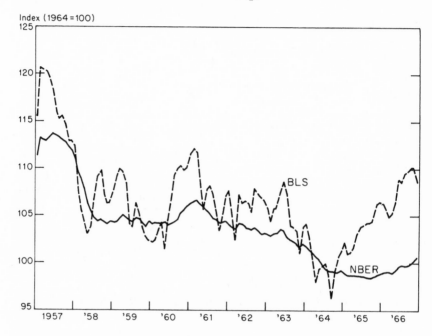

price), the two indexes show fairly similar cyclical patterns (except
that the NB index rose little in 1965 and 1966). The more rapid secular fall of the NB index is due exclusively to this difference in the last
two years.

The NB price index for coal, the only other fuel covered by our
study, is based upon prices paid by large transportation companies.
The NB index falls about one-half per cent a year until 1964 and then
rises substantially, whereas the BLS index falls about three-quarters
per cent a year until 1965. The NB index, which is based largely upon
long-term contracts, does not have the seasonal fluctuations evident in
the BLS index. The two indexes differ so much in coverage that no
useful comparison of details is possible.

TABLE 6-4

Petroleum and Products: Comparison of BLS and NBER Price Indexes

	BLS	NBER
Trend		
Monthly Percentage Rate of Increase	−.064	−.098
Cycle		
Average Monthly Percentage Rates of Change		
Peak to Trough	−.180	−.164
Trough to Peak	.161	−.045
Average Monthly Percentage Rates of Change		
Corrected for Trend		
Peak to Trough	−.040	−.035
Trough to Peak	.227	.069
Short Run		
Correlation of First Differences of Logarithms		
Monthly	.431	
Quarterly	.497	
Semiannually	.779	
Variances of First Differences of Logarithms	2.528	.156

RUBBER AND PRODUCTS

On average the BLS and NB indexes agree tolerably on rubber products (Figure 6-3 and Table 6-5). The agreement in tires, which are not shown separately, was close for the decade but not for shorter periods, and in synthetic rubber the NB index fell more rapidly. The NB index conforms more closely to business fluctuations and displays much smaller short-run fluctuation. The short-run fluctuations of the two indexes, however, are completely uncorrelated: the BLS index exhibits large and sudden price changes, often with complete reversals within a month or two, which are totally absent from the NB series.

PAPER, PULP AND ALLIED PRODUCTS

The agreement between the BLS and NB price indexes for paper and pulp products is broadly satisfactory, but poor in two respects (Figure 6-4 and Table 6-6). Neither price index has a strong trend, but the

Figure 6-3

Rubber and Products: Comparison of BLS and NBER Price Indexes of
Product Groups

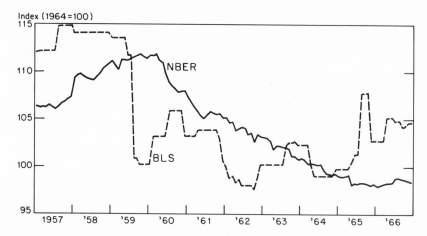

TABLE 6-5

Rubber and Products: Comparison of BLS and NBER Price Indexes

	BLS	NBER
Trend		
Monthly Percentage Rate of Increase	−.099	−.112
Cycle		
Average Monthly Percentage Rates of Change		
Peak to Trough	.046	−.028
Trough to Peak	−.099	.007
Average Monthly Percentage Rates of Change		
Corrected for Trend		
Peak to Trough	.275	−.015
Trough to Peak	−.035	.072
Short Run		
Correlation of First Differences of Logarithms		
Monthly	−.011	
Quarterly	−.113	
Semiannually	−.205	
Variances of First Differences of Logarithms	1.955	.161

Figure 6-4

Paper, Pulp and Allied Products: Comparison of BLS and NBER Price
Indexes of Product Groups

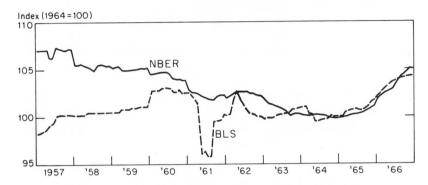

TABLE 6-6

Paper, Pulp and Allied Products: Comparison of BLS and NBER Price
Indexes

	BLS	NBER
Trend		
Monthly Percentage Rate of Increase	.015	−.049
Cycle		
Average Monthly Percentage Rates of Change		
Peak to Trough	−.013	−.194
Trough to Peak	.139	.091
Average Monthly Percentage Rates of Change		
Corrected for Trend		
Peak to Trough	−.028	−.113
Trough to Peak	.107	.125
Short Run		
Correlation of First Differences of Logarithms		
Monthly		.120	
Quarterly		.240	
Semiannually		.493	
Variances of First Differences of Logarithms	.493	.089

NB index falls almost two-thirds of 1 per cent per year while the BLS index drifts upward slightly. The NB index is also considerably more sensitive to business down-turns and omits the four-month break in prices in 1961 reported by the BLS.

CHEMICALS AND ALLIED PRODUCTS

The NB composite index for all chemicals falls more rapidly than the BLS index, but in other respects the series agree fairly well (see Figure 6-5 and Table 6-7). The differences in trends varied substantially among categories of chemicals: by .8 per cent a year, for industrial chemicals; by .6 per cent a year, for paints and materials; by 1.4 per cent a year for plastics; by zero, for ethical pharmaceutical preparations. The trend-corrected NB price indexes consistently conformed better than the BLS indexes to cyclical changes for each of these four commodity classes.

Figure 6-5

Chemicals and Allied Products: Comparison of BLS and NBER Price Indexes of Product Groups

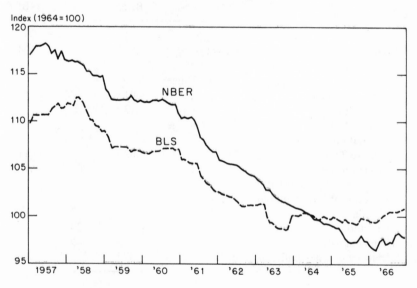

TABLE 6-7

Chemicals and Allied Products: Comparison of BLS and NBER Price Indexes

	BLS		NBER
Trend			
Monthly Percentage Rate of Increase	−.113		−.188
Cycle			
Average Monthly Percentage Rates of Change			
Peak to Trough	−.004		−.160
Trough to Peak	−.077		−.097
Average Monthly Percentage Rates of Change			
Corrected for Trend			
Peak to Trough	.124		−.006
Trough to Peak	.002		.062
Short Run			
Correlation of First Differences of Logarithms			
Monthly		.233	
Quarterly		.548	
Semiannually		.608	
Variances of First Differences of Logarithms	.129		.131

THE COMPREHENSIVE INDEX

The comprehensive NBER index, with commodities combined on the basis of their 1958 aggregate values, is presented in Figure 6-6 (and see also Table 6-8), together with the corresponding BLS index. The BLS index of nonfarm prices is also shown, to indicate the difference in price behavior of "all" industrial goods and the commodities in our sample.

The finding that the NB prices have a tendency to fall secularly relative to BLS prices is so general in the individual series that, of course, it is found in the comprehensive indexes: the difference is about .4 per cent per year. The difference in trend does not become significant or persistent until after 1961.

The cyclical patterns of the two indexes are similar. Both series rise moderately in cyclical expansions; they fall .13 (BLS) and .21 (NB) per cent per month during contractions. (The decline of the BLS index

Figure 6-6

All Industrial Commodities: Comparison of BLS and NBER Price Indexes
of Product Groups

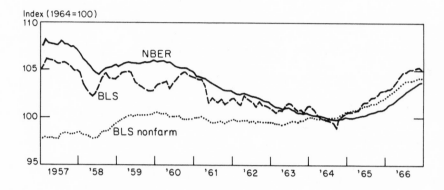

TABLE 6-8

Comparison of the Comprehensive BLS Index with the Corresponding
NBER Index for All Industrial Commodities

	BLS		NBER
Trend			
Monthly Percentage Rate of Increase	−.026		−.060
Cycle			
Average Monthly Percentage Rates of Change			
Peak to Trough	−.129		−.205
Trough to Peak	.118		.079
Average Monthly Percentage Rates of Change			
Corrected for Trend			
Peak to Trough	−.082		−.140
Trough to Peak	.117		.111
Short Run			
Correlation of First Differences of Logarithms			
Monthly		.378	
Quarterly		.576	
Semiannually		.728	
Variances of First Differences of Logarithms	.202		.042

in 1959 and early 1960 is attributable to the large break reported in BLS rubber and petroleum prices.)

The short-run movements of the two comprehensive indexes differ substantially. Even at this aggregate level the BLS index has larger, jerkier movements, and its variance of monthly changes is much larger

Figure 6-7

Nonmetallic Mineral Products: Comparison of BLS and NBER Price Indexes of Product Groups

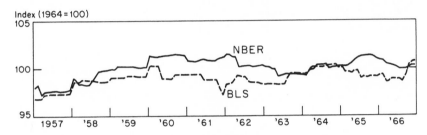

TABLE 6-9

Nonmetallic Mineral Products: Comparison of BLS and NBER Price Indexes

	BLS	NBER
Trend		
Monthly Percentage Rate of Increase	.013	.015
Cycle		
Average Monthly Percentage Rates of Change		
Peak to Trough	.083	.012
Trough to Peak	.019	.062
Average Monthly Percentage Rates of Change		
Corrected for Trend		
Peak to Trough	.053	−.060
Trough to Peak	−.006	.023
Short Run		
Correlation of First Differences of Logarithms		
Monthly	.305	
Quarterly	.123	
Semiannually	−.040	
Variances of First Differences of Logarithms	.124	.081

The Behavior of Industrial Prices

Figure 6-8

Electrical Machinery and Equipment: Comparison of BLS and NBER Price
Indexes of Product Groups

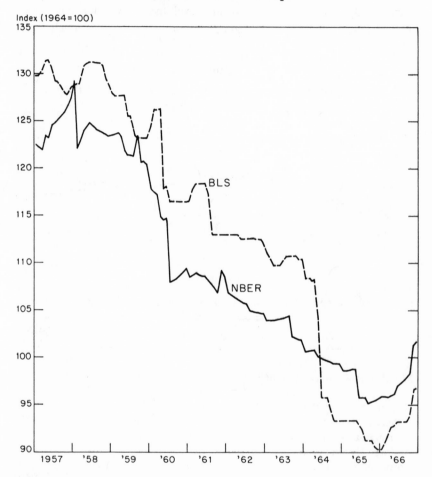

than that of the NB index. The timing of movements is also only
moderately close.

It is a traditional characteristic of index numbers which purport to
represent broad categories of transactions that they are remarkably unresponsive to changes in coverage and method of computation. Irving

TABLE 6-10

Electrical Machinery and Equipment: Comparison of BLS and NBER Price Indexes

	BLS	NBER
Trend		
Monthly Percentage Rate of Increase	−.344	−.262
Cycle		
Average Monthly Percentage Rates of Change		
Peak to Trough	−.123	−.352
Trough to Peak	−.113	−.134
Average Monthly Percentage Rates of Change		
Corrected for Trend		
Peak to Trough	.138	−.041
Trough to Peak	.247	.114
Short Run		
Correlation of First Differences of Logarithms		
Monthly	.170	
Quarterly	.253	
Semiannually	.333	
Variances of First Differences of Logarithms	1.597	1.110

Fisher italicized his conclusion: "All index numbers which are not freakish or biased practically agree with each other".[3] Measured by this exacting standard of difference, the NB and BLS indexes differ appreciably.

[3] *The Making of Index Numbers,* Boston, 1922, p. 360.

Figure 6-9

Lumber and Wood Products: Comparison of BLS and NBER Price Indexes
of Product Groups

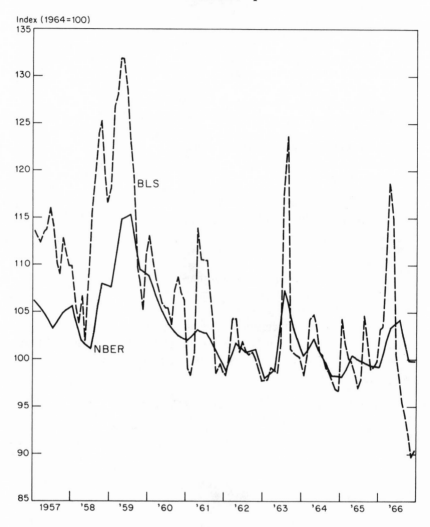

TABLE 6-11

Lumber and Wood Products: Comparison of BLS and NBER Price Indexes

	BLS		NBER
Trend			
Monthly Percentage Rate of Increase	−.148		−.063
Cycle			
Average Monthly Percentage Rates of Change			
Peak to Trough	−.850		−.214
Trough to Peak	−.096		.090
Average Monthly Percentage Rates of Change			
Corrected for Trend			
Peak to Trough	−.680		−.166
Trough to Peak	−.011		.114
Short Run			
Correlation of First Differences of Logarithms			
Monthly		.411	
Quarterly		.507	
Semiannually		.800	
Variances of First Differences of Logarithms	16.513		.894

7

The Dispersion
of Price Movements

The Unique Price, as we observed, is a myth. Differences among prices paid or received are almost universal. They arise for good cost reasons: economies of lot size, differences in quality tolerances. They arise also, at times, because of systematic price discrimination. They arise because it is uneconomic—still another cost basis—to collect full, continuous information on prices.

For at least some, and possibly all, of these reasons the relative movements of prices paid or received do not march together with fixed cadence. The individual price relatives which constitute a price index almost invariably display some dispersion. This dispersion can arise from differences in timing of purchases or sales, as well.[1] An annual average of the standard deviations of these monthly movements is reported with each of our price series in Appendix C. The average value of this standard deviation for ammonia, for example, is 1.145: with a normal distribution some two-thirds of the individual ammonia prices change each month by the average amount of the change in the index (.403 per cent in absolute value) ±1.145 per cent. Measures of the dispersion of price movements are the subject of the present chapter.

THE DETERMINANTS OF DISPERSION

If there were a unique price, there would be a unique price change from one date to the next. The converse is less simple. It would be

[1] For example, if a seller raises his price 5 per cent on January 1 but an irregular buyer does not purchase again until March, almost any interpolation or linking procedure will give a different time profile to seller's than to buyer's price.

possible that there was no dispersion of movement even with dispersion of prices, at a given time, because the differentials due to transportation costs, quality, lot size, etc., were stable. The dispersion in prices due to incomplete knowledge, however, would lead to dispersion of price movements. If seller A has a price 3 per cent higher than B today, and yet makes sales because of incomplete price search by buyers, it is unlikely that A and B will change prices simultaneously and in identical proportion, and impossible if *they* have incomplete knowledge of all prices. Hence the theory of information, which is concerned with dispersion of prices, is also relevant to the dispersion of price movements. We now adapt it to this end.

The buyer who seeks the best price and supplier at time t will also seek the best price at time $(t + 1)$. He will search the market—the potential suppliers—until the marginal gain from further search is no larger than the cost. Since the cost of search is much the same for a large buyer and a small buyer, we expect the larger buyer to search more intensively; therefore obtaining a lower price. We also expect the price movements of large buyers to have less dispersion than those of small buyers.[2]

The dispersion of prices is probably also a function of the number of sellers. The reason one must say "probably" is that the intractable problem of oligopoly appears. As the number of sellers increases from one to many, one expects the probability of independent price behavior by the several sellers to rise—and in good part precisely because it becomes more expensive to police any agreements on price.

The dispersion of prices is also dependent upon the rate of change of prices in the market. If "the" conditions of supply and demand were

---

[2] In period 1 let the prices asked by sellers be uniformly distributed between 0 and 1, so after n searches a buyer on average encounters a minimum price of $1/(n + 1)$, with variance $n/(n + 1)^2(n + 2)$. (For a derivation, see G. Stigler, *The Organization of Industry*, Homewood, Ill., 1968, pp. 173–74.)

In period 2 let the distribution of asking prices shift upward by k, so the mean rises by k and the variance is unchanged. The mean price change is k, and the variance of the price change is

$$\sigma^2_{P_{t+1} - P_t} = \frac{2n}{(n + 1)^2(n + 2)}.$$

The variance of the price change is smaller, the larger n (the number of price searches made by a buyer); and n is larger, the larger the buyer. If the prices at the two dates are correlated, as usually they will be, the variance of the price change is smaller the larger the correlation between prices at the two dates.

to remain the same forever, buyers would gradually learn of the existence of lower prices (and sellers, of higher prices) and shift to the lower price sellers (and sellers to higher price buyers) until dispersion was eliminated. Changes in supply and demand conditions not only prevent this asymptotic approach to complete knowledge but also reduce the rewards from intensive search in any period.

Some Empirical Investigations

For any one commodity, we expect the standard deviation of individual price changes about the mean (index) change ($\sigma_{\Delta p}$) to be larger, the larger the fluctuations in the (mean) price in the market. This effect should be the same with both price increases and price decreases, so we take the standard deviation of the index of prices σ_p as our measure of price change. We accordingly fit to each industry's semiannual data an equation,

$$\sigma_{\Delta p} = a + b\sigma_p,$$

with the expectation that b is positive. The standard deviations pertain to the same period, e.g., $\sigma_{\Delta p}$ is based upon the six changes (from December 1964) in the first six months of 1965 and σ_p is based upon the fluctuations of the index during these six months.

The results strongly support the expectation: without exception the regression coefficients for the seventy commodities are positive. Moreover, the regression coefficients are, in general, highly significant: sixty of the seventy t-ratios are in excess of two, and forty are in excess of four.[3] The elasticity of the variance of price relatives with respect to the variance of the price index is usually between .3 and .8.

We also investigate the comparative dispersion of price relatives in different industries. It is then possible to introduce the average concentration ratio (C) for producers of the commodity and the number of price reporters (N). This latter variable is positively, but probably loosely, related to the number of buyers of a commodity because we collected our data by presenting the same commodity list to each company when requesting data. Here the regression equation takes the form

$$\sigma_{\Delta p} = a + b\sigma_p + cC + dN$$

Here we expect that $b > 0, c < 0, d > 0$.

---

[3] Most of the products with low t-ratios have only a small number of price series.

The regression equation derived from the data for all seventy products is:

$$\sigma_{\Delta p} = \underset{(.203)}{.620} + \underset{(.073)}{.432\,\sigma_p} - \underset{(.0028)}{.0062\,C} + \underset{(.0041)}{.018\,N,}$$

$$R^2 = .404 \qquad df = 66$$

where the standard errors are given in parentheses under the regression coefficients. The results are gratifyingly kind to our expectations:

(1) The larger the fluctuations in the rate of change of a price index, the larger the dispersion of the rates of change of the individual price series (where the latter variable is an average of 119 monthly measures). The fluctuations of average prices serve to render obsolete the knowledge of prices in the market, and hence to lead to price dispersion.

(2) The dispersion of price series is smaller, the higher the concentration ratio for sellers (where C is the share in total sales of the four largest producers in 1958). High concentration implies fewer sellers, and a lesser task of obtaining information on market prices.

(3) The dispersion is greater, the larger the number of price series (measured at February 1962). The strength of the relationship is a little surprising. The number of price series in our sample is no doubt positively correlated with the true number of buyers, but this correlation may not be large. Still, the larger the number of buyers, the larger is the informational problem in the market. The argument is symmetrical for buyers and sellers.

When the standard deviation of prices $(\sigma_{\Delta p})$ and of price index changes (σ_p) are measured over each year, and the various years are treated as dummy variables, the regression coefficients are virtually the same as in the equation above. There is a modest tendency for the variance of prices to rise over the early years of the period, but this probably reflects the rising number of price series available in these years.[4]

[4] The equation, with the T's representing dummy variables for the years denoted by subscripts, becomes:

$$\sigma_{\Delta p} = \underset{(.026)}{.488\,\sigma_p} - \underset{(.0013)}{.0048\,C} + \underset{(.0018)}{.0162\,N} + \underset{(.116)}{.399\,T_{1957}} + \underset{(.115)}{.499\,T_{1958}}$$

$$+ \underset{(.114)}{.478\,T_{1959}} + \underset{(.114)}{.573\,T_{1960}} + \underset{(.113)}{.611\,T_{1961}} + \underset{(.112)}{.734\,T_{1962}}$$

$$+ \underset{(.113)}{.762\,T_{1963}} + \underset{(.113)}{.757\,T_{1964}} + \underset{(.112)}{.765\,T_{1965}} + \underset{(.113)}{.659\,T_{1966}}$$

$$R^2 = .390$$

TABLE 7-1

The Effect of Antitrust Complaints Upon the Level of Prices

Commodity	Date of Complaint or Indictment	Average Price: 3 Months after Complaint [a]		Average Price: 9 Months after Complaint [a]	
		Direct	Adjusted [b]	Direct	Adjusted [b]
Carbon steel sheet	7/64	100.00	100.04	99.73	99.72
Aluminum conductor cable	10/62	96.92	98.88	88.55	91.93
Gasoline (mid-Atlantic)	4/65	100.38	100.50	98.79	99.12
Rubber belting	3/59	100.05	99.64	100.69	99.42
Chlorine	12/64	96.77	96.79	95.42	95.96
Soda ash	12/64	100.00	99.95	100.00	100.57
Tetracycline	8/61	95.90	n.a.	91.70	n.a.
Terramycin	8/61	93.23	n.a.	89.26	n.a.
Meprobamate	1/60	94.73	n.a.	96.15	n.a.

[a] The average price for same number of months preceding the date of complaint = 100.
[b] Adjusted prices are deflated by prices of other commodities of the same general category.
n.a. = data not available for adjustment.

PRICE BEHAVIOR AND ANTITRUST CASES

Although our choice of commodities for the present study was wholly unrelated to the problem of monopoly, it happens that nine of our commodities were involved in antitrust cases with convictions for price-fixing during the period of our study.[5] These cases are listed in Appendix E, and the commodities are given in Table 7-1. The cases are dated in the month when the complaint or indictment was filed.

We are obviously unequipped to discuss the economic merits of these cases, but we can assess the effects of bringing the cases on the level and the variance of prices. Does the bringing of the case lead to a reduction of prices? Two answers are given in Table 7-1. One is based upon the mean price index in the three and nine months preceding the

[5] There were also a few cases involving mergers (Section 7, Clayton Act) but they do not raise any conventional questions about price behavior. We also omit price-fixing cases involving a *regional* offense where we do not have data for a regional price index.

date of the charge (complaint or indictment) and the mean price in the succeeding three and nine months. A second answer is obtained if the pre- and post-complaint prices are adjusted for movements of similar commodities not involved in the case (using the price index of the other commodities of the same general category).

The only commodities whose prices fell appreciably after a case was brought were the pharmaceutical drugs (in this area we had no satisfactory comparable products whose prices might be used to adjust for changes in general market conditions) and aluminum cable. Perhaps even this degree of impact is all one can expect. Antitrust cases pay much more attention to attempts to collude than to success in raising prices.

The variance of movements of prices paid by buyers can be measured in the behavior of both the price index and the individual buyers' prices. For the price index, we compare the variance of the price index in the nine months preceding and succeeding the beginning of the complaint, corresponding to the longer period in which the level of the index has been studied. The variance of the price relatives of the individual buyers' prices is also calculated for nine month periods. We would expect both

TABLE 7-2

The Effects of Antitrust Complaints upon the Variance of Price Index and of Individual Buyer's Prices

	Variance of Price Index		Variance of Individual Buyer's Prices	
	9 Months		9 Months	
Commodity	Before	After	Before	After
Carbon steel sheet	.156	.301	.135	1.656
Aluminum conductor cable	23.325	9.610	5.420	6.966
Gasoline (mid-Atlantic)	1.590	.208	8.938	.384
Rubber belting	.113	.430	.093	.193
Caustic soda	.760	.313	3.107	2.588
Chlorine	.292	.975	1.912	2.532
Tetracycline	16.073	24.663	7.563	15.074
Terramycin	26.586	3.535	16.479	18.622
Meprobamate	2.446	.604	.677	.857

these variances to increase substantially after a complaint is brought if there had been collusion and if it was weakened or terminated when the complaint was brought.[6] The results are given in Table 7-2.

The results are thoroughly puzzling. In four cases (gasoline, aluminum cable, terramycin, and meprobamate) there were large *declines* in the variance of the price index over time after the case was brought; and in one case, tetracycline, a large increase. The variances of individual price relatives in the indexes were slightly more in keeping with our expectations. Only one variance, gasoline, fell appreciably and several rose modestly. The antitrust history appears to shed little light upon price behavior in our sample.

[6] See G. Stigler, "A Theory of Oligopoly", *Journal of Political Economy*, February 1964, pp. 44–61.

Transcriptional Editing

of Raw Data

DATA COLLECTION

Firms and agencies made information available to us in one of three ways. Some gave permission for us to transcribe the relevant information directly from the records; others made available photo-reproduced copies of the records; still others preferred to send (at a date subsequent to the interview) specially prepared tabulations of the relevant data. The last procedure was the option chosen by most of the cooperating private firms; about two-thirds of the cooperating public agencies either allowed us to make reproductions of the relevant records or to copy information directly from the original records.

Where possible we copied the information from the records. We could then exercise a degree of quality control over transcription errors and look for relevant notations which might not be recorded by a firm's own transcriber. (The average degree of quality control actually exercised by others may have been higher or lower than ours, but others' transcriptions were undoubtedly more variable in quality.) However, the transcription of the data for us was only the final step in the processing of data by the firms: most reporters apparently took the information from summary records maintained for their own use, not from original invoices. (The number of invoices which come through the purchasing department of a large industrial firm is very large. The invoices themselves are typically used for no internal purposes other than the clerical operations of checking arrival of shipments and arranging payment.) Thus there were one or more steps of data transcription prior to entering the information on the form sent to us. Clerical errors inevitably appeared in some of the data sent to us or copied by us. The larger of these errors were, hopefully, caught by our checks for internal consistency and our review of large price changes and unusual timing of price changes.

Errors may also have arisen due to reports of nontransaction prices. In a few cases we encountered hostility to our study from subordinates assigned the task of cooperating with us. Usually it took the form of noncooperation, but on occasion it may have led to erroneous price quotations. Indolence, as well as hostility, led in some cases to the reporting of list prices (including in one case, copies of Bureau of Labor Statistics prices). We of course accepted list prices where they were reported to be paid, but not where they were given simply because the true records were inaccessible.

EDITING OF DATA

The price series reported to us were subjected to scrutiny from several points of view. We attempted to be sure that each price series represented quotations on a single commodity at different points in time; ideally, there would be no change in physical specifications of the commodity, its point of delivery, its approximate lot size, or in any of the other terms of sale or purchase. We also eliminated series whose information content was slim. In addition, certain prices were adjusted to take account of additional information in the report from the informant. These adjustments are discussed in detail below.

Minimal Coverage Requirements

Certain requirements were imposed on each series to eliminate those with very small amounts of information. First, no series was utilized if it had a gap of more than sixteen months between adjacent observations. Whenever a gap of such magnitude appeared, the total series was treated for computational purposes as if it were two independent series. Second, each series was required to extend over at least twenty-four months (i.e., the last quotation had to refer to a date at least twenty-four months after the earliest). Third, the number of months in which a price quotation was recorded had to be at least four. (These latter two tests were applied to series *after* they had been broken into two or more series because of gaps of over sixteen months, if necessary.) A series which failed to meet these requirements of coverage was deleted from the study.

Requirements for Product Homogeneity

Clearly a price series is less valuable if there are changes in any of the specifications relevant to the price. Our editing procedure for this problem was as follows:

(1) Whenever a change in any of the specifications was discovered, the series was linked, if possible at that point. Linking could be accomplished only when information on the prices of both the old and new specifications were available on the same date. This information was usually not available.

(2) Whenever a change in specifications could not be linked in, the price series was marked as being subject to a specification change at that date. In further analysis, "the" series were treated as two different series, one ending with the last observation before the specification change, the other beginning with the first observations on or after the date of the change.

Often serious problems were faced in deciding whether there had been a specification change, and we called upon the respondent for additional information. In general, any of the following were treated as changes in specifications unless we were specifically assured by the informant that the change had no effect on price: any change in physical description; change in f.o.b. point; unquantified change in credit terms; change in services provided by seller as a condition of sale; sizable change in lot size or volume of purchase over a period of time. Usually our doubts could be cleared up by the price reporter. There remains, of course, the problem of unreported changes in specifications. Our main defense against unreported specification changes was to examine each series for large shifts in the level of prices, and to inquire specifically if there were changes in specifications at such times.

Quantity discounts are a particularly important and pervasive example of specification changes. Both the size of the individual order and the volume of annual purchases may affect the price for each buyer. Quantity discount schedules usually deal with a single aspect of the problem.

Thus the steel industry charges extra for orders of less than 20,000 pounds of a given type of steel but amalgamations of orders are often allowed, and amalgamations of shipments to several plants of the buyer may be allowed. The procedures used to deal with quantity discounts were:

(1) As part of general instructions, informants were asked to identify (but may not always have done so) any changes in volume or lot size which they considered to have an effect on price. These were generally marked as specification changes.

(2) Movements from one known or published quantity discount bracket to another either were marked as specification changes, if there was a once-and-for-all shift, or only observations within a bracket were kept in any one series. No attempt was made to compare prices in different quantity discount brackets.

(3) Volume changes beyond the stated quantity discount schedule were not recorded as a specification change or eliminated from consideration unless the change were of the order of magnitude of two-fold or more. Such large changes called for a consultation with the informant.

We seldom got price reports for very small quantity purchases, for two evident reasons: purchases were less likely to be continuous; and the records are not as well kept. Therefore our price series under-represent prices to buyers of small quantities.

Internal Consistency of the Data:
Special Editing by Frequency of Data

Although we sought to obtain data at monthly intervals, this was not always possible. Some firms' records were not sufficiently detailed and other firms bought on a purchase contract specifying a price (or formula to be used for computing a price) to be used for some period of time. All data were classified by a frequency code, being classified as (1) monthly series, (2) averages of prices paid over a period (annual, semi-annual, or quarterly), (3) observations on prices in purchases at regular discrete intervals (again, annually, semi-annually, monthly); (4) as contract prices prevailing over a period, or (5) as irregular data. This coding was essential for correct processing and interpretation of the data.

Contract data, if not subject to escalation provisions, report prices which are firm over the specified period. Such contracts are recorded with the specified price treated as the price in each month covered by the contract. In the case of escalated contracts, the price is computed (by us) according to the formula, and the resulting figure recorded for each month of the contract. (Since all escalations required that a specified formula be applied to a published price, this can be done unambiguously.)

All data had to be combined eventually into a monthly index. In the absence of additional information, series which were not on a monthly basis after the above operations could not provide direct information about the behavior of price in the market for the months in which no prices were reported. Nevertheless, in numerous and important cases the series implied information on the missing months which was superior to the use of interpolation by other reporters' prices, which is the basic alternative method of using broken series. These cases are as follows:

(1) A particular series has one or more months with no data. The prices on either side of the gap are identical.

In this case, it is preferable to assume that the price for the missing months was the same as it was in the months before and after the gap than to believe that it rose and then fell, or fell and rose again, to exactly the level it was originally. We have accordingly filled in all such gaps. The slight bias toward price rigidity introduced by this procedure would appear to be more than counterbalanced by the loss of information entailed by not doing it.

(2) A series of prices, each averaged over a quarter or longer period, has two or more consecutive *averages* identical. In such a case, we assume that the same price prevailed in each month covered by the averages, and that the price was equal to the average. Again, it is vastly more probable that the price was constant than that two consecutive averages of fluctuating prices came to the same average.

(3) A single company submits data on an irregular basis for two or more closely related items—e.g., two sizes of brass rod. The dates given do not always coincide; where they do, it appears that one series is a multiple of the other, or differs by a constant amount. In such cases, the several series are combined employing the constant relationship to

make one series with fewer gaps. (Of course, the two series cannot be available only for identical dates or one series would not add to the information in the other.)

In many cases a firm submitted information on closely related items—items which fell under the same product classification used for purposes of constructing index numbers, for example, six sizes of window glass. Such series were combined into one prior to construction of index numbers. This gives any one company the same weight as any other company in an unweighted average. The only problem in the mechanics of combining arose when the series to be combined had observations at different dates but there was evidence that one or more series were not linear transformations of another. Here we had to choose between two alternatives in combining the series: Do two price series for closely related commodities from a particular firm behave more like each other than they behave like the average of all series from all reporters for the commodity in question? We chose to combine series on the basis of other series from the same reporter. For most of the multiple series, no problems arose, fortunately, for they were observations on the same time period for the different series.

The Construction of
the NBER Index Numbers

This section discusses the transformation of the edited data on individual commodities from the various informants into the NBER indexes for these commodities and commodity classes.

All indexes were constructed in such a way as to make the absolute level of each price series irrelevant. This decision was dictated by the nature of the data, and all subsequent interpretations and computations had to be made compatible with this. (The reason for this requirement is explained more fully below.) Different price series could be combined either by assuming that price series tended to differ by a constant number of dollars per physical unit of product, or by assuming that price series tended to differ by a constant percentage amount. It is not hard to find appropriate examples for each assumption. Price differences due only to freight differences, or due to quantity discounts expressed in dollars independent of the price per unit, would lead to absolute differentials. Price differences stemming from discounts of the more common variety, expressed as a percentage of the same base price, would represent percentage differentials.

Ultimately the choice of percentage differentials was forced upon us by a combination of factors. Some data were available only in the form of index numbers; certain firms insisted upon expressing their data this way, so that absolute levels of price were never disclosed. In other cases, we found the degree of product heterogeneity within some categories sufficiently great that we were reluctant to compare the dollar values of various items. These and other considerations argued for the calculation of indexes which preserve percentage differences rather than absolute differences between observations within a given series. The choice was reinforced by both computational ease and our intuition of the prevalence of parallel price movements of similar commodities in percentage terms.

Since we chose to preserve percentage or relative differences in individual series over time, it follows that the average taken of individual series at each point in time must be a geometric mean, not an arithmetic one. The only information contained in an individual firm's data, once it has been subject to multiplication by an arbitrary constant, is the relative change from month to month, so a meaningful index must preserve this change; and the geometric mean does. All computations were therefore performed as arithmetic operations on logarithms of the original data.

Since neither the time span covered nor the frequency of observation was the same for all series, it was necessary to adjust individual price series. The procedure was in two main steps. For each commodity group, the first step was to select out all those series which were either monthly data to begin with, or became so as a result of editing—mostly as a result of recording contract prices in each month of the period covered. An index of such monthly data was then constructed. Second, each series which was not monthly was interpolated, for missing observations, using the previously computed monthly index as a related series, where this was possible, and linear interpolation otherwise. The set of irregular or broken series thus interpolated into monthly series was then combined into an index of nonmonthly prices; and finally, the two monthly and nonmonthly indexes were combined into a single index weighted by the number of series in each. The mechanics of these operations are discussed in some detail below.

CONSOLIDATION OF MONTHLY SERIES
INTO A SINGLE INDEX

Since the various monthly price series begin and end in different months, they are combined by averaging the monthly relatives (first differences in logarithms) for each adjacent pair of months and linking these relatives to form a continuous series. The price index is simply the antilogarithms of the resulting series, with 1964 equal to 100.

INTERPOLATION OF NONMONTHLY SERIES

All series were interpolated so that they had no gaps in the months between the first and last observations. Interpolation in this case, for purposes of constructing an average, is an eminently reasonable procedure. We cannot afford to discard all the information contained in nonmonthly data. Milton Friedman has shown that an efficient interpolation procedure commends the use of an interpolating series that is well correlated with series to be interpolated; and, furthermore, that the interpolating series be followed more closely, the better it is correlated with the series to be completed.[1]

We adapted the Friedman procedure with the price data in logarithmic form. After the index of monthly series was computed, it was used as a related series to interpolate each of the nonmonthly series in turn. From all dates at which the monthly index and the nonmonthly series both had observations, the regression coefficient was computed. The initial step was to interpolate linearly in the nonmonthly series (thus imparting constant rates of change between observations), then to transfer the appropriate multiple (the correlation coefficient multiplied by the ratio of standard deviations is the multiplier) of the corresponding deviation of the monthly index from its constant rate of change trend to the series to be interpolated. This second component was superimposed on the linear interpolation already performed. Each nonmonthly series was so interpolated using the same "related" series; however, each such series had a regression coefficient of its own and, hence, the proportion of the variation in the monthly index which was imposed on the nonmonthly series differed. In the interpolation of one particular series, no attempt was made to use information from other nonmonthly series. The computational problems involved would have become formidable. When irregular price series were available for periods in which no monthly prices were available, we used linear interpolation.

After interpolation each of the nonmonthly series became a monthly series. In combining these series into a continuous index of nonmonthly prices, the differences in beginning and ending dates of individual series were handled exactly as with the true monthly series.

[1] *The Interpolation of Time Series by Related Series,* Technical Paper No. 16, New York, NBER, 1962.

For each commodity, the nonmonthly and monthly indexes were combined into a single index, which thereby utilized all available information, in the usual manner, i.e., using as weights the number of series. This formed the fundamental NBER index for each commodity.

COMBINATION OF INDEXES

The industrial price indexes in Chapter 6 are calculated with a conventional Laspeyres formula, using the BLS value of shipment weights for 1958. The BLS indexes are also recalculated, employing only commodity price indexes for which the NB has coverage.

The weighted commodity indexes in Chapter 4 are calculated by a similar procedure, using as weights the average quantities purchased by the individual price reporters in 1960–62.

Prices of Individual

Commodities and

Commodity Groups

The price indexes compiled in this study are presented here, together with Bureau of Labor Statistics price series. In the reporting of the NBER price series three basic numbers are presented:

1. The unweighted index of prices for the commodity
2. The annual average number of month-to-month pairs of price series on which the index is based.[1]
3. The annual average of standard deviations of month-to-month relative changes in individual prices from the average change in the index for the product. (See p. 40, footnote 3.)

The average number of reporters tells something of the statistical basis of the index. The standard deviation of the price changes is a measure of the cohesiveness of the price pattern: a value of zero would indicate strict proportionality and simultaneity in the price movements of the individual series.

These data are given for the sixty-four commodities for which we had an average of three or more reporters; other commodities' indexes are omitted because of promises of confidentiality. In addition group indexes are given.

---

[1] This number, it should be noted, is often a minimum count. When a state buys fuel oil for ten hospitals, we combine the individual prices into a single price index for that buyer.

TABLES: PRODUCT INDEXES

The products in Table 3-2 not presented here are omitted to preserve confidentiality.

Metals and Products
  Finished steel
    C-1 Carbon steel, sheet and strip—cold-rolled
    C-2 Carbon steel, sheet and strip—hot-rolled
    C-3 Tinplate
    C-4 Carbon steel plates
    C-5 Carbon steel, bars and rods—hot-rolled
    C-6 Carbon steel plain pipe
    C-7 Carbon steel wire
    C-8 Stainless steel sheet and strip
    C-9 Alloy steel bars—hot- and cold-rolled
  Nonferrous metal products
    Aluminum
    C-10 Ingot and shot
    C-11 Sheet and strip
    C-12 Wire and cable
    Copper
    C-13 Ingot
    C-14 Pipe and tubing
    C-15 Wire and cable—bare
    C-16 Insulated wire
    C-17 Magnet wire
    Zinc
    C-18 Zinc products
    Brass
    C-19 Bars and rods
Fuel and Related Products
  Petroleum and products
    C-20 Regular gasoline
    C-21 Diesel and distillate fuel No. 2
    C-22 Residual fuel oil No. 6
  Coal
    C-23 Coal, bituminous
Rubber and Products
  Tires
    C-24 Passenger car tires
    C-25 Truck and bus tires

  Synthetic rubber
    C-26 Synthetic rubber, SBR, hot and cold
    C-27 Neoprene
  Miscellaneous
    C-28 Belting, industrial
Paper, Pulp and Products
    C-29 Book, magazine, etc.
    C-30 Newsprint
    C-31 Coarse paper and bags (Kraft papers)
    C-32 Paperboard—unfabricated
    C-33 Paper boxes and shipping containers
    C-34 Bond
Chemicals and Allied Products
  Chemicals
    C-35 Sulfuric acid, bulk
    C-36 Caustic soda, liquid
    C-37 Titanium dioxide
    C-38 Chlorine—bulk
    C-39 Regular oxygen
    C-40 Ammonia
    C-41 Acetone
    C-42 Acetylene
    C-43 Benzene (benzol)
    C-44 Styrene monomer
    C-45 Ethyl alcohol
    C-46 Methyl alcohol
    C-47 Glycerine, natural and synthetic
    C-48 Phthalic anhydride
    C-49 Phenol
    C-50 Polyethylene
    C-51 Polystyrene
    C-52 Polyvinyl chloride
    C-53 Phenolic resins (plastics)
  Pharmaceutical preparations, ethical
    C-54 Antibiotics
    C-55 Tranquilizers
    C-56 Cardiac glycosides

Miscellaneous
  C-57 Paint
Nonmetallic Mineral Products
  C-58 Portland cement
  Flat glass
    C-59 Plate glass
    C-60 Safety glass and window glass

Electrical Machinery and Equipment
  C-61 Electric motors, excluding DC
  C-62 Batteries
Lumber and Wood Products
  C-63 Plywood
  C-64 Car flooring

TABLES: COMMODITY GROUPS

The commodity groups in Table 6-1 not presented here are omitted to preserve confidentiality.

C-65 Metals and Products
  C-66 Finished steel products
  C-67 Nonferrous products
    C-68 Primary refinery shapes [1]
    C-69 Mill shapes [2]
C-70 Fuel and Related Products
  C-71 Petroleum and products
C-72 Rubber and Products
  C-73 Tires
  C-74 Synthetic rubber
C-75 Pulp, Paper, and Allied Products

C-76 Paper, converted paper, and paperboard products [3]
C-77 Chemicals and Allied Products
  C-78 Industrial chemicals [4]
  C-79 Paints and paint materials [5]
  C-80 Pharmaceutical preparations, ethical
C-81 Nonmetallic Mineral Products
  C-82 Flat glass
C-83 Electrical Machinery and Equipment
C-84 Lumber and Wood Products
C-85 All Industrial Commodities

[1] Includes products in Tables C-10, C-13, and C-18.

[2] Includes products in Tables C-11, C-14, and C-19. Copper and brass sheet and strip are also included but are omitted from product tables to preserve confidentiality.

[3] Includes products in Tables C-29, C-30, C-31, C-33, and C-34.

[4] Includes products in Tables C-35, C-36, C-38 through C-46, and C-49. Sodium tripolyphosphate and acrylonitrile are also included but omitted from the product tables to preserve confidentiality.

[5] Includes products in Tables C-37, C-47, C-48, and C-57.

Appendix C

Table C-1. Carbon Steel, Sheet and Strip—Cold Rolled

(price indexes, 1964 = 100)

	1957	1958	1959	1960	1961	1962	1963	1964	1965	1966
BLS										
JANUARY	90.07	94.06	96.82	96.82	96.82	96.48	96.47	99.70	100.03	100.03
FEBRUARY	90.07	94.06	96.82	96.82	96.82	96.48	96.47	100.03	100.03	100.03
MARCH	90.07	94.06	96.82	96.82	96.82	96.48	96.47	100.03	100.03	100.03
APRIL	90.07	94.06	96.82	96.82	96.48	96.48	96.95	100.03	100.03	100.03
MAY	90.07	94.06	96.82	96.82	96.48	96.48	99.70	100.03	100.03	100.03
JUNE	90.07	93.86	96.82	96.82	96.48	96.48	99.70	100.03	100.03	100.03
JULY	94.00	93.86	96.82	96.82	96.48	96.48	99.70	100.03	100.03	100.03
AUGUST	94.06	96.82	96.82	96.82	96.48	96.48	99.70	100.03	100.03	100.03
SEPTEMBER	94.06	96.82	96.82	96.82	96.48	96.48	99.70	99.98	99.98	102.03
OCTOBER	94.06	96.82	96.82	96.82	96.48	96.48	99.70	99.98	100.03	102.05
NOVEMBER	94.06	96.82	96.82	96.82	96.48	96.47	99.70	100.03	100.03	102.05
DECEMBER	94.06	96.82	96.82	96.82	96.48	96.47	99.70	100.03	100.03	102.05
NBER										
JANUARY	91.75	95.83	96.34	96.12	95.89	96.51	97.60	99.30	100.36	98.77
FEBRUARY	91.95	96.03	96.29	96.17	95.81	96.53	97.63	99.39	100.03	98.76
MARCH	92.13	95.91	95.98	96.25	95.74	96.56	97.90	99.51	100.02	98.75
APRIL	92.28	96.53	96.32	97.02	95.91	96.58	98.45	99.63	99.81	98.74
MAY	92.39	95.65	96.44	96.30	96.14	96.87	99.27	99.64	99.60	98.77
JUNE	91.97	95.37	96.60	96.35	96.07	96.76	99.39	100.22	99.52	98.83
JULY	95.57	95.05	96.74	96.33	96.09	96.86	99.26	100.29	99.44	98.90
AUGUST	95.27	96.87	96.86	96.29	96.11	96.96	99.10	100.33	99.23	98.91
SEPTEMBER	95.18	97.28	96.74	96.26	96.54	97.08	98.97	100.37	99.03	99.97
OCTOBER	94.83	96.30	97.85	96.16	96.58	97.20	98.72	100.41	98.95	100.16
NOVEMBER	95.19	97.09	96.65	96.06	96.55	97.53	98.88	100.45	98.87	100.23
DECEMBER	95.53	96.41	97.56	95.98	96.49	97.56	99.16	100.48	98.78	100.29
NBER PRICE INDEX, ANNUAL AVERAGES:										
STD. DEV.*	1.0143	1.3242	1.1433	0.8993	0.4113	0.4462	1.0320	0.5234	0.6107	0.2230
NO. OF SERIES*	7.18	8.58	9.17	9.08	11.67	13.17	14.75	15.83	14.25	8.00

* See page 105.

Table C-2. Carbon Steel, Sheet and Strip—Hot Rolled

(price indexes, 1964 = 100)

	1957	1958	1959	1960	1961	1962	1963	1964	1965	1966
BLS										
JANUARY	91.49	95.33	96.93	96.93	96.93	96.93	96.93	100.00	100.00	99.99
FEBRUARY	91.49	95.33	96.93	96.93	96.93	96.93	96.93	100.00	100.00	99.99
MARCH	91.49	94.53	96.93	96.93	96.93	96.93	96.93	100.00	100.00	99.99
APRIL	91.49	94.53	96.93	96.93	96.93	96.93	97.49	100.00	100.00	99.99
MAY	91.48	94.53	96.93	96.93	96.93	96.93	100.00	100.00	100.00	99.99
JUNE	91.48	94.25	96.93	96.93	96.93	96.93	100.00	100.00	100.00	99.99
JULY	95.33	94.25	96.93	96.93	96.93	96.93	100.00	100.00	100.00	99.99
AUGUST	95.33	96.93	96.93	96.93	96.93	96.93	100.00	100.00	99.99	102.33
SEPTEMBER	95.33	96.93	96.93	96.93	96.93	96.93	100.00	100.00	99.99	102.33
OCTOBER	95.33	96.93	96.93	96.93	96.93	96.93	100.00	100.00	99.99	102.33
NOVEMBER	95.33	96.93	96.93	96.93	96.93	96.93	100.00	100.00	99.99	102.33
DECEMBER	95.33	96.93	96.93	96.93	96.93	96.93	100.00	100.00	99.99	102.33
NBER										
JANUARY	88.40	92.29	96.67	96.94	96.93	96.90	96.80	99.77	99.15	98.99
FEBRUARY	88.63	92.83	96.68	96.94	96.90	96.91	96.76	99.89	99.21	98.99
MARCH	88.87	93.37	96.69	96.94	96.89	96.94	96.73	100.01	99.27	98.98
APRIL	89.10	93.92	96.69	96.94	96.89	96.96	96.83	100.13	99.27	98.98
MAY	89.54	93.92	96.78	96.94	96.83	96.96	98.61	100.13	99.56	99.00
JUNE	89.97	93.92	96.86	96.94	96.78	96.96	99.17	100.13	99.85	99.06
JULY	93.84	93.92	96.86	96.94	96.73	96.96	99.45	100.13	100.15	99.12
AUGUST	93.82	99.74	96.83	96.94	96.70	97.02	99.51	100.13	100.13	99.41
SEPTEMBER	93.81	98.25	96.81	96.94	96.49	97.09	99.58	100.13	100.12	99.69
OCTOBER	93.79	96.79	96.87	96.95	96.50	97.14	99.65	100.13	100.10	99.96
NOVEMBER	93.89	96.75	96.94	96.94	96.62	96.97	99.69	99.85	99.64	99.96
DECEMBER	94.00	96.71	96.94	96.94	96.74	96.81	99.73	99.57	99.18	99.96
NBER PRICE INDEX, ANNUAL AVERAGES:										
STD. DEV.*	1.9171	1.7576	0.1674	0.0145	0.2504	0.2421	0.4836	0.3858	1.0256	0.3390
NO. OF SERIES*	20.00	20.00	21.58	22.00	21.58	22.33	22.75	23.67	23.67	20.58

* See page 105.

Table C-3. Tinplate

(price indexes, 1964 = 100)

	1957	1958	1959	1960	1961	1962	1963	1964	1965	1966
BLS										
JANUARY	92.29	96.34	100.01	100.01	100.01	100.01	100.00	100.00	100.00	102.57
FEBRUARY	92.29	96.34	100.01	100.01	100.01	100.01	100.00	100.00	100.00	102.57
MARCH	92.29	96.34	100.01	100.01	100.01	100.01	100.00	100.00	100.00	102.57
APRIL	92.29	96.34	100.01	100.01	100.01	100.01	100.00	100.00	100.00	102.57
MAY	96.34	96.34	100.01	100.01	100.01	100.01	100.00	100.00	100.00	102.57
JUNE	96.34	96.34	100.01	100.01	100.01	100.01	100.00	100.00	100.00	102.57
JULY	96.34	96.34	100.01	100.01	100.01	100.01	100.00	100.00	100.00	102.57
AUGUST	96.34	96.34	100.01	100.01	100.01	100.01	100.00	100.00	100.00	102.57
SEPTEMBER	96.34	96.34	100.01	100.01	100.01	100.01	100.00	100.00	100.00	102.57
OCTOBER	96.34	96.34	100.01	100.01	100.01	100.01	100.00	100.00	100.00	102.57
NOVEMBER	96.34	100.01	100.44	100.81	100.01	100.00	100.00	100.00	99.78	102.57
DECEMBER	96.34	100.01	105.19	100.69	100.01	100.00	100.00	100.00	102.57	102.57
NBER										
JANUARY	96.10	97.38	100.07	105.58	100.75	100.49	99.53	100.61	100.16	102.84
FEBRUARY	96.10	97.81	100.15	101.27	100.80	100.56	99.61	100.49	100.29	103.44
MARCH	96.01	97.80	100.28	101.32	100.89	100.47	99.75	100.39	100.48	103.30
APRIL	95.98	97.78	100.40	101.45	100.90	100.46	99.89	100.29	100.67	103.16
MAY	96.88	97.76	100.53	101.58	100.91	100.44	100.89	100.19	100.85	103.02
JUNE	96.58	97.77	100.40	101.56	100.94	100.35	100.95	100.06	100.69	103.26
JULY	97.51	97.77	100.28	101.12	100.96	100.25	101.00	99.93	101.25	103.50
AUGUST	97.18	98.53	100.15	101.01	100.98	100.16	101.06	99.12	101.09	103.74
SEPTEMBER	97.06	98.41	99.87	101.00	100.75	99.91	101.00	99.37	100.63	103.57
OCTOBER	96.83	98.59	100.44	100.90	100.51	99.61	100.93	99.63	100.17	103.82
NOVEMBER	96.61	99.60	104.81	100.81	100.28	99.36	100.87	99.89	99.71	104.07
DECEMBER	96.95	99.99	105.19	100.69	100.42	99.45	100.74	100.02	101.75	104.60
NBER PRICE INDEX, ANNUAL AVERAGES:										
STD. DEV.*	0.5289	0.4471	0.8646	0.7310	0.2003	0.2713	0.2911	0.3988	0.7003	0.6889
NO. OF SERIES*	3.73	4.00	4.00	4.00	4.92	5.00	5.00	5.00	5.00	4.92

* See page 105.

Table C-4. Carbon Steel Plates

(price indexes, 1964 = 100)

	1957	1958	1959	1960	1961	1962	1963	1964	1965	1966
BLS										
JANUARY	87.62	93.18	96.21	96.21	96.21	96.21	96.21	100.00	100.00	100.00
FEBRUARY	89.39	93.18	96.21	96.21	96.21	96.21	96.21	100.00	100.00	100.00
MARCH	89.39	93.18	96.21	96.21	96.21	96.21	96.21	100.00	100.00	102.33
APRIL	89.39	93.18	96.21	96.21	96.21	96.21	96.21	100.00	100.00	102.33
MAY	89.39	93.18	96.21	96.21	96.21	96.21	96.21	100.00	100.00	102.33
JUNE	89.39	93.18	96.21	96.21	96.21	96.21	96.21	100.00	100.00	102.33
JULY	93.18	93.18	96.21	96.21	96.21	96.21	96.21	100.00	100.00	102.33
AUGUST	93.18	96.21	96.21	96.21	96.21	96.21	96.21	100.00	100.00	102.33
SEPTEMBER	93.18	96.21	96.21	96.21	96.21	96.21	96.21	100.00	100.00	102.33
OCTOBER	93.18	96.21	96.21	96.21	96.21	96.21	100.00	100.00	100.00	102.33
NOVEMBER	93.18	96.21	96.21	96.21	96.21	96.21	100.00	100.00	100.00	102.33
DECEMBER	93.18	96.21	96.21	96.21	96.21	96.21	100.00	100.00	100.00	102.33
NBER										
JANUARY	86.37	93.26	96.45	96.45	96.48	96.36	96.32	99.72	100.07	100.73
FEBRUARY	87.28	93.26	96.46	96.46	96.48	96.23	96.33	99.85	100.02	100.94
MARCH	88.16	93.26	96.46	96.47	96.48	96.22	96.37	99.98	99.98	101.39
APRIL	89.04	93.26	96.45	96.47	96.48	96.22	96.41	100.11	99.95	101.60
MAY	88.88	93.26	96.44	96.48	96.48	96.24	96.46	100.13	99.89	101.62
JUNE	88.73	93.23	96.44	96.48	96.49	96.27	96.50	100.15	99.86	101.61
JULY	93.12	93.20	96.43	96.48	96.50	96.30	96.53	100.14	99.85	101.84
AUGUST	93.18	96.71	96.43	96.48	96.51	96.33	96.67	100.12	99.87	101.81
SEPTEMBER	93.22	96.55	96.42	96.48	96.52	96.35	96.81	100.10	99.87	101.77
OCTOBER	93.27	96.40	96.42	96.48	96.53	96.36	98.15	100.08	99.84	101.76
NOVEMBER	93.27	96.41	96.42	96.48	96.56	96.30	98.62	99.90	100.11	101.73
DECEMBER	93.26	96.43	96.43	96.48	96.61	96.28	98.91	99.71	100.38	101.73
NBER PRICE INDEX, ANNUAL AVERAGES:										
STD. DEV.**	0.7621	0.2539	0.0447	0.0338	0.0605	0.2315	0.4499	0.4097	0.4652	0.4007
NO. OF SERIES*	20.55	22.83	24.83	25.25	26.08	26.67	28.67	30.67	29.25	24.33

* See page 105.

Table C-5. Carbon Steel, Bars and Rods

(price indexes, 1964 = 100)

	1957	1958	1959	1960	1961	1962	1963	1964	1965	1966
BLS										
JANUARY	85.57	92.79	96.40	96.40	96.40	96.40	96.39	100.00	100.00	100.00
FEBRUARY	87.74	92.79	96.40	96.40	96.40	96.40	96.39	100.00	100.00	100.00
MARCH	87.74	92.79	96.40	96.40	96.40	96.40	96.39	100.00	100.00	100.00
APRIL	87.74	92.79	96.40	96.40	96.40	96.40	96.39	100.00	100.00	100.00
MAY	87.74	92.79	96.40	96.40	96.40	96.40	96.39	100.00	100.00	101.44
JUNE	87.74	92.79	96.40	96.40	96.40	96.40	96.39	100.00	100.00	101.44
JULY	92.79	92.79	96.40	96.40	96.40	96.40	96.39	100.00	100.00	101.44
AUGUST	92.79	96.40	96.40	96.40	96.40	96.40	96.39	100.00	100.00	101.44
SEPTEMBER	92.79	96.40	96.40	96.40	96.40	96.40	96.39	100.00	100.00	101.44
OCTOBER	92.79	96.40	96.40	96.40	96.40	96.40	100.00	100.00	100.00	101.44
NOVEMBER	92.79	96.40	96.40	96.40	96.40	96.39	100.00	100.00	100.00	101.44
DECEMBER	92.79	96.40	96.40	96.40	96.40	96.39	100.00	100.00	100.00	101.44
NBER										
JANUARY	85.10	93.24	96.91	97.40	97.42	97.21	96.92	100.20	99.52	99.48
FEBRUARY	88.86	93.28	97.12	97.40	97.42	97.27	96.92	100.21	99.53	99.25
MARCH	88.07	93.30	97.28	97.41	97.43	97.30	96.88	100.20	99.55	99.04
APRIL	87.29	93.32	97.43	97.42	97.25	97.34	97.09	100.20	99.53	98.83
MAY	87.34	93.31	97.41	97.43	97.24	97.32	97.08	100.09	99.53	98.56
JUNE	87.35	93.29	97.44	97.44	97.26	97.32	97.10	99.99	99.53	98.66
JULY	92.72	93.27	97.47	97.44	97.27	97.32	97.12	99.90	99.52	98.37
AUGUST	92.87	96.99	97.50	97.44	97.31	97.33	97.41	99.90	99.52	98.85
SEPTEMBER	93.03	96.91	97.45	97.44	97.32	97.32	97.72	99.90	99.53	99.37
OCTOBER	93.20	96.83	97.40	97.44	97.36	97.32	98.63	99.90	99.53	99.88
NOVEMBER	93.20	96.86	97.36	97.44	97.34	97.17	99.17	99.80	99.53	99.89
DECEMBER	93.22	96.89	97.37	97.44	97.32	97.04	99.69	99.70	99.52	99.89

NBER PRICE INDEX, ANNUAL AVERAGES:

	1957	1958	1959	1960	1961	1962	1963	1964	1965	1966
STD. DEV.*	1.1558	0.3255	0.3358	0.0257	0.1240	0.1958	0.5527	0.3037	0.2246	1.0113
NO. OF SERIES*	20.91	21.00	21.92	22.00	22.58	23.00	24.00	25.92	25.50	23.42

* See page 105.

Table C-6. Carbon Steel, Plain Pipe

(price indexes, 1964 = 100)

	1957	1958	1959	1960	1961	1962	1963	1964	1965	1966
BLS										
JANUARY	94.56	101.96	102.29	102.29	100.19	100.19	100.19	100.19	99.81	99.32
FEBRUARY	96.69	101.96	102.29	102.29	100.19	100.19	100.19	100.19	99.81	99.82
MARCH	97.22	101.96	102.29	102.29	100.19	100.19	100.19	100.19	99.81	99.82
APRIL	97.22	101.96	102.29	102.29	100.19	100.19	100.19	100.19	99.81	99.82
MAY	97.22	101.96	102.29	102.29	100.19	100.19	100.19	100.19	99.81	99.82
JUNE	97.22	101.96	102.29	102.29	100.19	100.19	100.19	100.19	99.81	99.82
JULY	101.96	101.96	102.29	100.19	100.19	100.19	100.19	99.81	99.81	99.82
AUGUST	101.96	105.49	102.29	100.19	100.19	100.19	100.19	99.81	99.81	99.82
SEPTEMBER	101.96	105.49	102.29	100.19	100.19	100.19	100.19	99.81	99.81	99.82
OCTOBER	101.96	102.29	102.29	100.19	100.19	100.19	100.19	99.81	99.70	99.82
NOVEMBER	101.96	102.29	102.29	100.19	100.19	100.19	100.19	99.81	99.70	99.82
DECEMBER	101.96	102.29	102.29	100.19	100.19	100.19	100.19	99.81	99.82	99.82
NBER										
JANUARY	92.39	99.58	105.08	103.93	102.21	100.84	99.06	99.74	100.09	101.10
FEBRUARY	93.08	99.59	105.15	103.69	102.19	100.77	99.01	99.63	100.18	100.95
MARCH	93.78	99.60	105.22	103.46	102.18	100.70	98.95	99.52	100.27	100.83
APRIL	94.48	99.62	105.29	103.22	102.16	100.60	98.85	99.63	100.49	100.71
MAY	95.27	99.64	104.96	103.09	102.22	100.69	98.84	99.92	100.47	100.64
JUNE	96.06	99.65	104.63	102.96	102.25	100.77	98.84	100.00	100.45	100.59
JULY	96.83	99.66	104.31	102.83	101.85	100.86	98.83	100.07	100.44	100.53
AUGUST	97.63	100.90	104.23	102.94	101.85	100.43	98.89	100.14	100.48	100.58
SEPTEMBER	98.44	102.16	104.15	103.04	101.85	100.00	98.92	100.21	100.57	100.63
OCTOBER	99.26	103.43	104.08	103.14	101.85	99.58	99.21	100.28	100.67	100.68
NOVEMBER	99.37	104.31	104.37	102.76	101.94	99.41	99.38	100.37	100.83	100.68
DECEMBER	99.47	104.70	104.23	102.48	101.93	99.23	99.48	100.48	100.99	100.68
NBER PRICE INDEX, ANNUAL AVERAGES:										
STD. DEV.*	1.0875	0.6905	1.2770	0.8730	0.3592	1.0355	0.7469	1.1491	0.5804	0.2723
NO. OF SERIES*	17.55	18.00	18.92	20.00	19.92	21.00	21.67	22.00	21.83	19.08

* See page 105.

Table C-7. Carbon Steel, Wire
(price indexes, 1964 = 100)

	1957	1958	1959	1960	1961	1962	1963	1964	1965	1966
BLS										
JANUARY	86.98	96.93	100.25	100.25	100.25	100.25	100.24	100.24	99.83	101.25
FEBRUARY	89.82	96.93	100.25	100.25	100.25	100.25	100.24	100.24	99.83	101.25
MARCH	92.66	96.93	100.25	100.25	100.25	100.25	100.24	100.24	99.83	101.25
APRIL	92.66	96.93	100.25	100.25	100.25	100.25	100.24	100.24	99.83	101.25
MAY	92.66	96.93	100.25	100.25	100.25	100.25	100.24	100.24	99.83	101.25
JUNE	92.66	96.93	100.25	100.25	100.25	100.25	100.24	99.83	99.83	101.25
JULY	96.93	96.93	100.25	100.25	100.25	100.25	100.24	99.83	100.55	101.25
AUGUST	96.93	100.25	100.25	100.25	100.25	100.25	100.24	99.83	101.25	101.25
SEPTEMBER	96.93	100.25	100.25	100.25	100.25	100.25	100.24	99.83	101.25	101.25
OCTOBER	96.93	100.25	100.25	100.25	100.25	100.25	100.24	99.83	101.25	101.25
NOVEMBER	96.93	100.25	100.25	100.25	100.25	100.24	100.24	99.83	101.25	101.25
DECEMBER	96.93	100.25	100.25	100.25	100.25	100.24	100.24	99.83	101.25	101.25
NBER										
JANUARY	104.40	111.55	112.81	112.01	109.95	107.23	105.52	101.64	96.52	100.41
FEBRUARY	105.85	111.98	112.33	111.99	109.98	107.04	105.16	101.51	95.83	100.83
MARCH	106.49	112.20	112.15	111.70	109.89	106.85	104.80	101.56	95.88	101.25
APRIL	107.14	112.43	112.15	111.79	109.79	106.66	104.44	101.19	95.92	101.68
MAY	107.80	112.84	112.15	110.79	109.68	106.47	104.05	100.82	95.97	102.11
JUNE	108.49	113.26	112.15	110.52	109.47	106.28	103.68	100.33	96.01	102.54
JULY	107.83	113.78	112.12	110.24	109.10	106.07	103.25	99.94	96.16	101.42
AUGUST	108.48	112.47	112.12	109.96	108.72	105.86	102.96	99.91	96.24	103.92
SEPTEMBER	109.13	112.63	112.10	109.69	108.35	105.58	102.68	99.34	96.33	103.92
OCTOBER	109.79	112.79	112.08	109.79	107.99	105.66	102.39	98.63	96.43	104.47
NOVEMBER	110.45	112.96	112.06	109.89	107.62	105.77	102.14	97.92	96.52	104.47
DECEMBER	111.12	113.12	112.03	109.92	107.43	105.88	'01.89	97.22	96.52	104.47
NBER PRICE INDEX, ANNUAL AVERAGES:										
STD. DEV.*	1.4431	0.7307	0.1738	0.4096	0.3842	0.4296	0.8607	0.9417	0.4069	1.6645
NO. OF SERIES*	5.09	6.00	6.00	6.00	5.83	6.00	6.17	7.00	6.08	3.67

* See page 105.

Table C-8. Stainless Steel, Sheet and Strip

(price indexes, 1964 = 100)

	1957	1958	1959	1960	1961	1962	1963	1964	1965	1966
BLS										
JANUARY	113.71	118.25	118.25	114.22	114.22	110.41	107.10	101.97	98.89	98.71
FEBRUARY	113.71	118.25	118.25	114.22	114.22	110.41	107.10	101.13	98.89	98.71
MARCH	113.71	118.25	115.37	114.22	114.22	110.41	107.10	101.13	98.89	98.71
APRIL	113.71	118.25	114.76	114.22	114.22	110.41	107.10	101.13	98.89	98.71
MAY	113.71	118.25	114.22	114.22	114.22	110.41	107.10	101.13	98.89	98.71
JUNE	113.71	118.25	114.22	114.22	110.64	110.41	107.10	99.15	98.89	98.71
JULY	118.25	118.25	114.22	114.22	110.41	109.80	107.10	99.15	98.89	98.71
AUGUST	118.25	118.25	114.22	114.22	110.41	109.80	107.10	99.15	98.71	98.71
SEPTEMBER	118.25	118.25	114.22	114.22	110.41	109.80	104.86	99.15	98.71	98.71
OCTOBER	118.25	118.25	114.22	114.22	110.41	108.10	102.72	99.15	98.71	98.71
NOVEMBER	118.25	118.25	114.22	114.22	110.41	107.10	101.97	98.89	98.71	100.76
DECEMBER	118.25	118.25	114.22	114.22	110.41	107.10	101.97	98.89	98.71	102.18
NBER										
JANUARY	109.02	110.51	110.51	109.23	108.72	104.80	103.79	101.04	100.41	98.58
FEBRUARY	109.02	110.51	110.51	109.23	108.74	104.80	102.93	101.13	100.74	98.11
MARCH	109.02	110.51	110.15	109.23	108.76	104.80	100.83	99.86	101.06	97.64
APRIL	108.27	110.51	110.15	109.23	108.59	104.80	100.84	99.44	101.38	97.17
MAY	108.27	110.51	110.15	108.53	107.06	104.80	100.86	99.53	100.86	97.15
JUNE	108.27	110.51	110.15	108.55	104.80	104.80	100.87	99.62	100.34	97.11
JULY	110.51	110.51	110.15	108.58	104.80	104.82	100.87	99.70	99.82	97.11
AUGUST	110.51	110.51	110.15	108.61	104.80	104.83	100.87	99.78	99.31	97.11
SEPTEMBER	110.51	110.51	110.15	108.64	104.80	104.85	100.87	99.86	98.79	97.11
OCTOBER	110.51	110.51	110.15	108.66	104.80	104.86	100.87	99.93	99.70	96.70
NOVEMBER	110.51	110.51	110.15	108.66	104.80	104.88	100.87	100.01	99.38	96.50
DECEMBER	110.51	110.51	110.15	108.69	104.80	104.89	100.95	100.09	99.06	96.09
NBER PRICE INDEX, ANNUAL AVERAGES:										
STD. DEV.*	0.3040	0.0000	0.0446	0.2288	0.3656	0.0146	0.4524	0.3631	1.0418	0.5952
NO. OF SERIES*	1.82	2.00	2.92	3.50	4.92	5.00	5.08	6.00	6.00	2.25

* See page 105.

Table C-9. Alloy Steel Bars—Hot and Cold Rolled

(price indexes, 1964 = 100)

	1957	1958	1959	1960	1961	1962	1963	1964	1965	1966
BLS										
JANUARY	90.39	95.82	98.50	98.50	98.50	98.50	98.49	100.24	99.27	103.20
FEBRUARY	90.83	95.82	98.50	98.50	98.50	98.50	98.49	100.24	99.27	104.15
MARCH	91.25	95.82	98.50	98.50	98.50	98.50	98.49	100.24	99.67	104.15
APRIL	91.25	95.82	98.50	98.50	98.50	98.50	98.49	100.24	99.75	104.15
MAY	91.25	95.82	98.50	98.50	98.50	98.50	98.49	100.24	99.75	104.15
JUNE	91.43	95.82	98.50	98.50	98.50	98.50	98.49	100.24	99.75	104.84
JULY	93.82	95.82	98.50	98.50	98.50	98.50	98.49	100.24	103.20	104.84
AUGUST	93.82	98.50	98.50	98.50	98.50	98.50	98.49	100.24	103.20	105.09
SEPTEMBER	93.82	98.50	98.50	98.50	98.50	98.50	98.49	100.24	103.20	105.12
OCTOBER	95.82	98.50	98.50	98.50	98.50	98.50	100.24	99.27	103.20	105.19
NOVEMBER	95.82	98.50	98.50	98.50	98.50	98.49	100.24	99.27	103.20	105.24
DECEMBER	95.82	98.50	98.50	98.50	98.50	98.49	100.24	99.27	103.20	105.85
NBER										
JANUARY	91.93	96.07	98.31	98.31	98.21	98.21	97.70	100.27	99.94	100.42
FEBRUARY	92.37	96.07	98.31	98.31	98.21	98.21	97.82	100.30	99.94	100.42
MARCH	92.56	96.07	98.31	98.31	98.21	98.21	97.94	99.94	99.94	100.42
APRIL	92.56	96.07	98.31	98.31	98.21	98.21	97.94	99.94	99.94	100.42
MAY	92.56	96.07	98.31	98.31	98.21	98.21	97.94	99.94	99.94	101.00
JUNE	92.56	96.07	98.31	98.31	98.21	98.21	97.91	99.94	99.93	101.90
JULY	96.07	96.07	98.31	98.31	98.21	98.21	97.88	99.94	100.52	101.90
AUGUST	96.07	98.31	98.31	98.31	98.21	98.12	97.85	99.94	100.51	101.90
SEPTEMBER	96.07	98.31	98.31	98.31	98.21	98.03	97.82	99.94	100.49	101.90
OCTOBER	96.07	98.31	98.31	98.31	98.21	97.94	100.18	99.94	100.48	101.90
NOVEMBER	96.07	98.31	98.31	98.31	98.21	97.94	100.21	99.94	100.46	102.80
DECEMBER	96.07	98.31	98.31	98.31	98.21	97.82	100.24	99.94	100.45	102.80
NBER PRICE INDEX, ANNUAL AVERAGES:										
STD. DEV.*	0.0438	0.0377	0.0000	0.0000	0.0140	0.0613	0.1204	0.0479	0.1227	0.1100
NO. OF SERIES*	2.00	2.00	2.92	3.00	3.00	3.83	5.00	5.00	5.00	2.25

* See page 105.

Table C-10. Aluminum, Ingot and Shot

(price indexes, 1964 = 100)

	1957	1958	1959	1960	1961	1962	1963	1964	1965	1966
BLS										
JANUARY	106.14	107.10	103.08	112.28	108.11	99.52	93.41	97.72	103.22	107.09
FEBRUARY	104.14	104.81	103.08	112.28	108.11	99.52	93.82	97.72	104.21	107.09
MARCH	104.95	104.81	103.08	112.28	108.11	99.52	93.82	99.21	104.21	107.09
APRIL	103.73	100.56	103.08	112.28	106.07	99.52	93.82	99.21	105.18	107.09
MAY	103.11	100.56	103.08	112.28	106.07	99.52	94.81	99.21	107.09	107.09
JUNE	102.08	100.56	105.09	110.32	106.07	99.52	94.81	100.53	107.09	107.09
JULY	104.74	100.56	107.04	110.32	106.07	99.52	95.41	100.53	107.09	107.09
AUGUST	108.53	103.08	107.04	110.10	105.02	99.52	95.41	100.53	107.09	107.09
SEPTEMBER	107.51	103.08	107.04	108.11	100.53	96.41	95.41	100.53	107.09	107.09
OCTOBER	106.49	103.08	107.04	108.11	100.53	96.41	97.72	100.53	107.09	107.09
NOVEMBER	106.49	103.08	107.04	108.11	100.53	97.04	97.72	101.52	107.09	107.09
DECEMBER	107.10	103.08	107.04	108.11	100.53	93.41	97.72	102.78	107.09	107.09
NBER										
JANUARY	110.34	104.83	102.95	112.76	106.68	100.43	94.98	98.68	102.97	107.61
FEBRUARY	107.06	104.00	104.09	113.09	106.13	100.06	95.51	98.82	103.42	107.53
MARCH	105.61	102.44	104.48	113.08	105.98	99.81	95.83	98.92	103.17	107.02
APRIL	105.12	100.94	104.99	112.51	105.99	99.74	96.28	99.24	105.29	106.87
MAY	105.59	100.36	105.03	112.04	105.40	99.99	96.10	99.34	107.01	107.06
JUNE	104.19	100.22	105.91	110.91	105.60	100.51	96.32	99.47	106.96	107.48
JULY	103.26	98.78	108.25	110.06	104.49	100.82	96.88	100.09	108.82	107.25
AUGUST	105.50	98.62	109.26	109.38	103.90	100.10	96.97	100.31	108.84	107.30
SEPTEMBER	106.84	100.09	109.24	109.06	103.25	99.63	97.06	100.36	109.17	107.21
OCTOBER	105.62	100.28	109.33	108.78	102.34	97.96	98.37	101.03	109.06	106.62
NOVEMBER	106.07	100.51	109.58	108.48	102.07	97.19	98.62	101.22	108.93	105.98
DECEMBER	105.54	103.20	109.93	107.18	100.84	96.77	99.05	102.53	108.89	106.32
NBER PRICE INDEX, ANNUAL AVERAGES:										
STD. DEV.**	2.1567	2.3075	1.0922	1.3405	1.2065	1.3850	1.3131	0.7470	1.3383	1.1194
NO. OF SERIES*	8.18	10.00	10.83	12.17	14.92	17.00	18.00	17.33	15.42	11.67

NOTE: This commodity is among those showing a "reversal of trend" (see page 42); the trend was fitted to the period ending May 1963.
* See page 105.

Table C-11. Aluminum, Sheet and Strip

(price indexes, 1964 = 100)

	1957	1958	1959	1960	1961	1962	1963	1964	1965	1966
BLS										
JANUARY	107.97	113.53	108.41	114.00	114.87	113.15	103.02	104.56	100.07	94.47
FEBRUARY	107.97	113.53	108.41	114.00	114.87	113.15	103.02	104.56	100.07	94.47
MARCH	107.97	113.53	108.41	114.00	114.87	113.15	103.02	102.04	100.07	94.47
APRIL	107.97	109.26	108.41	114.00	114.87	113.15	103.02	101.94	100.07	94.47
MAY	107.97	108.58	108.41	114.00	114.87	113.15	103.02	101.94	92.13	94.47
JUNE	107.97	108.58	108.41	114.00	114.87	113.15	103.02	97.35	94.47	94.47
JULY	107.97	107.02	108.41	114.00	114.87	113.15	102.85	97.35	94.47	94.47
AUGUST	113.53	107.02	108.41	114.87	114.87	113.15	102.85	97.35	94.47	94.47
SEPTEMBER	113.53	108.41	108.41	114.87	114.87	113.15	102.85	96.70	94.47	94.47
OCTOBER	113.53	108.41	108.41	114.87	113.15	105.17	104.05	96.70	94.47	94.35
NOVEMBER	113.53	108.41	108.41	114.87	113.15	105.17	104.56	99.45	94.47	94.35
DECEMBER	113.53	108.41	108.41	114.87	113.15	105.17	104.56	100.07	94.47	94.35
NBER										
JANUARY	128.62	129.24	124.69	127.19	123.40	117.16	102.67	101.93	98.06	111.01
FEBRUARY	128.62	129.24	124.64	128.86	122.95	116.47	102.64	100.88	98.83	110.76
MARCH	128.62	129.24	124.82	130.44	122.20	116.57	102.51	100.05	99.85	110.40
APRIL	128.62	123.71	125.01	131.92	122.28	116.43	102.24	99.81	100.88	110.81
MAY	128.62	123.45	125.19	133.37	121.79	116.29	102.50	99.56	102.03	111.21
JUNE	128.62	123.45	125.38	134.04	120.82	116.21	102.28	98.97	102.08	111.62
JULY	128.62	123.45	125.56	135.72	120.14	116.38	102.09	99.69	104.20	111.78
AUGUST	128.62	124.29	125.75	135.99	119.47	116.56	102.14	99.66	105.54	111.78
SEPTEMBER	130.86	124.29	125.93	135.57	118.28	110.50	102.01	99.87	105.36	111.94
OCTOBER	130.86	125.61	126.12	134.17	116.87	108.17	102.14	99.87	105.11	111.94
NOVEMBER	130.86	125.61	126.31	129.97	117.44	108.45	102.32	99.86	104.87	111.94
DECEMBER	130.86	125.61	125.63	124.61	116.67	108.58	102.99	99.85	104.63	111.94
NBER PRICE INDEX, ANNUAL AVERAGES:										
STD. DEV.*	0.0076	0.4435	0.4087	2.4135	0.9077	1.0520	0.9306	0.7247	1.7803	0.9048
NO. OF SERIES*	2.00	2.00	2.92	3.50	4.58	6.58	7.00	7.00	6.58	3.42

NOTE: This commodity is among those showing a "reversal of trend" (see page 42); the trend was fitted to the period ending October 1964.
* See page 105.

Table C-12. Aluminum, Wire and Cable
(price indexes, 1964 = 100)

	1957	1958	1959	1960	1961	1962	1963	1964	1965	1966
BLS										
JANUARY	118.35	112.76	99.34	102.16	104.42	108.93	101.03	92.80	103.97	108.48
FEBRUARY	117.21	112.76	99.34	102.16	104.42	108.93	101.03	96.18	103.97	108.48
MARCH	117.21	112.76	99.34	102.16	104.42	108.93	101.03	100.70	104.42	108.48
APRIL	117.21	112.76	99.34	102.16	104.42	108.59	101.03	100.70	106.22	108.48
MAY	117.21	112.76	98.33	102.16	104.42	108.59	96.52	100.70	106.22	112.76
JUNE	117.21	112.76	98.33	102.16	104.42	108.59	87.62	101.03	108.48	112.76
JULY	117.21	112.76	97.76	102.16	104.42	108.59	87.62	101.03	108.48	112.76
AUGUST	122.82	112.76	97.76	104.42	107.80	108.59	88.07	101.37	108.48	112.76
SEPTEMBER	122.82	112.76	97.76	104.42	109.60	108.59	91.11	101.37	108.48	112.76
OCTOBER	112.76	112.76	97.76	104.42	108.93	108.59	92.80	101.37	108.48	112.76
NOVEMBER	112.76	112.76	97.76	104.42	108.93	108.59	92.80	101.37	108.48	112.76
DECEMBER	112.76	108.36	97.76	104.42	108.93	108.59	92.80	101.37	108.48	112.76
NBER										
JANUARY	146.72	125.63	114.66	121.87	122.92	114.26	96.24	99.15	106.11	106.75
FEBRUARY	146.72	124.79	114.18	121.87	120.73	113.63	95.88	99.53	106.30	108.05
MARCH	145.24	124.79	112.53	122.31	117.77	110.52	95.43	99.93	103.62	112.10
APRIL	143.76	124.79	118.05	122.01	117.03	108.91	93.26	100.02	103.80	113.29
MAY	142.28	123.45	118.85	122.00	116.47	107.50	92.77	100.02	105.61	113.29
JUNE	140.42	122.45	118.46	122.29	115.91	107.16	93.21	100.02	105.02	113.29
JULY	131.16	115.70	118.22	122.09	115.74	102.53	92.08	100.26	105.69	113.29
AUGUST	130.60	116.19	118.22	122.47	115.76	102.18	91.72	100.07	104.32	113.29
SEPTEMBER	130.04	116.19	117.92	123.68	115.79	101.16	92.53	99.97	104.41	113.29
OCTOBER	129.48	116.07	118.06	124.30	115.68	100.60	93.25	100.16	104.41	113.29
NOVEMBER	130.79	116.07	118.20	124.72	115.69	100.29	93.54	100.34	104.50	113.29
DECEMBER	132.27	116.07	118.63	124.54	115.30	99.90	93.91	100.53	104.59	113.29
NBER PRICE INDEX, ANNUAL AVERAGES:										
STD. DEV.*	0.9660	1.2870	1.5340	0.4741	0.3435	1.6413	1.8587	0.8605	1.7325	0.8016
NO. OF SERIES*	1.45	2.92	4.00	3.50	3.42	5.92	5.67	5.00	4.42	2.42

NOTE: This commodity is among those showing a "reversal of trend" (see page 42); the trend was fitted to the period ending July 1963.
* See page 105.

Table C-13. Copper Ingot

(price indexes, 1964 = 100)

	1957	1958	1959	1960	1961	1962	1963	1964	1965	1966
BLS										
JANUARY	110.83	77.07	89.94	103.05	89.69	95.88	95.88	95.88	105.15	111.34
FEBRUARY	104.64	76.54	93.03	103.05	89.69	95.88	95.88	95.88	105.15	111.34
MARCH	98.46	76.27	98.64	102.06	89.69	95.88	95.88	98.97	105.15	111.34
APRIL	98.46	76.54	97.67	102.06	94.08	95.88	95.88	98.97	105.15	111.34
MAY	97.93	76.70	97.67	102.06	95.88	95.88	95.88	98.97	111.34	111.34
JUNE	97.93	80.14	97.42	102.06	95.88	95.88	95.88	98.97	111.34	111.34
JULY	90.21	79.89	94.33	102.06	95.88	95.88	95.88	98.97	111.34	111.34
AUGUST	88.04	81.96	92.78	102.06	95.88	95.88	95.88	98.97	111.34	111.34
SEPTEMBER	83.00	81.91	96.34	102.06	95.88	95.88	95.88	98.97	111.34	111.34
OCTOBER	82.73	85.05	96.34	101.02	95.88	95.88	95.88	105.15	111.34	111.34
NOVEMBER	83.00	90.19	102.41	92.78	95.88	95.88	95.88	105.15	114.43	111.34
DECEMBER	82.73	89.59	102.76	92.78	95.88	95.88	95.88	105.15	111.34	111.34
NBER										
JANUARY	102.05	80.31	86.13	105.61	91.19	93.20	94.30	95.52	106.87	113.42
FEBRUARY	107.25	75.82	91.13	107.12	89.00	92.95	94.55	95.46	105.79	116.21
MARCH	101.13	72.04	94.09	106.99	90.01	92.87	94.89	96.00	107.90	114.63
APRIL	97.76	72.76	97.15	104.55	90.87	92.55	95.25	98.48	107.56	115.88
MAY	96.03	73.27	96.94	104.16	92.59	92.12	95.63	98.67	109.59	116.75
JUNE	95.52	73.47	96.94	103.68	94.63	92.15	95.93	99.45	110.13	114.87
JULY	96.23	77.45	96.47	102.76	94.53	92.63	95.84	98.93	113.14	116.49
AUGUST	86.74	72.45	93.12	103.64	94.31	92.89	95.74	99.41	112.50	117.74
SEPTEMBER	86.43	78.78	95.31	103.52	94.05	93.12	95.66	99.71	113.30	113.18
OCTOBER	82.35	79.90	98.48	100.52	93.79	93.40	95.63	104.95	114.87	117.29
NOVEMBER	82.86	84.49	104.48	100.17	93.54	93.64	95.61	105.36	115.88	122.23
DECEMBER	79.09	87.25	105.10	95.99	93.31	93.97	95.55	108.05	113.35	118.60

NBER PRICE INDEX, ANNUAL AVERAGES:

	1957	1958	1959	1960	1961	1962	1963	1964	1965	1966
STD. DEV.*	N.A.	N.A.	0.3253	0.8559	1.5111	0.7961	0.5459	0.8004	1.5265	2.9303
NO. OF SERIES*	1.00	1.00	1.50	4.58	7.67	8.00	8.00	8.00	7.83	6.08

* See page 105.

Table C-14. Copper, Pipe and Tubing
(price indexes, 1964 = 100)

BLS	1957	1958	1959	1960	1961	1962	1963	1964	1965	1966
JANUARY	111.04	98.08	102.96	110.07	97.77	92.71	95.74	89.35	109.35	122.73
FEBRUARY	108.09	98.08	104.38	110.07	97.77	96.44	95.51	89.35	109.35	125.82
MARCH	105.16	98.08	106.63	110.07	94.31	96.36	95.51	94.82	109.35	130.10
APRIL	105.16	98.08	106.63	110.07	91.03	96.36	93.91	96.41	109.35	137.13
MAY	105.16	97.17	106.63	110.07	94.21	96.81	95.19	97.19	115.00	138.94
JUNE	105.16	97.07	106.63	109.14	95.64	94.23	94.12	97.51	114.94	142.90
JULY	101.11	97.48	103.41	109.14	98.07	91.59	97.31	100.05	114.94	142.90
AUGUST	99.99	98.19	102.91	109.14	98.86	90.18	97.31	104.28	117.30	145.46
SEPTEMBER	97.77	97.88	105.19	108.39	101.26	88.26	94.37	104.28	117.30	135.60
OCTOBER	97.77	98.90	105.91	102.98	99.63	90.41	90.15	107.72	117.30	139.59
NOVEMBER	101.02	101.54	105.91	106.33	96.73	92.82	89.28	109.68	121.59	139.59
DECEMBER	101.02	102.96	110.07	99.21	93.05	92.82	89.35	109.35	119.80	139.59
NBER										
JANUARY	110.68	101.78	105.58	109.97	101.30	104.21	101.12	95.64	107.74	129.72
FEBRUARY	108.86	101.76	106.02	110.13	101.03	103.88	101.97	95.32	107.84	132.32
MARCH	107.08	101.73	106.59	110.38	101.15	103.30	100.80	95.65	106.41	135.60
APRIL	106.14	101.98	106.92	110.63	101.16	102.67	99.02	95.95	104.42	139.79
MAY	105.21	102.22	107.22	110.82	101.51	102.05	99.64	96.19	107.45	141.56
JUNE	104.00	102.49	107.54	110.39	102.03	101.28	99.71	96.11	106.00	142.74
JULY	103.14	102.46	107.51	109.12	102.12	100.22	100.00	95.76	115.09	141.74
AUGUST	102.42	102.44	107.98	107.56	102.22	100.00	100.08	103.16	120.90	140.69
SEPTEMBER	101.88	102.83	108.92	105.60	101.81	99.17	96.25	104.90	122.22	140.04
OCTOBER	101.86	103.55	108.72	102.52	102.17	97.40	96.22	106.40	123.61	141.81
NOVEMBER	101.83	104.47	109.47	100.79	102.44	101.18	96.04	107.31	126.72	143.61
DECEMBER	101.81	105.20	109.80	101.87	103.51	100.32	97.11	107.62	126.88	144.07

NBER PRICE INDEX, ANNUAL AVERAGES:

	0022300	.0223	10.	COPPER	WIRE AN	D CABLE	- BARE			
STD. DEV.** NO. OF SERIES*	0.4094	0.1948	0.2386	1.2610	0.9675	1.7809	2.0836	2.0370	4.4667	1.6138

NOTE: This commodity is among those showing a "reversal of trend" (see page 42); the trend was fitted to the period ending January 1964.
* See page 105.

Table C-15. Copper, Wire and Cable—Bare

(price indexes, 1964 = 100)

	1957	1958	1959	1960	1961	1962	1963	1964	1965	1966
BLS										
JANUARY	105.47	80.25	88.26	100.64	91.70	96.28	96.60	96.60	106.05	118.96
FEBRUARY	100.89	80.25	90.55	100.18	91.70	96.28	96.60	96.60	106.05	120.81
MARCH	96.30	80.25	93.99	100.18	91.70	96.51	96.60	98.21	106.05	120.81
APRIL	96.30	80.25	93.99	100.18	91.70	96.51	96.60	98.91	106.75	122.19
MAY	96.30	80.25	94.45	100.18	93.99	96.51	96.60	99.13	117.35	126.57
JUNE	96.30	80.25	94.45	100.18	96.28	96.51	96.60	99.13	117.35	126.57
JULY	88.51	82.55	91.47	100.64	96.28	96.60	96.60	99.13	117.35	126.57
AUGUST	88.28	83.67	91.47	100.64	96.28	96.60	96.60	99.13	117.35	126.57
SEPTEMBER	85.07	85.96	93.99	100.64	96.28	96.60	96.60	99.13	117.35	126.57
OCTOBER	85.07	85.96	93.99	100.64	96.28	96.60	96.60	103.75	121.27	126.57
NOVEMBER	85.07	88.26	100.64	93.99	96.28	96.60	96.60	105.13	121.50	126.57
DECEMBER	85.07	88.26	100.64	93.99	96.28	96.60	96.60	105.13	118.96	126.57
NBER										
JANUARY	108.13	88.27	92.22	102.19	96.11	98.03	95.45	97.87	106.72	119.88
FEBRUARY	106.85	85.07	92.96	102.02	95.40	96.71	95.45	97.36	107.08	121.91
MARCH	101.17	83.85	94.93	102.42	94.69	95.44	95.58	96.84	107.45	122.74
APRIL	99.92	82.75	97.33	101.45	93.99	95.88	95.79	96.58	107.80	123.57
MAY	98.64	82.56	97.47	102.19	95.87	96.33	95.85	97.73	110.28	124.71
JUNE	97.26	82.84	97.99	101.59	95.36	96.71	95.91	98.95	110.77	125.84
JULY	95.11	83.11	98.21	100.98	96.54	96.15	96.11	99.98	112.02	129.51
AUGUST	94.54	84.81	98.29	101.21	96.57	95.60	96.71	98.54	112.20	129.29
SEPTEMBER	93.16	85.31	98.48	101.40	96.95	95.17	97.24	100.41	112.37	141.81
OCTOBER	90.86	87.37	98.72	100.47	97.26	95.24	97.43	104.70	113.45	141.58
NOVEMBER	89.91	90.73	99.81	99.46	97.51	95.31	96.35	104.68	115.16	141.58
DECEMBER	89.05	91.49	100.97	97.84	97.77	95.38	98.39	106.35	117.69	141.58
NBER PRICE INDEX, ANNUAL AVERAGES:										
STD. DEV.*	1.6088	1.8978	0.7788	1.8137	1.1110	0.9506	0.9742	1.1130	0.9709	2.3271
NO. OF SERIES*	17.27	18.00	17.75	19.00	16.50	4.00	3.92	4.75	4.58	2.00

NOTE: This commodity is among those showing a "reversal of trend" (see page 42); the trend was fitted to the period ending May 1958.

* See page 105.

Table C-16. Copper, Insulated Wire
(price indexes, 1964 = 100)

	1957	1958	1959	1960	1961	1962	1963	1964	1965	1966
BLS										
JANUARY	113.37	98.32	102.31	114.28	92.28	102.25	93.45	97.36	107.32	118.88
FEBRUARY	107.62	98.32	102.31	113.01	92.54	98.52	93.45	97.67	107.32	119.67
MARCH	111.32	94.53	98.51	105.47	92.54	95.61	93.69	94.03	107.04	118.66
APRIL	111.32	82.04	99.05	105.47	92.54	93.68	93.69	97.91	107.04	122.20
MAY	111.32	82.04	105.74	104.59	95.72	94.76	96.49	98.82	110.77	128.95
JUNE	107.19	86.14	105.22	98.03	95.27	95.15	96.49	98.68	114.12	131.15
JULY	106.73	86.16	104.18	91.24	95.27	96.18	95.35	98.68	114.95	131.15
AUGUST	106.57	86.16	104.18	90.83	98.61	96.18	95.35	99.70	114.95	131.15
SEPTEMBER	102.18	97.34	104.18	93.01	98.61	95.65	98.33	101.28	115.82	131.15
OCTOBER	93.72	97.34	109.74	93.01	98.61	95.65	97.28	103.21	116.74	131.15
NOVEMBER	94.76	102.31	114.28	91.45	98.61	94.57	97.28	105.32	117.67	131.15
DECEMBER	96.66	102.31	114.28	91.45	102.39	93.45	98.01	107.32	118.56	131.15
NBER										
JANUARY	0.00	96.08	101.80	104.16	100.81	98.12	94.67	96.25	105.66	127.55
FEBRUARY	0.00	93.03	102.07	103.75	100.70	98.01	94.62	96.47	106.03	126.94
MARCH	0.00	93.53	102.21	103.74	100.55	97.50	94.26	96.69	106.75	128.13
APRIL	0.00	94.04	102.01	103.73	99.07	96.51	94.64	97.12	109.31	131.53
MAY	124.39	94.29	101.81	103.17	98.95	96.47	95.01	97.27	108.77	133.49
JUNE	120.44	94.54	100.86	102.74	98.64	95.42	95.21	100.07	118.71	143.40
JULY	116.61	94.80	101.01	102.38	98.52	95.42	95.56	100.02	118.33	144.26
AUGUST	112.91	95.05	101.16	102.33	98.39	95.41	95.60	101.53	117.95	143.06
SEPTEMBER	109.32	95.31	101.33	102.45	98.76	95.64	95.85	101.78	118.63	143.20
OCTOBER	105.85	95.57	101.49	102.57	98.68	95.57	95.68	102.55	119.31	143.35
NOVEMBER	102.49	95.82	101.53	102.28	98.60	95.50	95.87	104.94	119.81	143.50
DECEMBER	99.23	96.08	101.13	102.23	98.53	95.45	96.03	105.30	118.70	143.50
NBER PRICE INDEX, ANNUAL AVERAGES:										
STD. DEV.*	N.A.	0.2686	0.8397	0.9977	0.7946	0.8412	0.9486	1.3719	2.1900	3.1839
NO. OF SERIES*	1.00	1.67	4.00	5.50	7.58	8.75	9.83	10.42	10.50	8.00

NOTE: This commodity is among those showing a "reversal of trend" (see page 42); the trend was fitted to the period ending April 1958.

* See page 105.

Table C-17. Copper, Magnet Wire

(price indexes, 1964 = 100)

	1957	1958	1959	1960	1961	1962	1963	1964	1965	1966
BLS										
JANUARY	101.72	101.72	101.72	101.72	93.09	98.63	98.63	98.63	102.33	121.01
FEBRUARY	101.72	101.72	101.72	101.72	93.09	98.63	98.63	98.63	102.74	120.38
MARCH	101.72	101.72	101.72	101.72	93.09	98.63	98.63	99.66	102.74	120.38
APRIL	101.72	101.72	101.72	101.72	93.09	98.63	98.63	99.66	102.74	124.49
MAY	101.72	101.72	101.72	101.72	96.79	98.63	98.63	99.66	104.81	127.27
JUNE	101.72	101.72	101.72	101.72	98.63	98.63	98.63	99.66	110.36	127.27
JULY	101.72	101.72	101.72	89.51	97.03	98.63	98.63	99.66	110.36	127.27
AUGUST	101.72	101.72	101.72	89.51	95.44	98.63	98.63	99.66	110.36	126.58
SEPTEMBER	101.72	101.72	101.72	89.51	93.83	98.63	98.63	99.66	110.36	126.58
OCTOBER	101.72	101.72	101.72	89.51	93.83	98.63	98.63	101.03	114.98	126.58
NOVEMBER	101.72	101.72	101.72	93.09	93.83	98.63	98.63	101.03	118.46	126.58
DECEMBER	101.72	101.72	101.72	93.09	98.63	98.63	98.63	103.09	116.25	127.27
NBER										
JANUARY	117.86	104.11	113.67	121.07	103.29	106.29	103.78	97.47	107.64	121.08
FEBRUARY	113.45	104.73	114.04	120.84	102.84	106.64	103.02	97.34	107.50	122.88
MARCH	109.04	105.36	114.41	120.65	103.50	107.00	99.56	97.52	108.52	122.42
APRIL	108.81	106.09	113.91	120.47	105.13	107.36	99.41	97.69	109.55	125.55
MAY	108.57	107.29	113.16	119.02	105.79	107.72	99.26	97.71	110.58	126.46
JUNE	108.33	108.50	112.40	110.32	105.05	107.12	99.10	97.73	114.68	126.14
JULY	106.69	107.23	112.76	109.01	103.10	107.24	98.81	98.82	115.18	127.28
AUGUST	107.05	107.02	113.12	107.69	102.59	107.36	98.51	101.62	116.11	127.52
SEPTEMBER	107.39	109.65	119.51	107.38	103.16	107.49	98.22	102.48	117.06	127.24
OCTOBER	107.26	111.06	120.11	106.40	103.74	105.98	98.35	103.35	120.67	127.78
NOVEMBER	107.13	112.44	120.71	105.21	107.26	106.10	98.06	103.87	121.44	130.06
DECEMBER	106.99	113.29	121.30	104.24	107.85	106.22	97.77	104.39	122.20	130.83
NBER PRICE INDEX, ANNUAL AVERAGES:										
STD. DEV.*	0.6237	1.0209	0.6892	1.3217	0.7647	0.5777	0.8014	0.8699	1.2716	0.9575
NO. OF SERIES*	2.82	4.00	4.00	4.83	5.00	5.00	5.92	6.00	5.25	3.17

* See page 105.

Table C-18. Zinc Products

(price indexes, 1964 = 100)

	1957	1958	1959	1960	1961	1962	1963	1964	1965	1966
BLS										
JANUARY	98.59	73.95	84.51	95.07	84.51	88.03	84.55	95.58	106.90	106.90
FEBRUARY	98.59	73.95	84.51	95.07	84.51	88.03	84.55	95.58	106.90	106.90
MARCH	98.59	73.95	80.99	95.07	84.51	88.03	84.55	95.58	106.90	106.90
APRIL	98.59	73.95	80.99	95.07	84.51	85.12	84.55	99.92	106.90	106.90
MAY	84.51	73.95	80.99	95.07	84.51	85.12	84.55	99.92	106.90	106.90
JUNE	80.99	73.95	80.99	95.07	84.51	84.55	85.12	99.92	106.90	106.90
JULY	73.95	73.95	80.99	95.07	84.51	84.55	88.03	99.92	106.90	106.90
AUGUST	73.95	73.95	80.99	95.07	84.51	84.55	92.09	99.92	106.90	106.90
SEPTEMBER	73.95	73.95	80.99	95.07	84.51	84.55	92.09	99.92	106.90	106.90
OCTOBER	73.95	80.99	88.03	95.07	84.51	84.55	92.09	99.92	106.90	106.90
NOVEMBER	73.95	84.51	91.55	95.07	84.51	84.55	92.09	106.90	106.90	106.90
DECEMBER	73.95	84.51	91.55	91.55	88.03	84.55	95.58	106.90	106.90	106.90
NBER										
JANUARY	100.12	77.47	85.95	94.62	84.34	86.67	84.48	95.93	107.50	108.04
FEBRUARY	100.12	77.71	86.96	96.84	86.21	86.79	84.42	95.98	107.63	107.93
MARCH	100.12	78.10	84.61	96.55	86.54	86.75	84.51	96.49	107.72	107.96
APRIL	100.97	77.64	84.15	97.46	86.23	85.96	84.70	98.96	107.80	108.00
MAY	91.07	76.81	84.03	98.15	85.71	85.75	84.96	98.51	107.93	108.00
JUNE	83.83	76.65	84.03	98.46	84.85	85.50	85.30	99.79	107.90	108.00
JULY	77.67	76.50	84.20	98.15	84.35	84.04	86.80	100.58	108.20	108.06
AUGUST	77.59	76.50	84.52	98.45	84.20	84.18	86.80	100.56	107.94	108.06
SEPTEMBER	77.53	76.50	87.07	98.46	84.47	84.25	90.03	100.21	108.00	108.06
OCTOBER	77.60	78.73	89.09	98.36	84.53	84.35	92.97	101.36	108.07	108.06
NOVEMBER	77.60	82.09	91.72	98.55	84.62	84.37	93.37	104.65	108.09	108.06
DECEMBER	77.72	83.29	91.50	95.61	87.09	84.35	93.99	105.99	108.14	108.06
NBER PRICE INDEX, ANNUAL AVERAGES:										
STD. DEV.*	1.1335	1.2056	1.8288	1.1997	1.4747	0.7310	1.0303	1.1292	0.4856	0.0652
NO. OF SERIES*	5.82	6.00	6.50	9.58	11.75	12.00	13.00	12.50	11.83	9.58

NOTE: This commodity is among those showing a "reversal of trend" (see page 42); the trend was fitted to the period ending July 1957.

* See page 105.

Table C-19. Brass, Bars and Rods

(price indexes, 1964 = 100)

	1957	1958	1959	1960	1961	1962	1963	1964	1965	1966
BLS										
JANUARY	110.44	85.66	85.66	99.15	93.37	97.22	97.50	93.09	109.34	116.50
FEBRUARY	106.86	85.66	88.13	99.15	93.37	97.22	97.50	92.54	109.34	116.50
MARCH	102.46	85.38	89.79	99.15	91.71	97.22	95.57	96.12	109.34	117.88
APRIL	98.05	85.38	89.79	99.15	91.71	97.22	95.57	97.22	109.34	118.71
MAY	96.12	80.70	89.79	99.15	93.37	97.22	95.57	97.50	112.65	136.88
JUNE	95.85	80.70	89.79	99.15	97.22	96.95	89.24	97.50	112.65	131.93
JULY	90.34	81.25	88.41	99.15	97.22	96.95	89.24	97.50	112.65	131.93
AUGUST	87.31	79.87	87.31	99.15	97.22	96.95	89.79	102.18	115.40	134.40
SEPTEMBER	85.10	79.87	90.89	99.15	97.22	96.95	89.79	102.18	115.13	132.75
OCTOBER	85.10	79.87	92.27	99.15	97.22	96.95	89.79	105.49	115.13	134.40
NOVEMBER	88.96	82.63	98.05	96.67	97.22	96.95	89.79	109.34	118.98	139.91
DECEMBER	88.96	85.66	98.05	96.67	97.22	96.95	93.09	109.34	116.50	139.91
NBER										
JANUARY	109.51	87.56	91.58	98.27	93.70	96.62	94.82	95.44	108.13	112.62
FEBRUARY	102.94	86.18	90.82	98.21	90.84	96.56	95.44	96.62	107.93	112.97
MARCH	102.94	84.78	90.83	98.15	91.20	96.44	95.28	96.74	107.49	113.11
APRIL	102.94	85.05	90.79	98.18	91.27	96.32	94.43	97.65	107.05	113.67
MAY	95.92	84.28	90.76	98.26	93.38	96.07	94.46	98.06	109.78	116.81
JUNE	92.54	84.55	90.47	98.35	95.20	95.95	93.65	98.15	109.72	117.17
JULY	92.83	82.52	84.06	98.24	95.23	95.76	93.84	99.81	110.09	119.85
AUGUST	87.89	82.47	84.00	98.08	95.23	95.62	90.92	101.79	110.37	120.22
SEPTEMBER	88.17	83.14	86.25	96.74	95.24	95.49	91.32	102.17	111.04	120.22
OCTOBER	86.30	83.82	87.37	94.98	95.24	95.30	92.81	102.12	111.31	120.22
NOVEMBER	88.62	89.14	96.37	94.69	95.24	95.17	93.82	105.57	112.19	120.22
DECEMBER	88.90	93.10	98.34	94.58	95.24	94.95	94.05	105.89	112.28	120.22
NBER PRICE INDEX, ANNUAL AVERAGES:										
STD. DEV.*	1.7613	1.5639	2.0219	0.3946	0.5337	0.2595	0.7751	0.8571	0.7330	0.6405
NO. OF SERIES*	2.36	3.67	4.00	4.17	5.33	8.00	8.00	8.00	7.17	2.67

NOTE: This commodity is among those showing a "reversal of trend" (see page 42); the trend was fitted to the period ending August 1958.
* See page 105.

Table C-20. Regular Gasoline

(price indexes, 1964 = 100)

BLS	1957	1958	1959	1960	1961	1962	1963	1964	1965	1966
JANUARY	111.50	110.57	105.69	99.70	111.22	105.51	103.57	102.65	100.53	106.15
FEBRUARY	116.56	106.24	106.24	101.36	110.57	101.45	101.36	101.64	98.69	104.95
MARCH	116.56	104.49	107.90	104.77	110.39	98.96	103.57	99.15	99.33	104.12
APRIL	116.56	103.66	108.64	105.51	107.16	107.07	104.68	97.30	100.81	105.32
MAY	116.01	102.46	107.90	101.91	105.41	106.80	108.09	100.44	103.11	107.81
JUNE	115.09	103.66	104.86	105.69	108.82	107.44	109.84	100.90	104.31	111.22
JULY	113.06	107.26	104.95	108.27	109.28	106.89	108.82	101.36	104.31	110.67
AUGUST	113.06	109.84	108.36	110.85	107.62	105.51	104.03	99.52	104.31	111.86
SEPTEMBER	114.08	109.84	107.81	111.22	105.04	109.19	104.31	95.92	103.75	111.86
OCTOBER	112.88	107.44	105.32	111.22	102.10	108.36	103.39	99.52	103.75	111.86
NOVEMBER	110.57	105.87	103.29	110.85	103.85	106.98	99.33	100.81	106.15	111.86
DECEMBER	110.57	105.23	100.71	110.85	105.51	105.51	103.39	100.81	106.15	109.01
NBER										
JANUARY	107.91	109.10	102.67	103.93	106.77	103.66	102.54	101.40	98.55	98.45
FEBRUARY	109.05	108.17	102.68	104.35	106.82	103.18	102.37	101.27	98.28	98.46
MARCH	109.14	108.03	103.11	104.55	106.75	102.87	102.54	100.83	98.24	98.52
APRIL	109.01	106.97	103.56	104.47	106.41	103.82	102.57	100.36	98.29	98.32
MAY	109.49	105.31	103.17	104.96	106.16	103.91	103.38	100.38	98.35	98.68
JUNE	110.12	104.66	103.27	104.59	105.57	103.76	103.40	99.87	98.17	99.36
JULY	110.05	104.14	103.59	105.06	105.06	103.86	102.69	99.55	98.19	99.58
AUGUST	110.30	103.87	104.18	105.21	104.67	103.64	102.44	99.39	97.98	99.62
SEPTEMBER	110.00	103.87	104.24	105.45	104.44	103.90	102.39	99.39	97.97	99.76
OCTOBER	109.86	103.56	103.82	106.04	103.90	103.60	102.12	99.29	98.05	99.94
NOVEMBER	109.61	102.81	103.79	106.01	103.90	103.16	101.48	99.06	98.13	100.49
DECEMBER	109.33	102.96	104.52	106.64	103.88	102.80	101.96	99.19	98.20	100.95
NBER PRICE INDEX, ANNUAL AVERAGES:										
STD. DEV.*	1.2554	1.8835	1.5675	1.5837	1.6429	2.0582	1.7600	1.7177	0.9183	1.0538
NO. OF SERIES*	23.64	29.08	32.92	44.58	50.00	52.75	57.00	57.67	55.00	47.50

* See page 105.

Table C-21. Diesel and Distillate Fuel No. 2

(price indexes, 1964 = 100)

	1957	1958	1959	1960	1961	1962	1963	1964	1965	1966
BLS										
JANUARY	120.60	113.62	120.24	112.63	113.71	115.68	113.97	110.39	108.15	109.23
FEBRUARY	126.69	110.48	124.81	108.07	118.81	117.11	115.14	106.99	108.15	110.84
MARCH	125.61	108.78	122.12	102.34	117.20	112.00	115.14	102.60	106.54	110.30
APRIL	125.17	105.92	117.65	101.17	112.18	108.42	112.27	99.74	103.95	108.33
MAY	122.93	104.75	113.71	100.01	105.02	104.93	107.89	96.43	103.95	105.74
JUNE	119.53	104.75	106.72	99.38	104.48	103.68	107.89	95.71	103.41	105.74
JULY	117.29	105.92	105.02	101.71	104.48	104.75	104.75	95.71	103.41	105.74
AUGUST	115.23	108.78	103.23	103.95	106.27	104.75	104.75	95.71	104.93	106.81
SEPTEMBER	114.69	111.74	100.37	106.27	106.27	104.75	103.41	95.71	106.63	108.42
OCTOBER	114.69	111.74	103.23	106.90	106.81	104.75	104.48	97.86	107.89	108.42
NOVEMBER	114.69	111.74	104.84	106.10	108.96	107.44	106.27	100.01	108.42	109.05
DECEMBER	114.69	113.97	110.48	107.26	112.36	110.84	106.54	103.14	109.23	110.93
NBER										
JANUARY	115.42	114.12	110.08	106.18	104.84	105.93	104.90	102.74	99.43	100.47
FEBRUARY	119.94	112.85	110.44	105.43	105.47	105.99	105.01	102.32	99.56	100.67
MARCH	117.80	111.26	110.87	104.66	106.10	105.94	105.28	102.22	99.46	100.90
APRIL	118.17	110.63	111.15	104.31	105.91	105.53	105.10	101.40	99.33	100.82
MAY	119.19	108.70	111.52	104.13	105.76	105.18	104.62	100.78	99.22	100.61
JUNE	119.46	107.76	109.64	103.19	105.79	104.35	104.14	100.17	99.32	100.83
JULY	118.33	106.41	108.30	101.73	105.38	102.90	103.19	98.32	99.23	101.22
AUGUST	117.71	105.78	108.28	101.96	104.90	103.02	102.92	98.18	99.48	101.13
SEPTEMBER	117.33	106.18	107.72	101.99	105.05	103.23	102.55	98.16	99.43	101.33
OCTOBER	117.27	107.07	107.41	102.97	105.26	103.26	102.47	98.19	99.73	101.36
NOVEMBER	115.74	108.27	105.19	103.24	105.56	102.85	102.07	98.31	99.78	101.83
DECEMBER	114.70	109.20	105.88	104.09	106.26	104.91	102.82	99.22	100.53	102.34
NBER PRICE INDEX, ANNUAL AVERAGES:										
STD. DEV.*	2.0355	2.1093	2.0981	1.7546	1.8995	1.9647	1.6530	1.7567	1.2512	1.1355
NO. OF SERIES*	43.73	47.92	49.92	61.67	69.75	78.33	81.33	87.42	88.67	77.25

* See page 105.

Table C-22. Residual Fuel Oil No. 6

(price indexes, 1964 = 100)

BLS	1957	1958	1959	1960	1961	1962	1963	1964	1965	1966
JANUARY	133.55	122.32	98.18	99.20	110.25	107.63	105.47	103.79	103.14	103.42
FEBRUARY	138.23	109.78	101.54	99.20	110.25	109.41	105.19	102.11	103.14	101.36
MARCH	138.23	105.19	101.54	97.52	110.25	108.28	104.26	100.80	102.85	100.51
APRIL	136.83	104.07	101.26	100.14	108.56	106.79	103.04	98.55	102.11	100.33
MAY	137.86	103.42	101.26	100.14	107.63	105.47	103.04	98.55	102.11	98.74
JUNE	136.83	103.42	97.80	105.19	106.97	105.47	101.64	98.55	102.11	98.74
JULY	133.55	103.42	97.80	106.41	106.97	105.47	101.64	98.55	102.29	98.74
AUGUST	130.46	105.10	96.96	108.84	106.97	105.47	101.64	98.55	102.48	98.74
SEPTEMBER	128.03	105.10	94.43	108.84	106.97	105.47	101.64	98.55	102.67	98.74
OCTOBER	125.13	95.84	94.43	110.25	106.97	105.47	100.98	99.20	102.85	101.45
NOVEMBER	125.13	97.52	96.12	110.25	107.81	105.47	102.01	101.08	103.70	100.80
DECEMBER	125.13	99.20	97.80	110.25	108.19	106.60	102.01	101.73	103.70	100.80
NBER										
JANUARY	127.60	118.85	103.29	101.58	106.29	103.77	102.63	101.42	99.96	99.68
FEBRUARY	129.30	114.11	103.37	101.41	106.39	103.81	102.55	101.54	99.92	99.72
MARCH	130.83	111.52	103.44	100.90	106.26	103.70	102.78	100.62	100.21	99.69
APRIL	129.69	110.09	103.50	100.36	105.88	103.87	103.23	100.42	100.02	99.60
MAY	129.65	108.77	103.11	100.74	105.17	103.33	103.00	100.40	99.94	99.40
JUNE	128.02	107.07	102.52	101.13	104.43	103.40	102.84	100.23	100.39	98.95
JULY	128.00	105.20	101.75	101.60	104.32	103.31	102.01	99.59	100.25	97.91
AUGUST	126.16	105.54	102.25	102.21	104.46	103.17	101.67	98.92	100.01	97.25
SEPTEMBER	125.51	105.12	102.24	103.06	104.50	103.18	101.76	98.99	99.95	97.11
OCTOBER	124.95	104.85	101.21	103.96	104.60	103.19	101.79	99.13	100.07	97.35
NOVEMBER	124.05	104.44	101.09	105.24	104.67	102.15	101.75	99.43	100.04	95.88
DECEMBER	124.45	104.68	100.97	105.64	105.02	102.21	101.66	99.31	100.00	95.67
NBER PRICE INDEX, ANNUAL AVERAGES:										
STD. DEV.*	2.5328	3.4421	2.6100	2.0862	1.5307	1.4197	1.1682	1.4759	0.9994	1.3863
NO. OF SERIES*	33.00	36.58	38.08	41.17	39.92	29.83	32.00	36.25	38.08	31.50

* See page 105.

Table C-23. Coal, Bituminous
(price indexes, 1964 = 100)

BLS	1957	1958	1959	1960	1961	1962	1963	1964	1965	1966
JANUARY	105.29	106.89	109.51	108.49	107.73	105.29	103.85	102.84	101.41	99.63
FEBRUARY	105.29	106.89	109.51	108.49	107.73	105.29	103.85	102.84	101.41	99.63
MARCH	102.92	106.89	106.72	108.49	106.47	105.29	103.85	99.89	98.88	99.63
APRIL	99.80	100.82	102.50	101.66	99.55	99.38	100.65	96.85	96.43	95.84
MAY	99.89	101.07	102.84	102.33	100.31	98.12	98.96	97.53	96.43	98.45
JUNE	100.82	102.84	104.61	104.11	101.49	98.96	100.22	98.03	97.36	98.96
JULY	102.50	104.36	106.05	105.12	103.01	99.80	101.32	98.45	97.95	99.47
AUGUST	104.36	106.47	107.73	106.97	104.36	101.57	102.00	98.96	98.37	100.22
SEPTEMBER	105.37	107.06	107.90	107.23	105.12	101.91	102.59	100.39	99.63	100.73
OCTOBER	106.05	107.31	108.16	107.48	104.87	103.09	102.59	101.41	99.63	100.73
NOVEMBER	106.89	107.56	108.49	107.73	105.29	103.68	102.59	101.41	99.63	102.84
DECEMBER	106.89	107.56	108.49	107.73	105.29	103.85	102.84	101.41	99.63	103.18
NBER										
JANUARY	101.74	103.33	103.65	104.39	101.88	100.95	100.90	100.35	100.02	102.98
FEBRUARY	102.52	103.06	103.89	104.27	102.13	100.99	100.56	100.01	101.10	103.05
MARCH	103.31	102.80	104.13	104.16	102.38	101.04	100.23	99.68	102.19	103.12
APRIL	104.10	102.53	104.37	104.04	102.64	101.09	99.90	99.35	103.30	103.19
MAY	104.53	102.76	104.34	104.27	102.50	100.66	99.60	99.61	103.12	104.50
JUNE	104.74	103.00	104.31	104.51	102.36	100.23	99.30	99.87	102.94	105.82
JULY	104.39	103.23	104.28	104.74	102.22	99.81	99.00	100.14	102.76	107.16
AUGUST	104.04	102.84	104.14	103.99	102.87	100.10	99.25	100.18	102.95	107.22
SEPTEMBER	103.69	102.46	103.99	103.25	103.53	100.39	99.49	100.23	103.31	107.28
OCTOBER	104.04	102.07	103.85	102.51	104.19	100.69	99.73	100.28	103.31	107.34
NOVEMBER	103.57	102.60	104.03	102.30	103.10	100.76	99.94	100.19	103.20	107.34
DECEMBER	103.45	103.12	104.21	102.09	102.02	100.83	100.15	100.11	103.09	107.34
NBER PRICE INDEX, ANNUAL AVERAGES:										
STD. DEV.*	0.9956	1.0897	1.0936	1.6840	1.6685	1.0671	0.6077	0.8159	1.2709	0.6992
NO. OF SERIES*	17.00	17.00	17.00	17.00	16.67	16.83	17.00	17.00	17.00	15.83

NOTE: The NBER index is based exclusively on prices paid by railroads.
* See page 105.

Table C-24. Passenger Car Tires
(price indexes, 1964 = 100)

BLS

	1957	1958	1959	1960	1961	1962	1963	1964	1965	1966
JANUARY	115.17	118.36	116.76	94.64	96.92	97.23	101.86	104.37	99.73	104.29
FEBRUARY	115.39	118.36	116.76	97.38	96.92	97.23	101.86	104.37	99.73	104.37
MARCH	115.39	118.36	116.76	97.38	96.92	97.91	101.86	104.37	99.73	104.37
APRIL	115.39	118.36	116.76	97.38	98.06	98.37	101.86	100.19	99.73	106.96
MAY	115.39	118.36	116.99	97.38	98.06	98.82	101.86	98.14	101.41	106.96
JUNE	115.39	118.36	116.99	97.38	98.06	98.82	101.86	98.14	101.41	106.96
JULY	115.39	118.36	116.99	97.38	98.06	98.82	103.91	98.14	114.79	106.96
AUGUST	118.81	116.76	94.64	97.38	98.06	98.82	104.37	98.14	114.79	106.96
SEPTEMBER	118.81	116.76	94.64	97.38	98.06	98.82	104.37	98.14	114.79	106.96
OCTOBER	118.81	116.76	94.64	97.38	98.06	98.82	104.37	98.14	104.37	106.96
NOVEMBER	118.81	116.76	94.64	97.38	98.06	100.72	104.37	98.14	104.37	107.87
DECEMBER	118.81	116.76	94.64	96.92	98.29	101.86	104.37	99.73	104.37	107.87

NBER

	1957	1958	1959	1960	1961	1962	1963	1964	1965	1966
JANUARY	108.87	111.00	113.78	110.99	106.82	106.33	103.96	100.98	98.99	99.37
FEBRUARY	108.87	111.77	112.68	111.22	106.60	106.18	103.84	101.27	99.01	99.58
MARCH	108.90	112.29	113.29	111.45	106.23	106.12	103.71	100.75	99.03	99.79
APRIL	108.94	112.16	113.21	110.56	105.72	104.49	103.12	100.81	99.41	100.18
MAY	108.92	111.74	113.08	110.22	105.20	104.68	103.11	100.57	99.42	100.52
JUNE	108.91	111.31	112.91	108.22	105.10	104.53	103.09	100.38	99.33	100.86
JULY	108.40	111.03	112.70	106.64	105.89	104.37	103.01	100.10	99.46	101.49
AUGUST	108.10	111.55	112.48	106.72	105.92	102.89	102.83	99.45	99.36	101.49
SEPTEMBER	107.95	112.08	112.27	106.81	106.00	102.91	102.78	98.89	99.25	101.49
OCTOBER	107.71	112.31	111.56	106.99	106.08	102.87	101.26	98.91	98.88	101.49
NOVEMBER	108.20	112.90	111.04	107.30	106.13	103.57	101.27	98.94	98.97	101.49
DECEMBER	108.76	113.51		107.51	106.18	104.34	101.53	98.96	99.05	101.49

NBER PRICE INDEX, ANNUAL AVERAGES:

	1957	1958	1959	1960	1961	1962	1963	1964	1965	1966
STD. DEV.*	1.1726	1.9579	1.8023	1.9150	1.3493	1.6030	1.9125	1.4335	0.7438	0.6883
NO. OF SERIES*	15.64	17.00	18.33	22.92	24.67	30.00	31.00	31.33	29.33	14.58

NOTE: This commodity is among those showing a "reversal of trend" (see page 42); the trend was fitted to the period ending August 1959.
* See page 105.

Table C-25. Truck and Bus Tires
(price indexes, 1964 = 100)

	1957	1958	1959	1960	1961	1962	1963	1964	1965	1966
BLS										
JANUARY	113.31	114.68	115.82	106.73	113.11	103.78	97.87	100.61	99.70	102.19
FEBRUARY	113.31	114.68	115.82	112.42	113.11	99.70	97.87	100.61	99.70	102.19
MARCH	113.31	114.68	115.82	112.42	113.11	100.15	97.87	100.61	99.70	102.19
APRIL	113.31	114.68	115.82	112.42	113.77	96.98	97.87	100.61	99.70	106.16
MAY	113.31	114.68	115.82	112.42	113.77	97.43	97.87	99.70	99.70	106.16
JUNE	113.31	114.68	109.02	112.42	113.77	95.15	97.87	99.70	102.19	106.16
JULY	113.31	114.68	109.02	121.72	113.77	95.15	97.87	99.70	102.19	104.58
AUGUST	116.97	117.42	109.02	121.72	113.77	95.15	100.84	99.70	102.19	104.58
SEPTEMBER	116.97	117.42	109.02	121.72	113.77	95.15	101.52	99.70	102.19	102.76
OCTOBER	116.97	117.42	106.73	121.72	113.77	95.15	101.52	99.70	102.19	102.76
NOVEMBER	116.97	117.42	106.73	121.72	110.82	96.98	101.52	99.70	102.19	102.76
DECEMBER	116.97	117.42	106.73	113.11	103.78	97.87	100.61	99.70	102.19	102.76
NBER										
JANUARY	102.31	108.72	109.21	110.29	108.15	103.52	100.14	100.54	98.19	96.64
FEBRUARY	102.11	108.48	109.21	110.30	107.28	103.33	100.34	100.62	98.28	96.65
MARCH	101.94	108.03	109.05	110.31	106.82	103.14	100.53	100.09	98.41	96.66
APRIL	101.78	107.77	109.96	110.32	105.96	102.87	100.72	100.17	98.53	96.67
MAY	102.00	107.69	109.32	110.33	105.87	102.65	100.61	100.23	98.62	96.88
JUNE	102.20	107.60	108.74	110.42	105.38	102.97	100.48	100.20	98.72	96.65
JULY	102.41	107.63	108.79	110.53	105.82	102.43	100.36	100.25	98.03	96.86
AUGUST	103.36	108.31	109.04	109.85	105.67	102.33	100.72	99.96	98.11	96.90
SEPTEMBER	104.34	108.99	109.28	109.62	105.19	102.22	100.98	99.76	98.19	96.95
OCTOBER	105.33	109.66	109.53	108.96	104.92	101.96	101.22	99.56	98.27	96.99
NOVEMBER	105.55	109.40	109.66	109.01	104.35	102.03	100.97	99.27	98.27	96.99
DECEMBER	105.66	109.14	109.75	108.93	104.12	100.28	100.93	99.34	98.27	96.99
NBER PRICE INDEX, ANNUAL AVERAGES:										
STD. DEV.*	0.9869	1.1508	1.1947	1.3858	1.4977	1.8508	0.9377	1.1266	1.4446	0.5152
NO. OF SERIES*	17.55	18.00	18.83	23.67	24.42	26.33	27.00	28.83	27.25	15.17

* See page 105.

Table C-26. Synthetic Rubber—SBR, Hot, Cold

(price indexes, 1964 = 100)

	1957	1958	1959	1960	1961	1962	1963	1964	1965	1966
BLS										
JANUARY	105.21	105.21	105.21	105.21	105.21	101.76	100.00	100.00	100.00	100.00
FEBRUARY	105.21	105.21	105.21	105.21	105.21	100.88	100.00	100.00	100.00	100.00
MARCH	105.21	105.21	105.21	105.21	105.21	100.00	100.00	100.00	100.00	100.00
APRIL	105.21	105.21	105.21	105.21	105.21	100.00	100.00	100.00	100.00	100.00
MAY	105.21	105.21	105.21	105.21	105.21	100.00	100.00	100.00	100.00	100.00
JUNE	105.21	105.21	105.21	105.21	105.21	100.00	100.00	100.00	100.00	100.00
JULY	105.21	105.21	105.21	105.21	105.21	100.00	100.00	100.00	100.00	100.00
AUGUST	105.21	105.21	105.21	105.21	105.21	100.00	100.00	100.00	100.00	100.00
SEPTEMBER	105.21	105.21	105.21	105.21	105.21	100.00	100.00	100.00	100.00	100.00
OCTOBER	105.21	105.21	105.21	105.21	104.78	97.29	100.00	100.00	100.00	100.00
NOVEMBER	105.21	105.21	105.21	105.21	104.78	96.41	100.00	100.00	100.00	100.00
DECEMBER	105.21	105.21	105.21	105.21	101.69	100.00	100.00	100.00	100.00	100.00
NBER										
JANUARY	108.78	108.78	110.58	121.92	109.93	107.08	107.70	102.26	100.16	95.07
FEBRUARY	108.78	108.56	111.24	120.88	108.52	104.01	107.27	99.78	100.04	95.09
MARCH	109.90	108.56	111.74	121.84	106.96	104.80	104.36	99.85	99.78	95.12
APRIL	108.33	107.88	112.56	119.77	107.52	104.77	100.54	99.93	99.52	95.02
MAY	110.79	108.33	113.86	118.95	106.49	105.91	103.64	100.25	91.30	93.47
JUNE	108.78	108.33	115.01	118.14	106.21	107.19	103.89	99.59	93.59	92.81
JULY	107.65	108.78	116.49	116.48	105.80	108.12	103.45	100.65	94.15	93.30
AUGUST	108.78	108.11	117.50	114.84	108.58	109.05	102.67	99.62	94.71	93.14
SEPTEMBER	109.90	107.43	119.01	113.22	107.91	110.12	101.79	99.56	94.92	92.51
OCTOBER	109.01	108.78	120.55	111.63	107.13	103.79	100.43	98.99	95.37	91.89
NOVEMBER	109.90	109.28	120.67	111.16	108.93	107.71	101.09	99.51	94.02	91.27
DECEMBER	108.33	110.08	120.80	110.58	105.09	106.32	98.16	100.03	94.54	90.66
NBER PRICE INDEX, ANNUAL AVERAGES:										
STD. DEV.*	1.1574	0.5404	1.2623	1.8994	1.6449	3.5240	2.8345	1.8131	1.7570	0.7608
NO. OF SERIES*	2.00	2.17	3.00	3.00	3.83	4.00	4.00	4.00	4.00	3.00

* See page 105.

Table C-27. Neoprene

(price indexes, 1964 = 100)

	1957	1958	1959	1960	1961	1962	1963	1964	1965	1966
BLS										
JANUARY	100.08	100.08	100.08	100.08	100.08	100.00	100.00	100.00	100.00	100.00
FEBRUARY	100.08	100.08	100.08	100.08	100.08	100.00	100.00	100.00	100.00	100.00
MARCH	100.08	100.08	100.08	100.08	100.08	100.00	100.00	100.00	100.00	100.00
APRIL	100.08	100.08	100.08	100.08	100.08	100.00	100.00	100.00	100.00	100.00
MAY	100.08	100.08	100.08	100.08	100.08	100.00	100.00	100.00	100.00	100.00
JUNE	100.08	100.08	100.08	100.08	100.08	100.00	100.00	100.00	100.00	100.00
JULY	100.08	100.08	100.08	100.08	100.08	100.00	100.00	100.00	100.00	100.00
AUGUST	100.08	100.08	100.08	100.08	100.08	100.00	100.00	100.00	100.00	100.00
SEPTEMBER	100.08	100.08	100.08	100.08	100.08	100.00	100.00	100.00	100.00	100.00
OCTOBER	100.08	100.08	100.08	100.08	100.08	100.00	100.00	100.00	100.00	100.00
NOVEMBER	100.08	100.08	100.08	100.08	100.08	100.00	100.00	100.00	100.00	100.00
DECEMBER	100.08	100.08	100.08	100.08	100.08	100.00	100.00	100.00	100.00	100.00
NBER										
JANUARY	100.55	100.49	100.25	100.49	99.94	99.76	99.88	100.00	99.88	99.84
FEBRUARY	100.44	100.49	100.37	100.49	99.76	99.74	100.00	100.00	99.68	100.43
MARCH	100.44	100.41	100.49	100.29	99.82	99.66	100.00	100.00	100.00	99.94
APRIL	100.44	100.52	100.49	100.25	99.82	99.92	99.84	99.62	99.80	99.37
MAY	100.44	100.52	100.49	100.25	99.76	99.80	99.84	100.04	99.80	99.82
JUNE	100.44	100.52	100.49	100.25	99.76	99.80	99.80	100.04	99.76	100.06
JULY	100.44	100.52	100.49	100.25	99.90	99.80	99.88	100.04	99.52	99.88
AUGUST	100.20	100.49	100.49	99.78	99.95	99.90	100.07	100.09	100.15	100.06
SEPTEMBER	100.60	100.49	100.49	99.70	99.90	100.00	100.07	100.09	99.76	99.99
OCTOBER	100.49	100.49	100.49	100.17	99.71	99.88	99.92	100.19	99.84	100.01
NOVEMBER	100.37	100.41	100.49	99.78	99.81	100.04	100.04	100.00	99.44	99.86
DECEMBER	100.60	100.49	100.49	99.78	99.81	100.00	100.04	100.04	99.60	99.87
NBER PRICE INDEX, ANNUAL AVERAGES:										
STD. DEV.*	0.1021	0.0542	0.0618	0.2051	0.1546	0.2027	0.1858	0.2543	0.5323	0.4089
NO. OF SERIES*	2.00	2.92	3.00	3.00	4.50	5.92	6.00	6.00	6.00	4.25

* See page 105.

Table C-28. Rubber Belting, Industrial
(price indexes, 1964 = 100)

	1957	1958	1959	1960	1961	1962	1963	1964	1965	1966
BLS										
JANUARY	85.93	87.43	87.43	90.85	94.44	94.44	96.10	99.26	103.72	103.52
FEBRUARY	85.93	87.43	87.43	90.85	94.44	94.44	96.10	99.26	103.72	106.16
MARCH	85.93	87.43	87.43	90.85	94.44	94.44	97.08	99.26	103.72	106.16
APRIL	85.93	87.43	87.43	90.85	94.44	94.44	98.12	99.26	102.22	106.16
MAY	85.93	87.43	87.43	90.85	94.44	96.10	98.12	99.26	102.22	106.16
JUNE	85.93	87.43	87.43	90.85	94.44	96.10	98.12	99.26	102.22	106.16
JULY	85.93	87.43	87.43	90.85	94.44	96.10	98.12	99.26	102.22	106.16
AUGUST	87.43	87.43	87.43	90.85	94.44	96.10	98.12	99.26	102.22	106.16
SEPTEMBER	87.43	87.43	89.87	94.44	94.44	96.10	99.26	99.26	102.22	106.16
OCTOBER	87.43	87.43	90.85	94.44	94.44	96.10	99.26	100.71	102.22	106.16
NOVEMBER	87.43	87.43	90.85	94.44	94.44	96.10	99.26	102.22	102.22	106.16
DECEMBER	87.43	87.43	90.85	94.44	94.44	96.10	99.26	103.72	102.22	106.16
NBER										
JANUARY	96.29	96.55	96.07	98.29	101.20	101.51	101.26	100.98	98.52	98.62
FEBRUARY	96.33	96.52	96.08	98.35	101.29	101.51	101.38	100.74	98.45	98.55
MARCH	96.37	96.49	96.10	98.41	101.37	101.51	101.51	100.50	98.38	98.47
APRIL	96.41	96.46	96.11	98.47	101.45	101.51	101.63	100.26	98.31	98.40
MAY	96.34	96.35	96.13	98.82	101.51	101.52	101.32	100.26	98.31	98.56
JUNE	96.26	96.24	96.16	99.18	101.56	101.53	101.01	100.26	98.31	98.73
JULY	96.18	96.13	96.19	99.54	101.62	101.55	100.71	100.26	98.31	98.89
AUGUST	96.37	96.17	96.61	100.09	101.60	101.48	100.71	99.95	98.24	99.24
SEPTEMBER	96.56	96.21	97.03	100.64	101.55	101.42	100.71	99.63	98.16	99.58
OCTOBER	96.75	96.24	97.45	101.20	101.55	101.36	100.71	99.32	98.08	99.93
NOVEMBER	96.68	96.18	97.73	101.20	101.54	101.32	100.80	99.05	98.26	99.93
DECEMBER	96.62	96.13	98.01	101.20	101.52	101.29	100.89	98.79	98.44	99.93
NBER PRICE INDEX, ANNUAL AVERAGES:										
STD. DEV.*	0.6799	0.3125	0.3157	0.7838	0.1666	0.0982	0.4620	0.6787	0.3852	0.7007
NO. OF SERIES*	17.00	17.00	17.00	17.00	16.33	14.83	15.00	14.83	14.92	13.08

NOTE: The NBER index is based exclusively on prices paid by railroads.
* See page 105.

Table C-29. Paper: Book, Magazine, Etc.

(price indexes, 1964 = 100)

	1957	1958	1959	1960	1961	1962	1963	1964	1965	1966
BLS										
JANUARY	89.87	92.99	93.13	96.42	97.71	97.56	98.01	98.60	100.40	103.41
FEBRUARY	89.87	92.99	93.13	96.42	97.71	97.73	98.01	98.60	100.40	104.00
MARCH	89.87	93.13	93.13	96.77	97.71	98.23	98.32	99.78	100.40	104.00
APRIL	89.87	93.13	94.84	97.32	97.71	98.70	98.60	100.03	100.62	104.20
MAY	92.61	93.13	94.84	97.90	97.71	98.82	98.60	100.37	100.62	105.17
JUNE	92.61	93.13	94.84	97.90	97.71	98.82	98.60	100.37	100.62	105.32
JULY	92.99	93.13	95.64	97.90	97.71	98.82	98.60	100.37	100.62	105.65
AUGUST	92.99	93.13	96.09	97.90	97.71	98.82	98.60	100.37	100.62	106.33
SEPTEMBER	92.99	93.13	96.09	97.90	97.56	98.82	98.60	100.37	100.62	106.33
OCTOBER	92.99	93.13	96.09	97.90	97.56	98.60	98.60	100.37	100.96	106.33
NOVEMBER	92.99	93.13	96.09	97.71	97.56	98.60	98.60	100.37	103.03	106.33
DECEMBER	92.99	93.13	96.09	97.71	97.56	98.60	98.60	100.40	103.03	106.33
NBER										
JANUARY	101.06	97.82	97.65	102.91	103.28	101.93	101.38	99.49	100.87	106.17
FEBRUARY	101.06	97.33	98.45	102.90	102.78	102.33	100.74	99.22	101.06	107.36
MARCH	101.06	97.46	98.42	102.99	102.82	102.30	100.68	99.18	101.06	107.38
APRIL	101.06	97.36	98.40	103.34	102.82	102.29	100.48	99.98	101.43	107.63
MAY	98.50	96.89	99.67	104.00	102.10	102.68	99.87	99.94	102.17	107.72
JUNE	98.50	96.79	99.62	104.10	102.09	102.67	99.83	99.92	102.18	108.03
JULY	99.10	96.79	101.00	104.26	102.41	102.69	99.49	100.18	102.43	108.10
AUGUST	98.33	97.31	101.71	103.64	101.95	102.31	99.37	100.24	103.13	108.52
SEPTEMBER	98.33	97.29	101.92	103.69	101.94	102.30	99.42	100.22	103.74	108.82
OCTOBER	98.29	97.14	102.46	103.74	101.77	101.51	99.34	100.20	103.78	109.02
NOVEMBER	97.79	97.93	102.75	103.22	101.93	101.87	99.25	100.69	104.49	109.11
DECEMBER	97.75	97.91	102.85	103.23	101.94	101.96	99.21	100.75	104.52	109.11
NBER PRICE INDEX, ANNUAL AVERAGES:										
STD. DEV.*	0.9226	0.8483	0.9526	0.7860	0.5762	0.6114	0.7914	0.6001	1.1164	0.9336
NO. OF SERIES*	12.36	17.00	19.00	20.50	21.33	22.75	24.42	26.08	26.33	22.83

* See page 105.

Table C-30. Newsprint

(price indexes, 1964 = 100)

	1957	1958	1959	1960	1961	1962	1963	1964	1965	1966
BLS										
JANUARY	96.92	100.12	100.12	100.12	100.12	100.12	100.12	100.12	98.63	98.63
FEBRUARY	96.92	100.12	100.12	100.12	100.12	100.12	100.12	100.12	98.63	98.63
MARCH	99.30	100.12	100.12	100.12	100.12	100.12	100.12	100.12	98.63	98.63
APRIL	100.12	100.12	100.12	100.12	100.12	100.12	100.12	100.12	98.63	100.12
MAY	100.12	100.12	100.12	100.12	100.12	100.12	100.12	100.12	98.63	100.12
JUNE	100.12	100.12	100.12	100.12	100.12	100.12	100.12	100.12	98.63	103.10
JULY	100.12	100.12	100.12	100.12	100.12	100.12	100.12	100.12	98.63	103.10
AUGUST	100.12	100.12	100.12	100.12	100.12	100.12	100.12	100.12	98.63	103.10
SEPTEMBER	100.12	100.12	100.12	100.12	100.12	100.12	100.12	100.12	98.63	103.10
OCTOBER	100.12	100.12	100.12	100.12	100.12	100.12	100.12	100.12	98.63	103.10
NOVEMBER	100.12	100.12	100.12	100.12	100.12	100.12	100.12	100.12	98.63	103.10
DECEMBER	100.12	100.12	100.12	100.12	100.12	100.12	100.12	98.63	98.63	103.10
NBER										
JANUARY	99.61	100.00	100.03	99.77	99.77	100.61	101.76	100.37	100.14	101.64
FEBRUARY	99.61	100.03	100.03	99.77	99.77	100.61	101.76	100.37	100.14	101.64
MARCH	99.61	100.03	100.03	99.77	99.77	100.61	101.76	100.37	100.14	101.64
APRIL	99.61	100.03	100.03	99.77	99.77	100.61	101.76	100.15	100.14	101.64
MAY	99.61	100.03	100.03	99.77	99.77	100.61	101.76	100.15	100.14	101.77
JUNE	99.61	100.03	100.03	99.77	99.77	100.61	101.76	100.15	100.14	101.92
JULY	99.95	100.03	99.77	99.77	99.77	101.76	100.37	99.74	100.63	102.07
AUGUST	99.95	100.03	99.77	99.77	100.61	101.76	100.37	99.74	100.63	102.07
SEPTEMBER	99.95	100.03	99.77	99.77	100.61	101.76	100.37	99.74	100.63	102.07
OCTOBER	99.95	100.03	99.77	99.77	100.61	101.76	100.37	99.74	100.63	102.07
NOVEMBER	99.95	100.03	99.77	99.77	100.61	101.76	100.37	99.74	100.63	102.24
DECEMBER	99.98	100.03	99.77	99.77	100.61	101.76	100.37	99.74	100.63	102.24
NBER PRICE INDEX, ANNUAL AVERAGES:										
STD. DEV.*	0.0990	0.0126	0.0643	0.0000	0.2076	0.2850	0.3442	0.1642	0.2224	0.3463
NO. OF SERIES*	8.91	9.00	9.00	9.00	9.00	9.00	9.17	10.00	9.00	8.42

* See page 105.

Table C-31. Coarse Paper and Bags, Kraft Papers

(price indexes, 1964 = 100)

	1957	1958	1959	1960	1961	1962	1963	1964	1965	1966
BLS										
JANUARY	103.80	108.16	106.45	106.07	107.36	113.19	94.71	97.37	103.19	110.47
FEBRUARY	103.80	108.16	106.45	106.07	107.36	114.77	95.09	98.14	104.43	111.29
MARCH	103.80	108.16	106.45	106.45	105.76	114.77	94.46	100.30	106.31	111.29
APRIL	103.80	108.16	106.45	106.07	102.85	114.77	94.46	100.30	106.31	112.20
MAY	103.80	106.45	105.97	108.18	104.79	107.52	96.20	98.87	107.06	112.20
JUNE	104.62	106.45	105.70	108.24	108.00	102.91	98.89	98.87	107.89	112.20
JULY	107.64	106.45	105.70	108.00	108.00	98.98	98.89	98.87	108.71	112.20
AUGUST	107.94	106.45	105.21	104.36	108.00	98.98	98.89	98.87	108.71	112.20
SEPTEMBER	107.94	106.45	105.21	104.36	106.49	97.76	98.89	98.87	108.71	112.20
OCTOBER	107.94	106.45	106.07	107.36	106.49	97.37	97.37	103.19	109.53	112.20
NOVEMBER	108.16	106.45	106.07	107.36	106.49	95.78	97.37	103.19	109.53	112.20
DECEMBER	108.16	106.45	106.07	107.36	113.24	94.71	97.37	103.19	109.74	112.20
NBER										
JANUARY	110.47	115.02	112.49	110.99	108.85	106.25	107.13	99.85	100.12	107.42
FEBRUARY	110.47	114.29	113.34	111.05	107.96	108.36	106.96	100.01	100.41	107.83
MARCH	110.47	114.33	113.35	111.06	107.98	108.36	106.87	99.84	100.55	107.87
APRIL	109.73	114.36	113.37	111.08	107.89	108.37	106.77	99.89	100.76	107.90
MAY	109.73	114.01	112.97	111.07	107.74	108.63	106.61	100.01	100.89	107.87
JUNE	116.60	114.05	112.99	111.16	107.65	108.64	106.51	100.06	100.94	107.91
JULY	116.63	114.06	112.27	111.27	107.64	108.59	105.77	100.12	101.65	107.87
AUGUST	116.74	113.96	111.11	108.30	106.25	107.57	104.86	100.05	107.15	111.64
SEPTEMBER	116.85	113.98	111.17	108.40	106.24	107.52	99.52	99.97	107.22	113.41
OCTOBER	116.85	113.99	111.23	108.51	106.24	107.48	99.60	99.97	107.28	113.30
NOVEMBER	114.95	112.46	110.87	108.78	106.23	107.27	99.68	100.11	107.28	113.23
DECEMBER	114.99	112.48	110.93	108.82	106.24	107.20	99.77	100.12	107.35	113.23
NBER PRICE INDEX, ANNUAL AVERAGES:										
STD. DEV.*	1.1867	0.6050	0.4593	0.6758	0.7145	0.7454	1.0462	0.6819	0.9275	1.3697
NO. OF SERIES*	3.91	4.58	5.00	19.67	23.83	23.50	23.83	24.00	23.58	20.83

NOTE: This commodity is among those showing a "reversal of trend" (see page 42); the trend was fitted to the period ending April 1964.

* See page 105.

Table C-32. Paperboard—Unfabricated
(price indexes, 1964 = 100)

	1957	1958	1959	1960	1961	1962	1963	1964	1965	1966
BLS										
JANUARY	103.90	103.99	103.91	103.83	100.74	93.05	97.61	100.06	99.91	100.31
FEBRUARY	103.90	103.99	103.91	103.83	98.97	93.05	97.61	100.06	99.91	100.31
MARCH	103.90	103.93	103.91	103.83	98.83	96.27	97.61	100.06	99.85	100.59
APRIL	103.90	103.89	103.91	103.83	98.21	97.24	97.61	100.06	99.85	100.69
MAY	103.90	103.88	103.91	103.83	98.07	97.32	97.61	100.06	99.85	100.76
JUNE	103.90	103.88	103.91	103.83	98.07	97.49	97.61	100.06	99.85	100.76
JULY	103.90	103.88	103.83	103.83	93.47	97.61	97.61	100.06	99.85	100.76
AUGUST	103.90	103.88	103.83	103.83	93.35	97.61	97.61	99.91	99.85	100.76
SEPTEMBER	103.90	104.02	103.83	103.83	93.06	97.61	97.61	99.91	100.00	100.76
OCTOBER	104.07	103.91	103.83	103.81	93.06	97.61	100.14	99.91	100.08	100.76
NOVEMBER	104.07	103.91	103.83	100.82	93.06	97.61	100.12	99.91	100.08	100.76
DECEMBER	104.07	103.91	103.83	100.82	93.06	97.61	100.06	99.91	100.08	100.76
NBER										
JANUARY	104.11	104.63	104.57	102.53	102.24	101.73	102.03	100.15	98.92	98.17
FEBRUARY	104.11	104.62	104.57	102.62	102.00	102.25	101.45	100.24	98.67	98.33
MARCH	104.11	104.60	104.98	102.73	101.76	102.52	100.86	100.33	98.39	98.51
APRIL	104.14	103.73	102.62	102.95	101.12	102.66	100.38	100.36	98.18	98.56
MAY	104.17	103.71	102.30	103.06	100.50	102.81	99.86	100.46	97.97	98.74
JUNE	104.19	103.70	102.38	103.18	99.69	102.96	99.35	100.55	97.76	99.07
JULY	104.12	104.18	102.26	102.67	99.64	102.88	99.45	100.31	97.94	98.58
AUGUST	104.04	104.44	102.48	102.39	99.71	102.78	99.62	100.00	98.15	98.51
SEPTEMBER	103.97	104.95	102.40	102.22	99.98	102.68	99.78	99.76	98.36	99.51
OCTOBER	103.90	104.89	102.27	102.33	100.71	102.58	99.87	99.53	98.09	98.88
NOVEMBER	103.83	104.85	102.47	102.49	101.07	102.49	99.96	99.28	98.26	98.88
DECEMBER	103.77	104.84	102.56	102.29	101.30	102.39	100.06	99.03	98.43	98.88
NBER PRICE INDEX, ANNUAL AVERAGES:										
STD. DEV.*	0.1637	1.0453	1.3523	1.3160	1.3602	0.6790	1.0335	0.5458	0.7103	0.7263
NO. OF SERIES*	2.36	3.92	5.00	6.00	6.75	7.00	7.00	7.00	7.00	5.50

* See page 105.

Table C-33. Paper Boxes and Shipping Containers

(price indexes, 1964 = 100)

	1957	1958	1959	1960	1961	1962	1963	1964	1965	1966
BLS										
JANUARY	99.70	100.49	101.60	104.91	105.07	100.81	102.54	103.02	98.84	100.89
FEBRUARY	99.70	100.49	101.60	104.91	105.07	100.81	102.62	103.17	98.84	101.05
MARCH	99.70	100.49	101.60	104.91	104.59	103.17	102.62	100.41	99.78	102.15
APRIL	99.70	100.49	101.60	104.91	104.28	104.12	102.62	100.41	99.94	102.15
MAY	99.70	101.60	101.60	104.91	92.13	104.12	102.62	98.84	99.94	101.91
JUNE	99.70	101.60	101.60	104.91	92.13	104.12	102.62	98.84	99.94	101.91
JULY	100.49	101.60	101.60	104.91	92.13	103.57	102.46	99.23	99.31	102.15
AUGUST	100.49	101.60	101.60	104.91	92.13	102.54	102.86	99.47	99.31	102.15
SEPTEMBER	100.49	101.60	101.60	104.91	101.12	102.54	102.86	99.47	99.47	102.23
OCTOBER	100.49	101.60	101.60	104.91	101.12	102.54	102.86	99.47	99.63	102.31
NOVEMBER	100.49	101.60	101.60	104.91	101.12	102.54	102.86	98.84	100.10	102.46
DECEMBER	100.49	101.60	101.60	104.91	101.36	102.54	102.86	98.84	100.34	102.46
NBER										
JANUARY	110.62	106.60	105.54	103.74	101.27	100.57	100.14	100.26	99.70	100.78
FEBRUARY	110.62	106.80	105.60	103.83	101.29	100.54	100.14	100.15	99.70	100.90
MARCH	110.62	107.00	105.66	103.92	101.32	100.75	100.14	100.04	99.97	101.26
APRIL	110.62	107.05	105.40	104.04	101.29	101.02	100.17	100.15	100.04	101.38
MAY	110.62	107.10	105.26	104.16	101.22	100.94	100.15	100.17	100.20	101.50
JUNE	110.62	106.60	105.26	104.01	101.01	100.84	100.14	100.19	100.27	101.62
JULY	110.36	106.06	105.23	103.66	100.73	100.75	100.17	100.15	99.93	101.94
AUGUST	110.10	106.27	105.20	103.61	100.68	100.81	100.18	100.10	98.50	102.23
SEPTEMBER	109.89	106.42	105.35	103.49	100.78	100.88	100.20	99.86	98.59	102.30
OCTOBER	109.70	106.40	105.26	103.42	101.53	100.72	100.65	99.83	99.07	102.98
NOVEMBER	110.70	106.20	105.01	103.26	101.56	100.61	100.67	99.57	99.27	103.66
DECEMBER	110.50	106.40	105.10	103.28	101.68	100.51	100.53	99.54	99.62	103.66
NBER PRICE INDEX, ANNUAL AVERAGES:										
STD. DEV.*	0.5179	1.1625	0.6803	1.1500	1.5315	1.1013	0.9269	0.9325	1.2777	0.9030
NO. OF SERIES*	7.36	10.50	13.58	19.67	28.50	30.17	31.42	33.25	32.08	19.17

* See page 105.

Table C-34. Bond Paper
(price indexes, 1964 = 100)

	1957	1958	1959	1960	1961	1962	1963	1964	1965	1966
BLS										
JANUARY	90.98	93.97	93.97	96.36	96.51	96.50	97.79	100.21	99.98	102.24
FEBRUARY	90.98	93.97	93.97	96.44	96.51	96.50	97.79	99.98	99.98	102.24
MARCH	90.98	93.97	93.97	96.51	96.51	96.50	97.79	99.98	99.98	102.24
APRIL	90.98	93.97	95.71	96.51	96.51	97.77	97.79	99.98	99.98	103.00
MAY	93.00	93.97	96.28	96.51	96.51	97.77	97.79	99.98	100.28	105.75
JUNE	93.57	93.97	96.28	96.51	96.51	97.79	97.79	99.98	100.70	105.75
JULY	93.69	93.97	96.28	96.51	96.51	97.79	97.79	99.98	100.70	106.00
AUGUST	93.97	93.97	96.36	96.51	96.51	97.79	97.79	99.98	100.70	106.00
SEPTEMBER	93.97	93.97	96.36	96.51	96.51	97.79	97.79	99.98	100.70	106.00
OCTOBER	93.97	93.97	96.36	96.51	96.51	97.79	98.82	99.98	102.09	106.00
NOVEMBER	93.97	93.97	96.36	96.51	96.51	97.79	99.40	99.98	102.24	106.43
DECEMBER	93.97	93.97	96.36	96.51	96.51	97.79	99.40	99.98	102.24	106.43
NBER										
JANUARY	104.53	105.13	108.54	109.46	105.45	104.53	103.67	100.75	100.40	101.50
FEBRUARY	104.53	104.76	109.09	109.32	105.24	104.47	101.49	100.61	100.64	101.56
MARCH	104.53	104.79	109.09	109.32	105.24	104.47	101.45	100.63	100.56	101.94
APRIL	104.53	104.82	109.07	109.32	105.23	104.47	101.40	100.00	100.51	102.58
MAY	99.89	104.26	109.75	107.96	105.09	104.60	101.27	100.11	100.72	102.63
JUNE	99.89	104.29	109.73	107.96	105.07	104.60	101.26	100.05	100.68	103.04
JULY	105.06	104.29	109.44	107.96	104.51	104.87	100.63	99.66	100.99	107.99
AUGUST	105.05	107.67	109.62	107.58	104.86	104.70	100.64	99.65	101.65	107.95
SEPTEMBER	105.40	107.93	109.67	107.58	104.82	104.70	100.68	99.65	100.80	107.98
OCTOBER	105.22	107.76	109.67	107.58	104.77	104.84	100.67	99.65	100.80	108.04
NOVEMBER	105.07	108.34	109.46	107.51	104.64	104.81	100.72	99.62	100.80	109.16
DECEMBER	105.10	108.43	109.46	107.51	104.64	104.81	100.72	99.62	100.80	108.52
NBER PRICE INDEX, ANNUAL AVERAGES:										
STD. DEV.*	1.5003	0.8665	0.5516	0.3496	0.9527	0.3930	0.9265	0.3904	1.0939	1.7843
NO. OF SERIES*	4.55	6.00	7.83	10.75	12.00	13.00	13.17	14.92	14.83	13.00

* See page 105.

Table C-35. Sulfuric Acid—Bulk

(price indexes, 1964 = 100)

	1957	1958	1959	1960	1961	1962	1963	1964	1965	1966
BLS										
JANUARY	100.00	100.00	100.00	100.00	100.00	100.00	100.00	100.00	104.03	108.77
FEBRUARY	100.00	100.00	100.00	100.00	100.00	100.00	100.00	100.00	104.03	108.77
MARCH	100.00	100.00	100.00	100.00	100.00	100.00	100.00	100.00	104.03	108.77
APRIL	100.00	100.00	100.00	100.00	100.00	100.00	100.00	100.00	104.03	108.77
MAY	100.00	100.00	100.00	100.00	100.00	100.00	100.00	100.00	104.03	115.26
JUNE	100.00	100.00	100.00	100.00	100.00	100.00	100.00	100.00	104.03	115.26
JULY	100.00	100.00	100.00	100.00	100.00	100.00	100.00	100.00	104.03	115.26
AUGUST	100.00	100.00	100.00	100.00	100.00	100.00	100.00	100.00	104.03	115.26
SEPTEMBER	100.00	100.00	100.00	100.00	100.00	100.00	100.00	100.00	104.03	115.26
OCTOBER	100.00	100.00	100.00	100.00	100.00	100.00	100.00	100.00	104.03	115.26
NOVEMBER	100.00	100.00	100.00	100.00	100.00	100.00	100.00	100.00	108.73	115.26
DECEMBER	100.00	100.00	100.00	100.00	100.00	100.00	100.00	100.00	108.73	115.26
NBER										
JANUARY	101.27	101.37	101.70	100.38	98.93	97.77	97.59	99.62	102.09	107.29
FEBRUARY	101.32	101.34	101.66	100.39	98.91	97.79	97.66	99.64	102.23	107.33
MARCH	101.32	101.42	101.55	100.44	98.87	97.82	97.68	99.71	102.23	107.35
APRIL	101.31	100.97	101.58	100.39	98.75	97.85	98.50	100.16	102.35	108.05
MAY	101.30	100.98	101.58	100.36	98.81	97.87	98.64	100.35	102.37	108.69
JUNE	101.36	100.98	101.63	100.33	98.87	97.88	98.56	100.12	102.37	109.66
JULY	101.34	101.01	101.58	100.27	98.83	97.83	98.54	100.08	102.46	110.32
AUGUST	101.36	100.94	101.59	100.28	98.83	97.84	98.50	100.07	102.69	110.43
SEPTEMBER	101.43	100.93	101.58	100.22	98.80	97.82	98.48	100.07	102.93	110.30
OCTOBER	101.45	100.94	101.55	100.19	98.80	97.78	98.44	100.11	104.63	111.62
NOVEMBER	101.40	100.91	101.49	100.20	98.78	97.71	98.42	100.06	104.80	111.62
DECEMBER	101.45	101.77	101.49	100.28	98.73	97.61	98.33	100.02	104.81	111.62
NBER PRICE INDEX, ANNUAL AVERAGES:										
STD. DEV.*	0.1456	0.9543	0.3216	0.4506	0.6426	0.4320	0.5830	1.5411	0.8886	1.6795
NO. OF SERIES*	21.00	25.83	26.92	29.33	32.83	34.00	37.92	39.92	37.58	31.33

* See page 105.

Table C-36. Caustic Soda—Liquid
(price indexes, 1964 = 100)

	1957	1958	1959	1960	1961	1962	1963	1964	1965	1966
BLS										
JANUARY	91.10	91.10	101.69	101.69	101.69	101.69	101.69	91.53	101.69	101.69
FEBRUARY	91.10	91.10	101.69	101.69	101.69	101.69	101.69	91.53	101.69	101.69
MARCH	91.10	91.10	101.69	101.69	101.69	101.69	101.69	101.69	101.69	101.69
APRIL	91.10	101.69	101.69	101.69	101.69	101.69	101.69	101.69	101.69	101.69
MAY	91.10	101.69	101.69	101.69	101.69	101.69	91.53	101.69	101.69	101.69
JUNE	91.10	101.69	101.69	101.69	101.69	101.69	91.53	101.69	101.69	101.69
JULY	91.10	101.69	101.69	101.69	101.69	101.69	91.53	101.69	101.69	101.69
AUGUST	91.10	101.69	101.69	101.69	101.69	101.69	91.53	101.69	101.69	101.69
SEPTEMBER	91.10	101.69	101.69	101.69	101.69	101.69	91.53	101.69	101.69	101.69
OCTOBER	91.10	101.69	101.69	101.69	101.69	101.69	91.53	101.69	101.69	101.69
NOVEMBER	91.10	101.69	101.69	101.69	101.69	101.69	91.53	101.69	101.69	101.69
DECEMBER	91.10	101.69	101.69	101.69	101.69	101.69	91.53	101.69	101.69	101.69
NBER										
JANUARY	111.05	109.63	108.65	108.47	106.46	105.11	101.64	98.00	100.35	98.93
FEBRUARY	111.10	109.63	108.65	108.47	106.46	105.14	99.50	97.71	100.38	98.84
MARCH	111.14	109.63	108.39	108.47	106.46	105.18	99.36	97.97	100.40	98.75
APRIL	109.21	109.63	108.39	108.47	106.46	105.16	99.05	100.23	100.19	98.66
MAY	109.26	109.63	108.39	108.02	106.46	105.14	98.90	100.60	99.93	98.33
JUNE	109.30	110.33	108.39	108.02	106.46	105.11	98.71	100.76	99.75	97.88
JULY	110.71	109.89	108.39	108.46	106.46	104.38	98.90	100.90	99.22	98.00
AUGUST	110.75	109.89	108.39	108.46	106.46	104.50	98.82	100.90	99.42	98.00
SEPTEMBER	110.79	109.89	108.39	108.46	106.31	105.17	98.79	100.81	99.54	98.00
OCTOBER	109.67	110.30	108.39	108.46	106.06	104.06	98.76	100.87	99.53	98.00
NOVEMBER	109.72	110.30	108.39	107.96	106.16	104.52	98.74	100.81	99.34	98.00
DECEMBER	109.76	110.30	108.39	107.96	106.16	104.37	98.74	100.44	99.25	98.00
NBER PRICE INDEX, ANNUAL AVERAGES:										
STD. DEV.*	1.7408	0.8679	0.4158	0.8538	0.4093	2.0583	1.5189	1.6609	1.1469	0.6002
NO. OF SERIES*	15.00	15.25	19.67	25.00	32.92	35.58	38.83	41.50	41.42	29.50

* See page 105.

Table C-37. Titanium Dioxide

(price indexes, 1964 = 100)

	1957	1958	1959	1960	1961	1962	1963	1964	1965	1966
BLS										
JANUARY	90.00	102.00	101.60	101.60	101.60	100.00	100.00	100.00	100.00	100.00
FEBRUARY	94.00	102.00	101.60	101.60	101.60	100.00	100.00	100.00	100.00	100.00
MARCH	94.00	102.00	101.60	101.60	101.60	100.00	100.00	100.00	100.00	100.00
APRIL	94.00	102.00	101.60	101.60	101.60	100.00	100.00	100.00	100.00	100.00
MAY	94.00	102.00	101.60	101.60	101.60	100.00	100.00	100.00	100.00	100.00
JUNE	94.00	102.00	101.60	101.60	101.60	100.00	100.00	100.00	100.00	100.00
JULY	94.00	102.00	101.60	101.60	101.60	100.00	100.00	100.00	100.00	100.00
AUGUST	94.00	102.00	101.60	101.60	101.60	100.00	100.00	100.00	100.00	100.00
SEPTEMBER	94.00	102.00	101.60	101.60	101.60	100.00	100.00	100.00	100.00	100.00
OCTOBER	94.00	102.00	101.60	101.60	101.60	100.00	100.00	100.00	100.00	100.00
NOVEMBER	94.00	102.00	101.60	101.60	100.00	100.00	100.00	100.00	100.00	100.00
DECEMBER	94.00	102.00	101.60	101.60	100.00	100.00	100.00	100.00	100.00	100.00
NBER										
JANUARY	105.14	108.25	105.29	105.29	104.33	101.83	101.15	100.37	99.60	97.31
FEBRUARY	105.54	108.26	105.29	105.29	104.33	101.83	101.10	100.22	99.50	97.31
MARCH	106.00	108.80	105.29	105.29	103.84	101.70	101.05	100.22	99.37	97.31
APRIL	106.56	108.81	105.29	105.29	103.44	101.64	101.07	100.20	99.37	97.31
MAY	107.30	107.11	105.29	105.29	103.39	101.55	100.95	100.19	99.44	97.31
JUNE	108.28	105.44	105.29	105.29	103.39	101.36	101.03	99.99	99.52	96.89
JULY	108.27	105.45	105.29	105.29	103.39	101.78	100.91	99.98	99.28	96.89
AUGUST	108.27	105.46	105.29	105.29	103.42	101.71	100.73	99.90	99.51	96.89
SEPTEMBER	108.26	105.47	105.29	105.29	102.76	101.65	100.67	99.83	99.53	96.81
OCTOBER	108.31	105.49	105.29	105.29	102.40	101.59	100.62	99.75	97.61	96.89
NOVEMBER	108.31	105.50	105.29	105.29	102.15	101.53	100.57	99.68	97.53	96.89
DECEMBER	108.25	105.56	105.29	105.29	102.39	101.46	100.52	99.60	97.51	96.89
NBER PRICE INDEX, ANNUAL AVERAGES:										
STD. DEV.*	0.7235	0.9425	0.0477	0.0000	0.7691	0.4839	0.2702	0.2952	0.5701	0.2819
NO. OF SERIES*	10.00	10.00	10.00	10.00	12.08	14.83	15.00	15.00	14.75	10.92

* See page 105.

Table C-38. Chlorine—Bulk

(price indexes, 1964 = 100)

	1957	1958	1959	1960	1961	1962	1963	1964	1965	1966
BLS										
JANUARY	96.92	96.92	96.92	96.92	100.00	100.00	100.00	100.00	100.00	100.00
FEBRUARY	96.92	96.92	96.92	96.92	100.00	100.00	100.00	100.00	100.00	100.00
MARCH	96.92	96.92	96.92	96.92	100.00	100.00	100.00	100.00	100.00	100.00
APRIL	96.92	96.92	96.92	100.00	100.00	100.00	100.00	100.00	100.00	100.00
MAY	96.92	96.92	96.92	100.00	100.00	100.00	100.00	100.00	100.00	100.00
JUNE	96.92	96.92	96.92	100.00	100.00	100.00	100.00	100.00	100.00	100.00
JULY	96.92	96.92	96.92	100.00	100.00	100.00	100.00	100.00	100.00	100.00
AUGUST	96.92	96.92	96.92	100.00	100.00	100.00	100.00	100.00	100.00	100.00
SEPTEMBER	96.92	96.92	96.92	100.00	100.00	100.00	100.00	100.00	100.00	100.00
OCTOBER	96.92	96.92	96.92	100.00	100.00	100.00	100.00	100.00	100.00	100.00
NOVEMBER	96.92	96.92	96.92	100.00	100.00	100.00	100.00	100.00	100.00	100.00
DECEMBER	96.92	96.92	96.92	100.00	100.00	100.00	100.00	100.00	100.00	100.00
NBER										
JANUARY	106.29	106.70	106.75	107.25	107.59	105.44	102.99	100.70	96.88	92.51
FEBRUARY	106.33	106.70	106.75	107.27	107.59	105.43	102.93	100.70	96.39	92.52
MARCH	106.38	106.70	106.75	107.28	107.59	105.43	102.87	100.71	96.30	92.54
APRIL	106.43	106.72	106.97	107.79	106.61	105.46	102.30	100.86	95.63	92.35
MAY	106.47	106.72	106.97	107.80	106.61	105.36	101.89	99.93	95.54	92.37
JUNE	106.51	106.72	106.97	107.81	106.61	105.35	101.83	99.93	95.19	92.17
JULY	106.55	106.72	106.97	107.49	106.61	105.35	101.68	99.89	94.50	92.17
AUGUST	106.59	106.72	106.97	107.51	106.61	104.88	101.73	99.85	94.41	92.17
SEPTEMBER	106.63	106.72	106.97	107.52	106.52	104.88	101.78	99.80	94.33	92.17
OCTOBER	106.72	106.72	106.95	107.51	106.52	104.38	101.82	99.76	94.24	92.17
NOVEMBER	106.76	106.72	106.95	107.53	106.52	104.37	101.87	99.71	94.16	92.17
DECEMBER	106.62	106.79	106.95	107.54	106.52	104.37	101.92	98.14	94.07	92.17
NBER PRICE INDEX, ANNUAL AVERAGES:										
STD. DEV.*	0.1685	0.0431	0.0680	0.3526	0.5649	0.7585	0.7244	1.0295	1.0447	0.5170
NO. OF SERIES*	10.55	10.92	11.00	17.42	22.83	24.00	24.00	25.08	26.00	17.50

* See page 105.

Table C-39. Regular Oxygen
(price indexes, 1964 = 100)

	1957	1958	1959	1960	1961	1962	1963	1964	1965	1966
BLS										
JANUARY	91.89	94.91	94.91	94.91	94.91	94.91	94.91	100.00	100.00	100.00
FEBRUARY	91.89	94.91	94.91	94.91	94.91	94.91	100.00	100.00	100.00	100.00
MARCH	91.89	94.91	94.91	94.91	94.91	94.91	100.00	100.00	100.00	100.00
APRIL	91.89	94.91	94.91	94.91	94.91	94.91	100.00	100.00	100.00	100.00
MAY	91.89	94.91	94.91	94.91	94.91	94.91	100.00	100.00	100.00	100.00
JUNE	91.89	94.91	94.91	94.91	94.91	94.91	100.00	100.00	100.00	100.00
JULY	91.89	94.91	94.91	94.91	94.91	94.91	100.00	100.00	100.00	100.00
AUGUST	94.91	94.91	94.91	94.91	94.91	94.91	100.00	100.00	100.00	100.00
SEPTEMBER	94.91	94.91	94.91	94.91	94.91	94.91	100.00	100.00	100.00	100.00
OCTOBER	94.91	94.91	94.91	94.91	94.91	94.91	100.00	100.00	100.00	100.00
NOVEMBER	94.91	94.91	94.91	94.91	94.91	94.91	100.00	100.00	100.00	100.00
DECEMBER	94.91	94.91	94.91	94.91	94.91	94.91	100.00	100.00	100.00	103.11
NBER										
JANUARY	103.44	108.34	106.56	108.10	108.97	111.81	107.34	101.00	106.63	103.60
FEBRUARY	103.69	108.26	111.07	108.10	109.39	111.57	111.26	100.40	106.20	104.18
MARCH	107.00	108.19	105.65	107.97	110.21	110.86	110.77	100.45	106.23	104.44
APRIL	107.26	108.11	106.06	109.37	111.51	110.21	110.25	100.41	105.83	103.63
MAY	107.39	108.19	106.54	108.44	111.86	113.48	109.33	100.51	106.08	103.73
JUNE	107.52	109.12	107.02	108.27	110.08	110.35	109.68	100.50	106.39	103.73
JULY	107.65	108.61	107.02	107.97	112.01	112.52	109.78	100.51	106.38	102.97
AUGUST	107.77	111.28	107.64	108.35	112.89	111.49	109.33	100.61	106.44	99.81
SEPTEMBER	107.90	108.19	107.70	108.52	109.93	109.74	107.50	100.53	106.51	100.59
OCTOBER	108.03	109.83	107.77	108.16	109.86	110.15	107.58	98.14	104.92	99.58
NOVEMBER	108.15	107.96	107.82	113.55	109.57	110.26	107.58	98.24	104.92	99.10
DECEMBER	108.25	106.91	107.88	107.11	109.44	108.94	107.53	98.71	104.92	99.39

NBER PRICE INDEX, ANNUAL AVERAGES:

	1957	1958	1959	1960	1961	1962	1963	1964	1965	1966
STD. DEV.*	0.5933	2.0342	2.0368	3.2260	2.3342	3.5408	2.1264	2.5312	2.3786	2.9706
NO. OF SERIES*	3.09	5.50	6.00	6.00	6.92	9.75	10.92	13.58	14.75	12.75

* See page 105.

Table C-40. Ammonia
(price indexes, 1964 = 100)

	1957	1958	1959	1960	1961	1962	1963	1964	1965	1966
BLS										
JANUARY	88.55	97.14	97.14	97.14	101.43	101.43	101.43	101.43	101.43	101.43
FEBRUARY	88.55	97.14	97.14	97.14	101.43	101.43	101.43	101.43	101.43	101.43
MARCH	88.55	97.14	97.14	97.14	101.43	101.43	101.43	101.43	101.43	101.43
APRIL	88.55	97.14	97.14	97.14	101.43	101.43	101.43	101.43	101.43	101.43
MAY	88.55	97.14	97.14	97.14	101.43	101.43	101.43	101.43	101.43	101.43
JUNE	88.55	97.14	97.14	97.14	101.43	101.43	101.43	101.43	101.43	101.43
JULY	88.55	97.14	97.14	97.14	101.43	101.43	101.43	101.43	101.43	101.43
AUGUST	88.55	88.55	92.84	97.14	101.43	92.84	92.84	92.84	92.84	92.84
SEPTEMBER	88.55	88.55	92.84	101.43	101.43	92.84	92.84	92.84	92.84	92.84
OCTOBER	92.84	92.84	94.99	101.43	101.43	101.43	101.43	101.43	101.43	92.84
NOVEMBER	92.84	92.84	94.99	101.43	101.43	101.43	101.43	101.43	101.43	92.84
DECEMBER	92.84	92.84	94.99	101.43	101.43	101.43	101.43	101.43	101.43	92.84
NBER										
JANUARY	105.28	114.36	109.29	107.61	108.60	108.06	104.86	100.45	98.25	94.87
FEBRUARY	105.28	114.36	108.26	107.72	108.53	107.99	103.85	100.45	97.20	94.87
MARCH	105.28	114.36	107.80	107.83	108.45	107.96	103.85	100.45	97.20	94.87
APRIL	105.28	114.36	107.35	107.94	108.37	107.94	103.85	100.45	97.20	94.37
MAY	105.28	114.36	106.89	108.05	108.30	107.91	103.85	100.45	97.20	94.87
JUNE	105.28	114.36	106.44	108.16	108.22	107.88	103.85	100.45	97.20	94.87
JULY	105.28	111.04	105.81	108.08	107.24	106.93	98.70	99.71	97.20	94.87
AUGUST	105.84	109.98	105.84	108.13	107.26	105.07	97.87	99.52	96.37	93.45
SEPTEMBER	106.40	108.92	105.87	108.19	107.23	105.07	97.87	99.52	96.37	93.31
OCTOBER	109.70	109.17	106.31	108.74	108.06	106.99	99.50	99.52	96.37	93.17
NOVEMBER	109.41	108.83	106.61	108.66	108.04	106.61	99.50	99.52	96.37	93.17
DECEMBER	109.13	108.57	106.91	108.58	108.01	105.88	99.50	99.52	96.37	93.17
NBER PRICE INDEX, ANNUAL AVERAGES:										
STD. DEV.*	0.5337	1.3182	1.1966	0.8456	1.3128	1.9218	1.8745	0.9343	0.7882	0.6689
NO. OF SERIES*	3.00	3.50	5.92	9.17	10.00	10.42	10.92	11.92	12.92	9.58

* See page 105.

Table C-41. Acetone

(price indexes, 1964 = 100)

BLS	1957	1958	1959	1960	1961	1962	1963	1964	1965	1966
JANUARY	123.08	130.77	130.77	130.77	123.08	107.69	100.00	100.00	100.00	100.00
FEBRUARY	123.08	130.77	130.77	130.77	123.08	107.69	100.00	100.00	100.00	100.00
MARCH	123.08	130.77	130.77	130.77	123.08	107.69	100.00	100.00	100.00	100.00
APRIL	123.08	130.77	130.77	130.77	123.08	107.69	100.00	100.00	100.00	100.00
MAY	123.08	130.77	130.77	130.77	123.08	100.00	100.00	100.00	100.00	100.00
JUNE	123.08	130.77	130.77	130.77	123.08	100.00	100.00	100.00	100.00	100.00
JULY	130.77	130.77	130.77	123.08	107.69	100.00	100.00	100.00	100.00	100.00
AUGUST	130.77	130.77	130.77	123.08	107.69	100.00	100.00	100.00	100.00	100.00
SEPTEMBER	130.77	130.77	130.77	123.08	107.69	100.00	100.00	100.00	100.00	100.00
OCTOBER	130.77	130.77	130.77	123.08	107.69	100.00	100.00	100.00	100.00	100.00
NOVEMBER	130.77	130.77	130.77	123.08	107.69	100.00	100.00	100.00	100.00	100.00
DECEMBER	130.77	130.77	130.77	123.08	107.69	100.00	100.00	100.00	100.00	100.00
NBER										
JANUARY	137.41	143.25	143.05	141.97	130.84	111.29	107.37	102.25	95.43	91.82
FEBRUARY	137.41	143.25	143.05	141.65	130.39	109.99	106.45	101.15	95.36	91.97
MARCH	137.33	143.25	143.05	141.33	129.95	109.75	106.47	100.60	95.31	92.11
APRIL	137.25	143.25	143.05	140.67	128.58	112.60	103.19	100.61	95.27	95.04
MAY	137.17	143.25	143.05	140.54	128.15	112.62	103.15	100.27	94.54	99.07
JUNE	137.35	143.36	143.96	139.36	123.41	112.63	103.01	100.11	94.49	99.22
JULY	143.18	143.34	143.05	135.28	114.35	112.62	101.84	100.19	94.45	101.59
AUGUST	143.25	143.43	143.05	135.61	113.47	111.71	101.66	100.19	94.58	103.02
SEPTEMBER	143.25	143.34	143.05	134.93	112.31	111.63	101.48	99.02	93.85	104.39
OCTOBER	143.25	143.25	143.05	134.26	110.83	111.62	100.50	98.63	93.98	103.67
NOVEMBER	149.84	143.25	143.05	133.59	110.68	111.57	100.33	98.50	94.11	104.39
DECEMBER	149.84	143.25	143.05	133.14	111.39	111.65	99.90	98.50	93.74	104.39
NBER PRICE INDEX, ANNUAL AVERAGES:										
STD. DEV.*	1.6537	0.8610	0.3513	1.3724	2.8051	1.6081	1.8817	1.4764	0.9436	3.8914
NO. OF SERIES*	6.91	8.83	9.00	9.92	10.83	11.00	11.92	12.92	13.00	10.75

* See page 105.

Table C-42. Acetylene

(price indexes, 1964 = 100)

	1957	1958	1959	1960	1961	1962	1963	1964	1965	1966
BLS										
JANUARY	88.06	92.32	92.32	92.32	92.32	92.32	92.32	100.00	100.00	100.00
FEBRUARY	88.06	92.32	92.32	92.32	92.32	92.32	100.00	100.00	100.00	100.00
MARCH	88.06	92.32	92.32	92.32	92.32	92.32	100.00	100.00	100.00	100.00
APRIL	88.06	92.32	92.32	92.32	92.32	92.32	100.00	100.00	100.00	100.00
MAY	88.06	92.32	92.32	92.32	92.32	92.32	100.00	100.00	100.00	100.00
JUNE	88.06	92.32	92.32	92.32	92.32	92.32	100.00	100.00	100.00	100.00
JULY	88.06	92.32	92.32	92.32	92.32	92.32	100.00	100.00	100.00	100.00
AUGUST	88.06	92.32	92.32	92.32	92.32	92.32	100.00	100.00	100.00	100.00
SEPTEMBER	92.32	92.32	92.32	92.32	92.32	92.32	100.00	100.00	100.00	100.00
OCTOBER	92.32	92.32	92.32	92.32	92.32	92.32	100.00	100.00	100.00	100.00
NOVEMBER	92.32	92.32	92.32	92.32	92.32	92.32	100.00	100.00	100.00	100.00
DECEMBER	92.32	92.32	92.32	92.32	92.32	92.32	100.00	100.00	100.00	102.65
NBER										
JANUARY	80.70	87.93	88.07	93.44	94.19	94.92	95.67	99.96	99.97	101.12
FEBRUARY	80.61	87.97	88.25	93.44	94.28	94.90	96.76	99.94	99.91	100.51
MARCH	80.80	87.74	88.41	93.44	94.37	94.88	98.29	99.92	99.84	99.90
APRIL	80.71	87.77	87.68	93.70	94.46	94.84	99.29	99.35	100.57	100.58
MAY	81.09	87.88	88.24	93.96	94.45	95.05	99.49	99.54	100.61	100.86
JUNE	81.46	87.99	91.95	94.21	94.45	95.26	99.68	99.74	100.66	101.14
JULY	81.84	88.10	92.53	94.47	94.45	95.47	99.88	99.93	100.70	101.42
AUGUST	80.30	88.71	93.04	94.56	94.44	95.77	99.80	100.21	100.78	101.81
SEPTEMBER	88.09	89.32	93.56	94.65	94.44	96.06	99.71	100.49	100.86	102.20
OCTOBER	88.09	88.68	93.19	94.54	94.97	94.38	100.27	100.76	100.90	102.61
NOVEMBER	86.93	88.47	93.27	94.42	94.95	94.70	100.16	100.31	100.97	102.61
DECEMBER	87.43	88.27	93.35	94.31	94.94	95.02	100.04	99.86	101.05	102.61
NBER PRICE INDEX, ANNUAL AVERAGES:										
STD. DEV.*	1.9196	0.9373	1.2526	0.6448	0.5151	1.0498	1.2913	1.1158	0.7971	1.3261
NO. OF SERIES*	18.18	19.67	20.00	20.00	20.00	20.83	21.00	21.00	21.00	18.83

* See page 105.

Table C-43. Benzene, Benzol

(price indexes, 1964 = 100)

	1957	1958	1959	1960	1961	1962	1963	1964	1965	1966
BLS										
JANUARY	144.00	144.00	124.00	136.00	136.00	124.00	100.00	100.00	100.00	108.00
FEBRUARY	144.00	144.00	124.00	136.00	136.00	112.00	100.00	100.00	100.00	108.00
MARCH	144.00	144.00	124.00	136.00	136.00	112.00	100.00	100.00	100.00	108.00
APRIL	144.00	144.00	124.00	136.00	136.00	100.00	100.00	100.00	104.00	108.00
MAY	144.00	144.00	124.00	136.00	136.00	100.00	100.00	100.00	104.00	108.00
JUNE	144.00	144.00	124.00	136.00	136.00	100.00	100.00	100.00	108.00	108.00
JULY	144.00	124.00	124.00	136.00	136.00	100.00	100.00	100.00	108.00	108.00
AUGUST	144.00	124.00	124.00	136.00	124.00	100.00	100.00	100.00	108.00	108.00
SEPTEMBER	144.00	124.00	124.00	136.00	124.00	100.00	100.00	100.00	108.00	108.00
OCTOBER	144.00	124.00	124.00	136.00	124.00	100.00	100.00	100.00	108.00	108.00
NOVEMBER	144.00	124.00	124.00	136.00	124.00	100.00	100.00	100.00	108.00	108.00
DECEMBER	144.00	124.00	124.00	136.00	124.00	100.00	100.00	100.00	108.00	108.00
NBER										
JANUARY	144.05	145.11	125.45	138.40	136.23	113.49	104.21	100.64	100.09	115.25
FEBRUARY	144.05	145.11	125.45	139.97	135.74	111.08	103.11	100.42	102.02	114.41
MARCH	144.05	145.11	126.42	139.43	138.18	110.02	102.71	100.19	102.24	114.58
APRIL	144.05	145.11	127.40	139.34	137.86	105.82	102.90	100.04	105.25	114.39
MAY	144.05	145.11	128.39	139.24	135.97	105.62	102.50	99.89	105.40	114.23
JUNE	144.05	145.11	130.19	140.81	135.62	106.37	102.40	99.74	105.56	114.07
JULY	144.22	130.90	128.82	141.02	131.51	106.63	102.36	99.70	106.24	113.12
AUGUST	144.39	126.00	128.14	139.80	132.04	104.12	101.62	99.67	107.40	113.30
SEPTEMBER	144.55	126.81	127.46	137.41	130.82	103.66	102.29	99.64	107.66	113.43
OCTOBER	144.74	126.27	126.79	137.42	128.95	105.50	101.90	99.83	107.59	113.80
NOVEMBER	144.93	126.59	126.13	137.44	127.83	103.41	101.51	100.03	107.58	113.48
DECEMBER	145.11	126.18	125.19	137.50	129.70	105.33	101.47	100.22	107.88	113.80
NBER PRICE INDEX, ANNUAL AVERAGES:										
STD. DEV.*	0.1373	1.3797	1.3811	2.4684	2.7991	3.8077	1.2343	0.4699	1.6959	1.6381
NO. OF SERIES*	4.73	5.42	6.50	7.50	8.00	8.92	9.00	11.75	12.00	9.75

NOTE: This commodity is among those showing a "reversal of trend" (see page 42); this trend was fitted to the period ending August 1964.

* See page 105.

Table C-44. Styrene Monomer
(price indexes, 1964 = 100)

	1957	1958	1959	1960	1961	1962	1963	1964	1965	1966
BLS										
JANUARY	195.24	151.43	138.10	132.38	137.14	119.05	114.29	114.29	93.33	86.67
FEBRUARY	195.24	137.14	138.10	132.38	137.14	119.05	114.29	114.29	93.33	86.67
MARCH	195.24	137.14	130.48	132.38	119.05	117.14	114.29	102.86	86.67	86.67
APRIL	195.24	137.14	130.48	132.38	119.05	117.14	114.29	102.86	86.67	98.10
MAY	195.24	137.14	130.48	132.38	119.05	117.14	114.29	102.86	86.67	98.10
JUNE	195.24	137.14	130.48	132.38	119.05	117.14	114.29	102.86	86.67	98.10
JULY	151.43	137.14	130.48	135.24	119.05	114.29	114.29	93.33	86.67	98.10
AUGUST	151.43	137.14	130.48	135.24	119.05	114.29	114.29	93.33	86.67	98.10
SEPTEMBER	151.43	137.14	130.48	135.24	119.05	114.29	114.29	93.33	86.67	98.10
OCTOBER	151.43	137.14	131.43	135.24	119.05	114.29	114.29	93.33	86.67	98.10
NOVEMBER	151.43	137.14	131.43	135.24	119.05	114.29	114.29	93.33	86.67	98.10
DECEMBER	151.43	137.14	131.43	135.24	119.05	114.29	114.29	93.33	86.67	98.10
NBER										
JANUARY	169.92	135.80	130.64	132.54	134.37	120.96	114.87	114.87	92.94	86.67
FEBRUARY	169.55	135.80	129.54	130.85	135.51	120.50	114.18	114.68	93.71	85.73
MARCH	169.92	135.52	129.26	131.71	123.89	118.54	114.65	105.78	88.04	85.92
APRIL	169.55	134.39	129.26	131.43	122.73	118.77	114.65	103.20	85.14	95.45
MAY	169.55	135.80	128.98	131.71	119.42	118.54	114.65	102.39	86.85	96.23
JUNE	169.92	136.36	128.98	131.71	119.87	117.19	114.18	97.84	85.54	95.85
JULY	141.81	135.79	129.81	134.15	120.10	115.61	114.18	94.44	85.73	95.45
AUGUST	133.90	136.35	129.53	134.44	119.63	115.28	113.95	93.89	85.73	95.45
SEPTEMBER	134.17	136.35	129.25	134.15	120.31	115.46	114.18	92.94	86.11	95.65
OCTOBER	134.71	136.62	130.62	134.71	119.49	114.80	115.77	93.71	85.73	96.04
NOVEMBER	134.44	136.06	131.18	133.86	120.50	114.44	114.87	93.52	85.92	95.45
DECEMBER	134.44	136.88	129.48	134.71	120.27	114.20	113.71	92.74	84.32	95.45
NBER PRICE INDEX, ANNUAL AVERAGES:										
STD. DEV.*	2.0728	0.6794	0.7464	0.9042	1.8063	0.9486	1.1271	2.5423	2.1500	1.4891
NO. OF SERIES*	3.45	4.00	4.00	4.00	4.83	5.00	5.00	5.92	6.00	5.92

* See page 105.

Table C-45. Ethyl Alcohol

(price indexes, 1964 = 100)

	1957	1958	1959	1960	1961	1962	1963	1964	1965	1966
BLS										
JANUARY	92.56	92.28	99.71	100.00	100.00	100.00	100.00	100.00	100.00	100.00
FEBRUARY	92.56	92.28	99.71	100.00	100.00	100.00	100.00	100.00	100.00	100.00
MARCH	92.56	92.28	99.71	100.00	100.00	100.00	100.00	100.00	100.00	100.00
APRIL	92.56	92.28	99.71	100.00	100.00	100.00	100.00	100.00	100.00	100.00
MAY	92.56	92.28	99.71	100.00	100.00	100.00	100.00	100.00	100.00	100.00
JUNE	92.56	92.28	99.71	100.00	100.00	100.00	100.00	100.00	100.00	100.00
JULY	92.28	92.28	99.71	100.00	100.00	100.00	100.00	100.00	100.00	100.00
AUGUST	92.28	92.28	99.71	100.00	100.00	100.00	100.00	100.00	100.00	100.00
SEPTEMBER	92.28	92.28	99.71	100.00	100.00	100.00	100.00	100.00	100.00	100.00
OCTOBER	92.28	100.09	100.00	100.00	100.00	100.00	100.00	100.00	100.00	100.00
NOVEMBER	92.28	100.09	100.00	100.00	100.00	100.00	100.00	100.00	100.00	100.00
DECEMBER	92.28	100.09	100.00	100.00	100.00	100.00	100.00	100.00	100.00	100.00
NBER										
JANUARY	90.96	90.96	102.22	102.22	102.22	102.17	100.40	100.97	97.68	96.95
FEBRUARY	90.96	90.96	102.22	102.22	102.22	102.13	100.55	100.95	97.68	96.95
MARCH	90.96	90.96	102.22	102.22	102.22	102.08	100.69	100.94	97.68	96.95
APRIL	90.96	90.96	102.22	102.22	102.22	102.04	100.84	100.92	97.51	96.95
MAY	90.96	90.96	102.22	102.22	102.22	102.00	100.98	100.90	97.51	96.95
JUNE	90.96	90.96	102.22	102.22	102.22	101.95	101.12	100.88	97.51	96.95
JULY	90.96	90.96	102.22	102.22	102.22	99.55	101.10	99.91	97.51	96.95
AUGUST	90.96	90.96	102.22	102.22	102.22	99.69	101.08	99.58	97.51	96.95
SEPTEMBER	90.96	90.96	102.22	102.22	102.22	99.83	101.06	99.24	97.51	96.95
OCTOBER	90.96	90.73	102.22	102.22	102.22	99.97	101.04	98.90	97.51	96.95
NOVEMBER	90.96	100.66	102.22	102.22	102.22	100.12	101.01	98.57	97.51	96.95
DECEMBER	90.96	100.59	102.22	102.22	102.22	100.26	100.99	98.24	97.51	96.95
NBER PRICE INDEX, ANNUAL AVERAGES:										
STD. DEV.*	0.0000	0.0963	0.1304	0.0000	0.0000	0.5842	0.2049	0.5780	0.1628	0.0996
NO. OF SERIES*	2.00	2.92	3.00	3.92	5.08	6.92	7.00	8.83	9.00	8.25

* See page 105.

Table C-46. Methyl Alcohol

(price indexes, 1964 = 100)

BLS

	1957	1958	1959	1960	1961	1962	1963	1964	1965	1966
JANUARY	108.33	108.33	86.67	100.00	100.00	100.00	100.00	100.00	100.00	89.67
FEBRUARY	108.33	108.33	86.67	100.00	100.00	100.00	100.00	100.00	100.00	89.67
MARCH	108.33	108.33	86.67	100.00	100.00	100.00	100.00	100.00	100.00	89.67
APRIL	108.33	108.33	100.00	100.00	100.00	100.00	100.00	100.00	89.67	89.67
MAY	108.33	108.33	100.00	100.00	100.00	100.00	100.00	100.00	89.67	89.67
JUNE	108.33	86.67	100.00	100.00	100.00	100.00	100.00	100.00	89.67	89.67
JULY	108.33	86.67	100.00	100.00	100.00	100.00	100.00	100.00	89.67	89.67
AUGUST	108.33	86.67	100.00	100.00	100.00	100.00	100.00	100.00	89.67	89.67
SEPTEMBER	108.33	86.67	100.00	100.00	100.00	100.00	100.00	100.00	89.67	89.67
OCTOBER	108.33	86.67	100.00	100.00	100.00	100.00	100.00	100.00	89.67	89.67
NOVEMBER	108.33	86.67	100.00	100.00	100.00	100.00	100.00	100.00	89.67	89.67
DECEMBER	108.33	86.67	100.00	100.00	100.00	100.00	100.00	100.00	89.67	89.67

NBER

	1957	1958	1959	1960	1961	1962	1963	1964	1965	1966
JANUARY	129.85	123.07	111.17	118.25	115.61	112.52	110.39	100.34	100.58	105.39
FEBRUARY	129.85	123.07	111.19	118.18	115.59	112.57	110.14	100.40	100.61	105.38
MARCH	129.85	123.01	111.21	118.04	115.64	112.63	109.88	100.01	100.71	105.38
APRIL	129.85	122.96	118.72	119.89	116.60	112.68	109.56	99.74	102.04	105.38
MAY	129.85	114.91	118.78	119.79	116.55	112.74	109.24	99.80	102.99	105.38
JUNE	129.85	109.09	118.68	119.71	116.50	112.79	108.93	99.87	103.09	105.39
JULY	129.80	109.11	118.57	119.66	115.43	112.72	108.73	99.90	103.36	106.60
AUGUST	129.02	109.14	118.67	119.07	115.46	112.06	107.78	99.93	104.41	106.60
SEPTEMBER	129.07	109.06	118.52	119.01	114.69	111.99	107.58	99.96	104.41	106.60
OCTOBER	127.77	109.14	118.48	118.95	113.84	111.92	106.63	99.99	104.41	106.60
NOVEMBER	129.11	109.06	118.37	118.90	112.99	111.51	105.79	100.02	104.40	106.60
DECEMBER	128.26	109.00	118.29	118.81	113.02	111.43	105.69	100.05	104.40	106.60

NBER PRICE INDEX, ANNUAL AVERAGES:

	1957	1958	1959	1960	1961	1962	1963	1964	1965	1966
STD. DEV.*	0.6310	2.1872	1.1522	0.6420	1.8428	0.5163	1.1866	0.8696	1.1823	0.4934
NO. OF SERIES*	7.55	8.00	10.33	12.42	14.83	15.00	15.92	17.83	18.17	13.33

* See page 105.

Table C-47. Glycerine—Natural and Synthetic
(price indexes, 1964 = 100)

	1957	1958	1959	1960	1961	1962	1963	1964	1965	1966
BLS										
JANUARY	124.68	124.23	123.78	130.46	121.56	110.43	82.37	97.96	100.19	102.41
FEBRUARY	124.68	123.78	123.78	130.46	121.56	110.43	82.37	97.96	100.19	102.41
MARCH	124.68	123.78	123.78	130.46	121.56	110.43	82.37	97.96	100.19	102.41
APRIL	124.68	123.78	123.78	130.46	121.56	110.43	82.37	102.41	100.19	105.97
MAY	124.68	123.78	123.78	130.46	111.32	101.52	82.37	102.41	100.19	105.97
JUNE	124.68	123.78	123.78	130.46	111.32	97.07	82.37	100.19	100.19	105.97
JULY	124.68	123.78	123.78	130.46	111.32	92.62	82.37	100.19	100.19	109.09
AUGUST	124.68	123.78	123.78	130.46	110.43	92.62	82.37	100.19	102.41	109.09
SEPTEMBER	124.68	123.78	123.78	130.46	110.43	92.62	82.37	100.19	102.41	109.09
OCTOBER	124.68	123.78	130.46	130.46	110.43	82.37	91.28	100.19	102.41	109.09
NOVEMBER	124.68	123.78	130.46	130.46	110.43	82.37	91.28	100.19	102.41	109.09
DECEMBER	124.68	123.78	130.46	130.46	110.43	82.37	91.28	100.19	102.41	109.09
NBER										
JANUARY	130.50	129.33	129.97	134.27	126.06	114.48	86.11	94.69	101.70	103.72
FEBRUARY	130.03	129.28	130.06	134.16	125.04	114.59	85.95	97.68	101.74	103.74
MARCH	130.89	129.41	130.11	133.99	124.97	114.70	85.95	97.11	101.53	103.83
APRIL	130.42	129.42	130.25	133.92	124.77	109.90	85.94	99.69	101.58	105.06
MAY	130.42	129.43	130.24	133.76	118.19	106.25	85.85	100.75	101.63	105.07
JUNE	130.42	129.44	130.38	133.60	116.40	100.85	85.06	101.78	101.67	106.10
JULY	130.44	129.50	130.36	133.73	115.58	98.83	84.91	101.46	102.24	107.50
AUGUST	130.45	129.56	130.29	133.86	115.07	97.29	84.78	101.50	102.83	107.45
SEPTEMBER	130.60	129.62	131.08	133.95	114.61	96.84	84.65	101.50	103.18	109.11
OCTOBER	130.48	129.68	132.46	133.95	114.62	87.49	87.36	101.26	103.47	109.77
NOVEMBER	130.50	129.74	132.90	134.19	114.51	85.24	89.00	101.27	103.33	109.95
DECEMBER	130.51	129.80	134.55	132.68	114.67	85.22	90.06	101.32	103.37	110.15
NBER PRICE INDEX, ANNUAL AVERAGES:										
STD. DEV.*	0.3416	0.1475	0.6648	0.6842	1.3239	2.3409	1.4985	1.3767	0.4582	0.9392
NO. OF SERIES*	6.55	8.00	9.83	10.00	10.92	11.00	11.00	11.00	11.92	10.25

NOTE: This commodity is among those showing a "reversal of trend" (see page 42); the trend is fitted to the period ending April 1963.
* See page 105.

Table C-48. Phthalic Anhydride

(price indexes, 1964 = 100)

	1957	1958	1959	1960	1961	1962	1963	1964	1965	1966
BLS										
JANUARY	180.65	180.65	180.65	146.24	172.04	133.33	124.73	103.23	98.92	77.42
FEBRUARY	180.65	180.65	146.24	146.24	172.04	133.33	124.73	103.23	90.32	77.42
MARCH	180.65	180.65	146.24	146.24	172.04	133.33	124.73	103.23	86.02	77.42
APRIL	180.65	180.65	146.24	146.24	172.04	133.33	103.23	103.23	86.02	86.02
MAY	180.65	180.65	146.24	146.24	172.04	133.33	103.23	103.23	86.02	86.02
JUNE	180.65	180.65	146.24	146.24	172.04	133.33	103.23	103.23	77.42	86.02
JULY	180.65	180.65	146.24	163.44	172.04	133.33	77.42	103.23	77.42	94.62
AUGUST	180.65	180.65	146.24	163.44	172.04	124.73	77.42	90.32	77.42	94.62
SEPTEMBER	180.65	180.65	146.24	163.44	154.84	124.73	77.42	90.32	77.42	94.62
OCTOBER	180.65	180.65	146.24	163.44	154.84	124.73	103.23	98.92	86.02	94.62
NOVEMBER	180.65	180.65	146.24	163.44	133.33	124.73	103.23	98.92	77.42	94.62
DECEMBER	180.65	180.65	146.24	163.44	133.33	124.73	103.23	98.92	77.42	94.62
NBER										
JANUARY	182.78	183.20	154.13	151.12	173.87	132.55	119.62	103.74	94.54	83.52
FEBRUARY	182.78	183.26	154.10	151.17	173.71	132.70	115.16	103.63	92.60	83.52
MARCH	182.78	183.32	154.07	151.22	172.98	132.85	111.57	103.52	91.42	83.52
APRIL	182.78	183.38	154.04	158.29	172.24	133.00	96.64	103.41	88.09	95.32
MAY	182.78	183.44	154.02	158.35	172.11	133.16	96.32	103.30	86.24	95.31
JUNE	182.78	183.50	153.99	158.40	171.98	133.31	90.15	101.98	85.14	95.33
JULY	182.84	183.47	154.04	165.76	172.18	131.69	86.10	95.35	82.92	98.81
AUGUST	182.90	183.44	154.09	165.61	165.32	128.27	84.41	94.81	82.92	98.81
SEPTEMBER	182.96	183.41	154.14	165.46	162.39	128.26	84.29	94.86	82.92	99.94
OCTOBER	183.02	183.37	154.19	165.32	146.04	125.68	93.54	98.41	83.52	103.25
NOVEMBER	183.08	183.34	154.24	165.17	138.49	124.90	93.41	98.46	83.52	103.25
DECEMBER	183.14	183.31	154.29	166.77	138.65	123.09	93.28	98.52	83.52	103.25
NBER PRICE INDEX, ANNUAL AVERAGES:										
STD. DEV.*	0.0401	0.0567	0.7621	1.5171	2.7575	2.0368	4.4721	3.0269	2.3081	1.2915
NO. OF SERIES*	5.27	6.00	6.00	6.00	6.83	7.00	7.00	8.83	8.50	8.00

* See page 105.

Table C-49. Phenol

(price indexes, 1964 = 100)

	1957	1958	1959	1960	1961	1962	1963	1964	1965	1966
BLS										
JANUARY	166.67	166.67	161.46	154.17	164.58	135.42	116.67	97.92	102.08	102.08
FEBRUARY	166.67	166.67	161.46	154.17	164.58	130.21	97.92	97.92	102.08	102.08
MARCH	166.67	166.67	161.46	154.17	164.58	130.21	97.92	97.92	102.08	102.08
APRIL	166.67	166.67	161.46	154.17	159.38	125.00	97.92	97.92	102.08	102.08
MAY	166.67	166.67	154.17	154.17	159.38	119.79	97.92	97.92	102.08	102.08
JUNE	166.67	166.67	154.17	154.17	159.38	119.79	97.92	97.92	102.08	102.08
JULY	166.67	166.67	154.17	154.17	159.38	116.67	97.92	97.92	102.08	102.08
AUGUST	166.67	166.67	154.17	154.17	151.04	116.67	97.92	102.08	102.08	102.08
SEPTEMBER	166.67	166.67	154.17	154.17	151.04	116.67	97.92	102.08	102.08	102.08
OCTOBER	166.67	166.67	154.17	154.17	151.04	116.67	97.92	102.08	102.08	102.08
NOVEMBER	166.67	161.46	154.17	154.17	151.04	116.67	97.92	102.08	102.08	102.08
DECEMBER	166.67	161.46	154.17	154.17	135.42	116.67	97.92	102.08	102.08	102.08
NBER										
JANUARY	144.64	148.54	145.66	140.05	141.46	126.07	100.15	100.15	97.47	96.53
FEBRUARY	144.64	148.54	145.66	140.05	141.46	126.62	100.15	101.33	97.47	96.61
MARCH	144.64	148.54	145.66	140.05	141.46	120.32	100.15	101.33	97.70	96.61
APRIL	144.64	148.54	145.66	140.05	141.46	118.80	100.15	99.94	97.70	95.73
MAY	144.64	148.54	145.66	140.05	141.46	119.42	100.15	99.68	97.70	96.59
JUNE	144.64	148.54	145.66	140.05	141.46	119.42	100.15	99.68	97.70	96.59
JULY	144.64	148.54	142.83	140.05	141.83	118.28	100.15	99.12	97.70	96.59
AUGUST	144.64	148.54	142.83	139.20	141.46	117.14	101.63	99.94	97.70	96.59
SEPTEMBER	144.64	148.54	142.83	139.20	136.39	116.91	100.88	99.71	97.70	98.00
OCTOBER	144.64	148.54	142.83	139.20	135.51	116.67	100.15	99.71	97.70	98.00
NOVEMBER	147.72	148.54	142.83	138.71	134.63	116.43	100.15	99.71	97.70	98.00
DECEMBER	147.72	148.54	142.83	138.71	134.11	117.36	101.35	99.71	97.70	96.27
NBER PRICE INDEX, ANNUAL AVERAGES:										
STD. DEV.*	0.2706	0.0650	0.5146	0.4218	1.2123	2.3705	1.5970	0.9926	0.4631	0.9535
NO. OF SERIES*	2.00	2.00	2.92	3.00	3.92	4.00	4.00	4.92	4.25	3.50

* See page 105.

Table C-50. Polyethylene

(price indexes, 1964 = 100)

	1957	1958	1959	1960	1961	1962	1963	1964	1965	1966
BLS										
JANUARY	111.10	111.10	111.10	111.10	100.00	100.00	100.00	100.00	100.00	100.00
FEBRUARY	111.10	111.10	111.10	111.10	100.00	100.00	100.00	100.00	100.00	100.00
MARCH	111.10	111.10	111.10	111.10	100.00	100.00	100.00	100.00	100.00	100.00
APRIL	111.10	111.10	111.10	111.10	100.00	100.00	100.00	100.00	100.00	100.00
MAY	111.10	111.10	111.10	111.10	100.00	100.00	100.00	100.00	100.00	100.00
JUNE	111.10	111.10	111.10	111.10	100.00	100.00	100.00	100.00	100.00	100.00
JULY	111.10	111.10	111.10	111.10	100.00	100.00	100.00	100.00	100.00	100.00
AUGUST	111.10	111.10	111.10	100.00	100.00	100.00	100.00	100.00	100.00	100.00
SEPTEMBER	111.10	111.10	111.10	100.00	100.00	100.00	100.00	100.00	100.00	100.00
OCTOBER	111.10	111.10	111.10	100.00	100.00	100.00	100.00	100.00	100.00	100.00
NOVEMBER	111.10	111.10	111.10	100.00	100.00	100.00	100.00	100.00	100.00	100.00
DECEMBER	111.10	111.10	111.10	100.00	100.00	100.00	100.00	100.00	100.00	100.00
NBER										
JANUARY	177.45	170.48	166.11	153.62	140.96	134.12	114.45	105.87	94.62	93.66
FEBRUARY	177.45	170.29	162.32	149.53	141.68	133.89	113.83	101.04	94.31	92.96
MARCH	168.57	166.07	166.89	151.03	141.35	131.44	111.02	102.42	94.44	93.13
APRIL	168.88	170.03	165.54	152.85	140.70	132.14	113.99	100.69	95.50	93.68
MAY	169.70	165.47	163.51	153.05	139.44	131.43	115.53	100.11	95.84	92.65
JUNE	170.53	169.44	164.13	149.14	138.60	129.94	118.23	99.79	94.64	92.21
JULY	170.96	165.86	163.05	138.63	137.95	129.15	115.58	101.21	95.98	93.54
AUGUST	169.16	165.72	161.97	138.84	138.56	128.71	109.21	100.49	93.48	92.66
SEPTEMBER	172.28	166.50	162.59	139.05	138.83	128.72	109.23	99.59	93.42	92.32
OCTOBER	169.95	169.43	163.20	139.66	139.17	129.97	107.52	96.77	94.06	93.75
NOVEMBER	168.37	165.74	160.61	140.16	139.63	130.41	108.16	96.14	93.85	94.84
DECEMBER	167.71	165.60	157.11	138.31	139.21	129.51	108.37	95.88	94.16	94.62

NBER PRICE INDEX, ANNUAL AVERAGES:

	1957	1958	1959	1960	1961	1962	1963	1964	1965	1966
STD. DEV.*	2.0462	3.0821	2.2489	2.2257	2.0811	2.3362	4.4240	4.4939	3.1525	2.2603
NO. OF SERIES*	3.27	4.00	4.00	4.17	6.83	7.92	7.92	8.92	8.92	8.08

* See page 105.

Appendix C

Table C-51. Polystyrene
(price indexes, 1964 = 100)

	1957	1958	1959	1960	1961	1962	1963	1964	1965	1966
BLS										
JANUARY	172.27	153.09	149.03	125.79	121.73	120.26	120.26	100.89	95.54	95.54
FEBRUARY	172.27	153.09	149.03	125.79	121.73	120.26	120.26	100.89	95.54	95.54
MARCH	172.27	149.03	125.79	125.79	121.73	120.26	120.26	100.89	95.54	95.54
APRIL	172.27	149.03	125.79	125.79	121.73	120.26	100.89	100.89	95.54	95.54
MAY	172.27	149.03	125.79	125.79	121.73	120.26	100.89	100.89	95.54	95.54
JUNE	169.51	149.03	125.79	125.79	121.73	120.26	100.89	100.89	95.54	95.54
JULY	169.51	149.03	125.79	125.79	121.73	120.26	100.89	100.89	95.54	95.54
AUGUST	169.51	149.03	125.79	125.79	121.73	120.26	100.89	100.89	95.54	95.54
SEPTEMBER	169.51	149.03	125.79	125.79	121.73	120.26	100.89	100.89	95.54	95.54
OCTOBER	169.51	149.03	125.79	125.79	120.26	120.26	100.89	100.89	95.54	95.54
NOVEMBER	153.09	149.03	125.79	125.79	120.26	120.26	100.89	95.54	95.54	95.54
DECEMBER	153.09	149.03	125.79	121.73	120.26	120.26	100.89	95.54	95.54	95.54
NBER										
JANUARY	172.03	160.53	150.97	133.07	120.98	118.48	118.49	103.45	96.89	91.09
FEBRUARY	178.08	163.33	148.20	136.06	122.78	119.93	118.61	102.84	94.97	90.74
MARCH	174.76	159.04	133.79	135.35	121.54	119.41	117.09	102.85	98.95	90.76
APRIL	175.77	160.30	134.71	134.39	122.16	119.51	112.62	102.16	92.72	93.32
MAY	172.39	160.83	135.28	136.46	122.16	118.48	111.76	101.57	94.44	93.59
JUNE	175.58	160.66	133.08	135.51	119.97	120.34	109.35	101.94	93.20	93.23
JULY	172.16	160.86	136.77	136.18	121.67	120.60	108.59	99.09	92.70	93.74
AUGUST	160.58	157.81	134.24	136.16	122.53	119.28	108.11	97.38	92.81	95.15
SEPTEMBER	161.50	160.18	143.30	136.13	121.41	119.05	107.20	98.76	92.90	95.81
OCTOBER	164.62	158.87	137.52	137.00	122.98	120.03	107.29	97.27	91.05	96.85
NOVEMBER	167.03	158.28	132.89	137.94	122.18	118.29	106.91	96.02	92.36	97.60
DECEMBER	161.16	156.62	133.16	121.81	119.74	117.66	106.35	96.67	90.18	95.60
NBER PRICE INDEX, ANNUAL AVERAGES:										
STD. DEV.*	0.4615	0.7862	2.7422	2.1757	2.4841	1.5219	1.9669	2.7434	3.8322	2.8374
NO. OF SERIES*	1.91	2.92	3.00	4.08	5.92	6.92	7.42	8.17	8.92	6.58

* See page 105.

Table C-52. Polyvinyl Chloride
(price indexes, 1964 = 100)

BLS	1957	1958	1959	1960	1961	1962	1963	1964	1965	1966
JANUARY	146.05	146.05	127.12	127.12	100.00	100.00	100.00	100.00	100.00	100.00
FEBRUARY	146.05	146.05	127.12	127.12	100.00	100.00	100.00	100.00	100.00	100.00
MARCH	146.05	146.05	127.12	127.12	100.00	100.00	100.00	100.00	100.00	100.00
APRIL	146.05	146.05	127.12	127.12	100.00	100.00	100.00	100.00	100.00	100.00
MAY	146.05	146.05	127.12	127.12	100.00	100.00	100.00	100.00	100.00	100.00
JUNE	146.05	146.05	127.12	127.12	100.00	100.00	100.00	100.00	100.00	100.00
JULY	146.05	146.05	127.12	127.12	100.00	100.00	100.00	100.00	100.00	100.00
AUGUST	146.05	135.17	127.12	127.12	100.00	100.00	100.00	100.00	100.00	100.00
SEPTEMBER	146.05	135.17	127.12	127.12	100.00	100.00	100.00	100.00	100.00	100.00
OCTOBER	146.05	135.17	127.12	127.12	100.00	100.00	100.00	100.00	100.00	100.00
NOVEMBER	146.05	135.17	127.12	127.12	100.00	100.00	100.00	100.00	100.00	100.00
DECEMBER	146.05	127.12	127.12	127.12	100.00	100.00	100.00	100.00	100.00	100.00
NBER										
JANUARY	154.96	152.97	142.08	140.85	121.62	105.42	101.30	99.42	98.51	91.28
FEBRUARY	156.64	153.26	141.39	139.39	121.03	103.64	100.60	99.71	98.11	90.30
MARCH	153.83	153.68	142.32	138.13	119.99	103.61	99.15	99.18	96.56	89.92
APRIL	154.11	154.66	141.74	138.83	119.72	103.03	97.65	101.72	95.32	89.69
MAY	156.64	153.12	141.13	137.66	116.26	103.03	100.10	102.65	93.96	89.83
JUNE	153.26	152.16	142.53	136.08	112.48	102.20	98.68	100.41	92.68	89.69
JULY	154.40	149.46	140.14	137.43	109.95	102.49	99.19	99.34	94.35	89.17
AUGUST	156.08	152.02	142.02	131.70	108.74	102.49	99.67	102.01	94.76	90.41
SEPTEMBER	153.83	153.39	143.02	129.01	106.12	102.36	99.67	101.78	94.44	90.73
OCTOBER	154.11	151.61	143.62	129.92	107.04	102.47	97.40	100.03	93.18	89.13
NOVEMBER	154.40	148.12	141.65	127.60	106.14	100.68	98.62	96.93	93.95	89.20
DECEMBER	152.12	151.43	142.78	125.85	106.36	100.75	99.07	96.80	93.82	88.91

NBER PRICE INDEX, ANNUAL AVERAGES:

	1957	1958	1959	1960	1961	1962	1963	1964	1965	1966
STD. DEV.*	1.5427	2.9914	2.0545	3.0942	2.4599	1.1330	2.3699	3.4550	2.7682	1.9101
NO. OF SERIES*	2.00	3.83	4.00	4.00	5.83	7.00	7.00	7.00	6.92	6.17

* See page 105.

Table C-53. Phenolic Resins, Plastics
(price indexes, 1964 = 100)

	1957	1958	1959	1960	1961	1962	1963	1964	1965	1966
BLS										
JANUARY	93.66	104.88	95.12	95.12	100.00	100.00	100.00	100.00	100.00	100.00
FEBRUARY	98.54	104.88	95.12	95.12	100.00	100.00	100.00	100.00	100.00	100.00
MARCH	98.54	104.88	95.12	95.12	100.00	100.00	100.00	100.00	100.00	100.00
APRIL	98.54	104.88	95.12	95.12	100.00	100.00	100.00	100.00	100.00	100.00
MAY	98.54	104.88	95.12	95.12	100.00	100.00	100.00	100.00	100.00	100.00
JUNE	98.54	104.88	95.12	95.12	100.00	100.00	100.00	100.00	100.00	100.00
JULY	98.54	95.12	95.12	95.12	100.00	100.00	100.00	100.00	100.00	100.00
AUGUST	98.54	95.12	95.12	95.12	100.00	100.00	100.00	100.00	100.00	100.00
SEPTEMBER	98.54	95.12	95.12	95.12	100.00	100.00	100.00	100.00	100.00	100.00
OCTOBER	98.54	95.12	95.12	95.12	100.00	100.00	100.00	100.00	100.00	100.00
NOVEMBER	104.88	95.12	95.12	95.12	100.00	100.00	100.00	100.00	100.00	104.88
DECEMBER	104.88	95.12	95.12	95.12	100.00	100.00	100.00	100.00	100.00	104.88
NBER										
JANUARY	103.86	106.36	102.32	102.57	104.49	100.21	101.16	100.02	100.02	100.02
FEBRUARY	103.86	106.36	102.44	102.57	104.49	100.21	101.28	100.02	100.02	100.02
MARCH	103.86	106.36	102.19	102.57	104.61	100.21	101.04	100.02	100.02	100.02
APRIL	103.86	106.36	102.44	102.57	104.49	100.21	101.16	100.02	100.02	100.02
MAY	103.86	106.11	102.57	102.57	104.49	100.21	101.16	100.02	100.02	100.02
JUNE	103.86	102.82	102.57	102.57	104.36	100.21	100.02	100.02	100.02	100.02
JULY	103.86	102.32	102.57	102.69	104.49	100.21	100.02	100.02	100.02	100.02
AUGUST	103.86	102.57	102.57	102.57	104.36	100.21	100.02	99.92	100.02	100.02
SEPTEMBER	103.86	102.44	102.57	102.57	104.49	100.21	100.14	99.92	100.02	100.97
OCTOBER	103.86	102.19	102.57	102.57	104.49	100.21	99.89	100.02	100.02	100.97
NOVEMBER	104.62	102.44	102.57	102.82	104.49	100.21	100.02	100.02	100.02	101.34
DECEMBER	106.36	102.44	102.69	103.19	104.36	100.21	100.02	100.02	100.02	102.54
NBER PRICE INDEX, ANNUAL AVERAGES:										
STD. DEV.*	0.3063	0.6480	0.1636	0.1615	0.3483	0.5742	0.5100	0.0366	0.0000	0.4149
NO. OF SERIES*	2.00	3.83	4.00	4.00	4.00	4.00	4.00	4.92	5.00	4.00

* See page 105.

Table C-54. Antibiotics

(price indexes, 1964 = 100)

BLS

	1957	1958	1959	1960	1961	1962	1963	1964	1965	1966
JANUARY	180.56	224.47	158.55	124.36	117.10	115.81	103.63	103.28	95.90	96.37
FEBRUARY	224.47	224.47	158.55	124.36	117.10	115.81	103.63	103.28	95.90	96.37
MARCH	224.47	224.47	158.55	124.36	115.93	115.57	103.63	103.28	95.90	96.37
APRIL	224.47	224.47	158.55	134.19	115.93	115.57	103.63	103.28	95.90	91.69
MAY	224.47	224.47	158.55	134.19	115.93	115.57	103.63	103.28	95.90	91.69
JUNE	224.47	224.47	158.55	134.19	115.93	115.57	103.40	97.66	95.90	90.40
JULY	224.47	224.47	158.55	134.19	115.81	102.93	103.40	97.66	95.90	90.40
AUGUST	224.47	224.47	158.55	134.19	115.81	102.69	103.40	97.66	95.78	88.99
SEPTEMBER	224.47	224.47	134.19	134.19	116.74	102.58	103.40	97.66	95.78	88.99
OCTOBER	224.47	158.55	134.19	134.19	116.74	102.58	103.28	97.66	96.37	88.99
NOVEMBER	224.47	158.55	134.19	124.36	116.74	102.58	103.28	97.66	96.37	88.99
DECEMBER	224.47	158.55	124.36	124.36	116.74	101.41	103.28	97.66	96.37	86.42

NBER

	1957	1958	1959	1960	1961	1962	1963	1964	1965	1966
JANUARY	200.75	220.93	177.51	127.37	130.64	119.77	107.77	101.41	97.05	90.87
FEBRUARY	200.75	220.93	177.51	127.37	130.41	119.77	107.57	101.37	97.00	90.86
MARCH	256.27	220.93	177.51	132.92	130.16	116.68	107.74	101.07	96.85	90.61
APRIL	256.27	220.93	161.71	134.63	128.97	114.37	107.82	100.44	96.61	90.05
MAY	256.27	220.93	161.71	134.63	128.83	113.83	107.90	100.17	96.57	89.61
JUNE	256.27	220.93	161.71	134.63	128.00	113.49	108.09	100.03	96.45	89.59
JULY	247.38	220.93	161.71	134.63	127.94	112.54	106.78	99.64	94.07	89.22
AUGUST	238.79	220.93	161.71	134.63	127.38	112.61	106.28	99.60	93.71	88.47
SEPTEMBER	254.44	177.51	149.95	132.97	121.85	112.27	105.50	99.41	93.61	88.31
OCTOBER	245.62	177.51	127.37	132.52	121.67	109.60	104.50	99.17	92.74	88.55
NOVEMBER	237.10	177.51	127.37	132.08	121.67	109.59	104.45	99.11	92.67	88.57
DECEMBER	228.86	177.51	127.37	131.72	121.64	109.58	102.65	98.59	92.19	88.59

NBER PRICE INDEX, ANNUAL AVERAGES:

	1957	1958	1959	1960	1961	1962	1963	1964	1965	1966
STD. DEV.**	3.9708	2.1179	4.0072	1.2332	2.5654	3.0262	3.3838	2.2294	2.3308	2.4754
NO. OF SERIES*	1.55	2.17	3.00	4.33	47.08	65.33	80.83	95.92	106.70	87.00

NOTE: The indexes of prices of antibiotics of the BLS and NBER before 1961 were constructed by extrapolating the indexes backward by the respective indexes of price of penicillin. For 1961 and after, the NBER index is a weighted group index employing rough estimates of weights for the following commodities: Chloromycetin, penicillin, tetracycline hydrochloride (achromycin, etc.), Terramycin and Declomycin.
* See page 105.

Table C-55. Tranquilizers
(price indexes, 1964 = 100)

BLS	1957	1958	1959	1960	1961	1962	1963	1964	1965	1966
JANUARY	100.00	100.00	100.00	100.00	100.00	100.00	100.00	100.00	100.00	100.00
FEBRUARY	100.00	100.00	100.00	100.00	100.00	100.00	100.00	100.00	100.00	100.00
MARCH	100.00	100.00	100.00	100.00	100.00	100.00	100.00	100.00	100.00	100.00
APRIL	100.00	100.00	100.00	100.00	100.00	100.00	100.00	100.00	100.00	101.40
MAY	100.00	100.00	100.00	100.00	100.00	100.00	100.00	100.00	100.00	101.40
JUNE	100.00	100.00	100.00	100.00	100.00	100.00	100.00	100.00	100.00	101.40
JULY	100.00	100.00	100.00	100.00	100.00	100.00	100.00	100.00	100.00	101.40
AUGUST	100.00	100.00	100.00	100.00	100.00	100.00	100.00	100.00	100.00	101.40
SEPTEMBER	100.00	100.00	100.00	100.00	100.00	100.00	100.00	100.00	100.00	101.40
OCTOBER	100.00	100.00	100.00	100.00	100.00	100.00	100.00	100.00	100.00	101.40
NOVEMBER	100.00	100.00	100.00	100.00	100.00	100.00	100.00	100.00	100.00	101.40
DECEMBER	100.00	100.00	100.00	100.00	100.00	100.00	100.00	100.00	100.00	101.40
NBER										
JANUARY	113.94	113.94	113.34	110.87	110.10	109.06	105.89	101.86	97.42	95.71
FEBRUARY	113.94	113.94	113.15	111.05	110.30	109.02	105.87	100.57	97.41	95.80
MARCH	113.69	113.94	112.92	110.87	110.49	109.04	105.84	101.49	96.83	95.80
APRIL	113.69	113.94	112.73	111.06	110.69	109.10	105.81	101.36	96.81	95.85
MAY	113.69	113.94	112.55	111.27	110.89	109.12	105.78	100.26	96.81	95.62
JUNE	113.69	113.94	112.37	111.45	111.06	109.16	105.75	100.13	96.85	95.59
JULY	113.69	113.94	112.57	111.39	110.38	109.29	104.58	99.91	96.35	94.88
AUGUST	113.69	113.94	112.77	111.32	109.76	109.26	104.52	99.78	96.35	94.93
SEPTEMBER	113.94	113.59	112.84	111.26	109.68	109.00	104.46	99.18	95.93	94.93
OCTOBER	113.94	113.59	113.05	111.21	109.55	108.97	104.33	98.55	95.84	93.77
NOVEMBER	113.94	113.59	113.25	111.16	109.50	108.95	103.81	98.46	95.84	93.77
DECEMBER	113.94	113.59	113.45	111.12	109.45	108.91	103.31	98.44	95.84	93.77
NBER PRICE INDEX, ANNUAL AVERAGES:										
STD. DEV.*	0.1297	0.0773	0.3610	0.5611	1.2449	0.7941	1.9992	2.0372	1.3372	1.2464
NO. OF SERIES*	7.00	9.83	16.75	23.92	36.75	49.83	54.08	61.75	68.25	59.58

NOTE: The NBER index is a weighted group index employing rough estimates of weights for the following commodities: meprobamate (Miltown, Equanil, etc.), Librium, Thorazine, Compazine and Stedazine.

* See page 105.

Table C-56. Cardiac Glycosides

(price indexes, 1964 = 100)

	1957	1958	1959	1960	1961	1962	1963	1964	1965	1966
BLS										
JANUARY	0.00	0.00	0.00	0.00	100.00	98.90	88.50	88.20	81.90	82.30
FEBRUARY	0.00	0.00	0.00	0.00	100.00	98.90	88.50	88.20	81.90	82.30
MARCH	0.00	0.00	0.00	0.00	99.00	98.70	88.50	88.20	81.90	82.30
APRIL	0.00	0.00	0.00	0.00	99.00	98.70	88.50	88.20	81.90	78.30
MAY	0.00	0.00	0.00	0.00	99.00	98.70	88.50	88.20	81.90	78.30
JUNE	0.00	0.00	0.00	0.00	99.00	98.70	88.30	83.40	81.90	77.20
JULY	0.00	0.00	0.00	0.00	98.90	87.90	88.30	83.40	81.90	77.20
AUGUST	0.00	0.00	0.00	0.00	98.90	87.70	88.30	83.40	81.80	76.00
SEPTEMBER	0.00	0.00	0.00	0.00	99.70	87.70	88.20	83.40	81.80	76.00
OCTOBER	0.00	0.00	0.00	0.00	99.70	87.60	88.20	83.40	82.30	76.00
NOVEMBER	0.00	0.00	0.00	0.00	99.70	87.60	88.20	83.40	82.30	76.00
DECEMBER	0.00	0.00	0.00	0.00	99.70	86.60	88.20	83.40	82.30	73.80
NBER										
JANUARY	112.32	112.32	115.64	112.16	112.79	110.89	105.49	101.26	95.92	94.91
FEBRUARY	112.32	112.32	115.64	112.22	112.76	110.64	105.52	102.73	96.04	94.72
MARCH	112.32	112.29	115.64	112.17	112.74	110.38	105.16	102.99	95.91	94.70
APRIL	112.32	112.26	115.64	112.11	112.71	110.13	104.92	104.44	95.78	94.70
MAY	112.32	112.22	115.64	112.05	113.20	110.75	104.83	104.42	95.87	94.70
JUNE	112.32	112.19	115.70	111.99	113.33	110.71	104.84	104.40	95.96	94.70
JULY	112.32	112.16	115.76	111.93	113.37	110.67	103.55	98.21	95.72	93.37
AUGUST	112.32	112.13	115.82	111.88	113.52	110.64	103.50	97.94	95.60	93.37
SEPTEMBER	112.32	112.10	115.88	110.98	112.94	110.15	103.45	96.21	95.18	93.21
OCTOBER	112.32	112.07	115.94	110.95	109.57	110.25	103.96	95.83	95.06	93.21
NOVEMBER	112.32	112.04	116.01	110.91	109.71	110.43	103.86	95.71	94.99	93.21
DECEMBER	112.32	112.04	116.07	110.88	109.86	110.79	103.78	95.87	94.92	93.21
NBER PRICE INDEX, ANNUAL AVERAGES:										
STD. DEV.*	0.0000	0.2091	0.5839	1.1231	1.7495	1.0571	1.9419	4.3670	0.8445	0.4813
NO. OF SERIES*	4.82	6.17	9.75	11.08	15.00	20.25	22.92	28.67	33.92	25.25

NOTE: The NBER index is a weighted group index employing rough estimates of weights for the following commodities: digitalis, digitoxin and digoxin.

* See page 105.

Table C-57. Paint

(price indexes, 1964 = 100)

	1957	1958	1959	1960	1961	1962	1963	1964	1965	1966
BLS										
JANUARY	92.88	96.10	95.95	96.03	98.57	99.02	99.17	100.59	100.07	101.12
FEBRUARY	92.88	96.10	96.10	96.03	99.10	99.02	99.17	100.07	100.44	101.12
MARCH	92.88	96.10	96.10	96.03	99.10	99.02	99.02	100.07	99.69	101.12
APRIL	92.88	96.10	96.03	96.03	99.10	99.02	99.02	100.07	99.69	101.42
MAY	93.33	96.10	96.03	96.03	99.10	99.17	98.35	100.07	100.97	101.42
JUNE	93.93	95.95	96.03	96.03	99.10	99.17	98.35	99.25	100.97	102.01
JULY	95.88	95.95	96.03	96.10	99.10	99.17	98.35	99.39	100.97	102.01
AUGUST	95.88	95.95	96.03	96.10	99.10	99.17	99.25	100.07	100.97	102.01
SEPTEMBER	95.88	95.95	96.03	96.10	99.10	99.17	99.25	100.07	100.97	102.01
OCTOBER	95.88	95.95	96.03	96.10	98.95	99.17	99.25	100.07	101.12	102.46
NOVEMBER	95.88	95.95	96.03	96.10	98.95	99.17	100.37	100.22	101.12	102.99
DECEMBER	96.10	95.95	96.03	97.52	98.95	99.17	100.59	100.07	101.12	103.66
NBER										
JANUARY	96.14	98.11	98.34	101.19	102.83	105.95	106.65	100.68	99.66	100.16
FEBRUARY	96.35	97.96	98.09	101.11	103.86	106.12	106.40	100.55	99.54	100.26
MARCH	96.56	97.81	97.84	101.04	104.89	106.30	106.14	100.42	99.42	100.36
APRIL	96.77	97.66	97.59	100.96	105.93	106.48	105.89	100.29	99.30	100.46
MAY	97.31	97.67	97.53	101.03	105.94	106.53	105.61	100.21	99.31	100.49
JUNE	97.86	97.69	97.48	101.09	105.96	106.58	105.33	100.13	99.32	100.52
JULY	98.41	97.70	97.42	101.15	105.97	106.64	105.05	100.05	99.33	100.55
AUGUST	98.31	97.70	97.57	101.67	105.96	106.19	104.55	99.81	99.46	100.92
SEPTEMBER	98.21	97.70	97.71	102.20	105.96	105.75	104.06	99.56	99.59	101.30
OCTOBER	98.12	97.70	97.86	102.72	105.95	105.31	103.58	99.32	99.73	101.68
NOVEMBER	98.11	97.91	98.96	102.76	105.95	105.75	102.60	99.43	99.87	101.68
DECEMBER	98.11	98.13	100.07	102.80	105.95	106.20	101.64	99.55	100.01	101.68
NBER PRICE INDEX, ANNUAL AVERAGES:										
STD. DEV.*	0.9364	0.3324	1.0550	1.1997	1.3619	0.8151	1.3550	1.1917	0.4469	0.8483
NO. OF SERIES*	17.00	17.00	17.00	17.00	18.67	16.17	16.92	17.00	16.83	16.75

* See page 105.

Table C-58. Portland Cement

(price indexes, 1964 = 100)

	1957	1958	1959	1960	1961	1962	1963	1964	1965	1966
BLS										
JANUARY	95.78	98.76	99.69	101.58	101.70	101.07	100.80	99.99	100.26	100.41
FEBRUARY	95.78	98.76	99.69	101.64	101.70	101.13	100.86	99.99	100.26	100.62
MARCH	95.75	98.76	99.69	101.64	101.70	101.22	100.77	99.99	100.26	100.62
APRIL	96.59	99.00	99.69	101.64	101.70	101.28	100.74	99.99	100.11	100.62
MAY	96.59	99.00	99.69	101.64	101.70	101.28	100.65	99.99	100.11	100.62
JUNE	96.62	98.94	99.69	101.64	101.70	101.07	100.59	99.99	100.11	100.59
JULY	96.62	98.94	99.69	101.64	101.70	101.04	100.59	99.99	100.11	100.59
AUGUST	96.62	98.94	99.69	101.61	101.70	101.07	100.26	99.99	100.11	100.59
SEPTEMBER	96.62	98.94	99.66	101.61	101.70	101.07	100.11	99.99	100.11	100.59
OCTOBER	96.62	98.94	99.66	101.61	101.61	100.98	99.96	99.99	100.32	100.59
NOVEMBER	96.62	98.88	99.66	101.61	100.26	100.98	99.96	100.05	100.32	100.59
DECEMBER	96.62	98.88	99.66	101.61	99.24	100.83	99.96	100.05	100.32	100.59
NBER										
JANUARY	91.04	94.62	96.30	98.97	99.54	100.71	100.75	100.20	99.82	101.14
FEBRUARY	91.59	94.82	96.30	99.12	99.56	100.78	100.79	100.16	99.99	101.15
MARCH	92.06	94.97	96.29	99.24	99.59	100.85	100.82	100.12	100.19	101.16
APRIL	92.53	95.12	96.29	99.35	99.62	100.95	100.73	100.09	100.53	101.11
MAY	92.58	94.99	96.29	99.42	99.62	100.96	100.82	100.07	101.24	100.92
JUNE	92.62	94.91	96.30	99.50	99.62	100.97	100.97	100.07	101.56	100.73
JULY	92.66	94.82	96.30	99.58	99.62	100.96	101.03	100.05	101.80	100.53
AUGUST	92.68	94.98	96.31	99.61	99.62	100.91	101.02	100.11	101.87	100.53
SEPTEMBER	92.70	95.16	96.31	99.64	99.62	100.88	101.02	99.73	101.93	100.53
OCTOBER	92.90	95.33	96.31	99.67	99.62	100.85	101.03	99.80	102.11	100.53
NOVEMBER	92.95	95.47	96.32	99.62	99.69	101.05	101.02	99.72	101.87	100.84
DECEMBER	93.01	95.62	96.32	99.57	99.70	101.13	100.95	99.87	101.43	100.84
NBER PRICE INDEX, ANNUAL AVERAGES:										
STD. DEV.*	0.4264	0.5426	0.2737	0.5442	0.0708	0.4849	0.4244	0.6895	0.9726	0.6042
NO. OF SERIES*	25.91	27.00	27.00	26.92	27.67	30.42	32.58	33.00	32.33	24.83

* See page 105.

Table C-59. Plate Glass
(price indexes, 1964 = 100)

	1957	1958	1959	1960	1961	1962	1963	1964	1965	1966
BLS										
JANUARY	107.97	107.97	107.56	107.79	105.30	102.73	100.06	100.06	99.34	97.19
FEBRUARY	107.97	107.97	107.56	107.79	105.30	102.73	100.06	100.06	96.47	97.19
MARCH	107.97	107.97	107.56	107.79	105.30	102.73	100.06	100.06	96.47	93.48
APRIL	107.97	107.97	107.56	107.79	105.30	102.73	100.06	100.06	96.47	92.77
MAY	107.97	107.97	107.56	105.30	105.30	102.73	100.06	100.06	97.19	92.77
JUNE	107.97	107.97	107.79	105.30	102.73	102.73	100.06	100.06	97.19	92.77
JULY	107.97	107.97	107.79	105.30	102.73	102.73	100.06	100.06	97.19	92.77
AUGUST	107.97	107.79	107.79	105.30	102.73	100.06	100.06	100.06	97.19	92.77
SEPTEMBER	107.97	107.56	107.79	105.30	102.73	100.06	100.06	100.06	97.19	94.20
OCTOBER	107.97	107.56	107.79	105.30	102.73	100.06	100.06	100.06	97.19	99.34
NOVEMBER	107.97	107.56	107.79	105.30	102.73	100.06	100.06	100.06	97.19	99.34
DECEMBER	107.97	107.56	107.79	105.30	102.73	100.06	100.06	99.34	97.19	99.34
NBER										
JANUARY	112.78	109.08	112.50	111.83	109.82	109.05	102.04	97.87	100.02	99.90
FEBRUARY	112.78	109.19	112.50	111.83	109.82	109.05	102.04	97.87	100.02	99.90
MARCH	105.89	107.65	113.74	111.47	109.10	107.15	100.58	100.88	99.65	98.60
APRIL	105.89	107.65	113.74	111.47	109.10	107.15	100.58	100.88	99.65	98.60
MAY	105.89	107.65	113.74	111.47	109.10	103.09	97.71	100.88	99.65	98.60
JUNE	105.89	109.89	113.74	111.47	109.10	103.09	97.71	100.88	99.65	98.60
JULY	105.89	109.89	113.74	111.47	109.10	103.09	97.71	100.88	99.65	98.60
AUGUST	105.42	112.18	113.30	111.83	109.05	102.04	97.47	99.75	99.65	98.60
SEPTEMBER	105.42	113.91	113.30	111.83	109.05	102.04	97.47	99.75	99.65	98.60
OCTOBER	105.42	113.91	113.30	111.83	109.05	102.04	97.47	99.75	99.65	98.60
NOVEMBER	105.42	113.91	113.30	111.83	109.05	102.04	97.47	99.75	99.65	98.60
DECEMBER	105.42	113.91	113.30	111.83	109.05	102.04	97.47	99.75	99.65	98.60
NBER PRICE INDEX, ANNUAL AVERAGES:										
STD. DEV.*	0.9588	1.9951	0.3851	0.3232	0.4907	1.1164	0.9334	0.8437	0.1310	0.1741
NO. OF SERIES*	3.82	4.00	4.00	4.00	4.58	5.75	5.92	6.00	6.00	4.75

* See page 105.

Table C-60. Safety Glass and Window Glass

(price indexes, 1964 = 100)

	1957	1958	1959	1960	1961	1962	1963	1964	1965	1966
BLS										
JANUARY	88.14	88.14	87.87	87.87	85.71	85.06	88.69	96.62	100.67	97.65
FEBRUARY	88.14	88.14	87.87	87.87	85.71	85.06	88.69	96.62	100.67	97.65
MARCH	88.14	88.14	87.87	87.87	85.71	85.06	88.69	98.34	100.67	97.65
APRIL	88.14	88.14	87.87	87.87	85.71	88.60	88.69	100.87	100.67	98.61
MAY	88.14	88.14	87.87	82.86	85.71	88.69	88.69	100.06	100.67	100.33
JUNE	88.14	88.14	87.87	82.86	85.06	88.69	88.69	100.06	100.67	99.98
JULY	88.14	88.14	87.87	82.86	85.06	88.69	88.69	100.06	97.13	99.98
AUGUST	88.14	88.14	87.87	85.71	85.06	88.69	94.07	101.68	98.30	98.63
SEPTEMBER	88.14	87.87	87.87	85.71	85.06	88.69	96.62	101.68	97.65	100.22
OCTOBER	88.14	87.61	87.87	85.71	85.06	88.69	96.62	101.68	97.65	100.83
NOVEMBER	88.14	87.61	87.87	85.71	85.06	88.69	96.62	101.68	97.65	102.41
DECEMBER	88.14	87.87	87.87	85.71	85.06	88.69	96.62	100.67	97.65	102.41
NBER										
JANUARY	106.96	103.28	98.88	97.14	93.95	94.82	95.17	97.13	100.90	100.98
FEBRUARY	106.96	101.59	98.73	96.42	93.95	94.54	95.17	97.52	100.90	100.17
MARCH	106.96	99.94	98.58	95.71	93.95	94.26	95.17	97.91	100.90	99.36
APRIL	106.96	99.94	98.58	95.71	94.73	94.50	95.17	97.91	100.90	99.36
MAY	106.96	99.94	98.58	95.71	95.51	93.03	93.72	100.71	100.96	99.36
JUNE	106.96	99.94	98.58	95.71	95.83	93.03	93.72	100.71	100.96	99.36
JULY	106.96	99.77	98.58	95.71	95.51	93.66	95.00	100.89	100.72	99.36
AUGUST	106.96	99.60	98.58	95.71	95.25	94.18	95.00	101.07	100.72	99.36
SEPTEMBER	106.96	99.43	98.58	95.71	94.99	94.70	95.00	101.26	100.72	99.36
OCTOBER	106.96	99.43	98.58	95.71	96.06	94.70	95.37	101.45	100.72	99.62
NOVEMBER	106.96	99.43	98.58	95.71	96.32	94.70	95.73	101.63	100.72	99.88
DECEMBER	106.96	99.43	98.58	95.71	96.58	94.70	96.10	101.82	100.72	100.14
NBER PRICE INDEX, ANNUAL AVERAGES:										
STD. DEV.*	0.0000	1.0805	0.2080	0.4160	0.7610	0.9646	0.8477	1.2933	0.2681	0.7434
NO. OF SERIES*	1.82	2.00	2.00	2.00	4.17	6.00	6.00	6.00	6.00	3.50

* See page 105.

Table C-61. Electric Motors—Excluding DC

(price indexes, 1964 = 100)

	1957	1958	1959	1960	1961	1962	1963	1964	1965	1966
BLS										
JANUARY	130.37	129.24	128.36	124.81	116.87	113.33	111.23	108.55	93.21	90.05
FEBRUARY	130.37	129.43	128.08	126.85	118.31	113.33	110.89	108.55	93.21	90.81
MARCH	130.82	129.43	128.08	126.85	118.62	113.33	109.90	108.26	93.21	91.40
APRIL	131.92	131.39	128.08	126.85	118.93	113.33	109.90	108.53	93.21	92.50
MAY	131.92	131.56	128.08	118.18	118.93	112.86	109.90	104.18	93.21	92.50
JUNE	131.25	131.79	125.99	118.61	118.93	112.97	110.56	95.56	92.07	92.84
JULY	129.66	131.79	125.99	116.87	117.64	112.97	110.95	95.56	90.90	92.84
AUGUST	129.66	131.70	124.53	116.87	113.33	112.97	111.11	95.56	90.90	92.84
SEPTEMBER	129.04	131.70	123.65	116.87	113.33	112.97	111.11	94.42	90.90	92.84
OCTOBER	128.46	131.45	123.65	116.87	113.33	112.86	111.11	94.42	90.35	93.47
NOVEMBER	128.34	129.93	123.65	116.87	113.33	112.86	110.64	93.21	90.35	96.46
DECEMBER	129.04	129.15	123.65	116.87	113.33	112.53	110.53	93.21	90.05	96.63
NBER										
JANUARY	122.52	129.20	123.50	117.87	108.47	106.79	103.88	100.59	98.02	95.81
FEBRUARY	122.19	122.02	123.61	117.52	108.67	106.56	103.93	100.69	98.01	95.82
MARCH	121.85	122.85	122.72	117.27	108.89	106.34	103.98	100.79	98.08	95.67
APRIL	123.45	123.94	122.31	114.85	108.74	106.12	104.03	100.79	98.24	95.85
MAY	123.19	124.41	121.34	114.56	108.59	105.91	104.08	100.08	98.19	96.06
JUNE	124.55	124.83	121.34	114.74	108.55	105.68	104.13	99.93	95.61	96.92
JULY	124.84	124.40	121.36	107.89	108.13	105.63	104.29	99.77	95.63	97.21
AUGUST	125.22	123.97	121.32	108.07	107.72	104.90	104.42	99.68	95.65	97.52
SEPTEMBER	125.60	123.84	123.38	108.24	107.37	104.85	102.15	99.54	95.02	97.88
OCTOBER	125.91	123.72	120.57	108.58	106.80	104.81	102.10	99.34	95.21	98.24
NOVEMBER	126.57	123.57	120.70	108.92	109.11	104.76	101.98	99.41	95.37	101.31
DECEMBER	127.41	123.42	120.38	109.27	108.53	104.73	101.89	99.39	95.53	101.69
NBER PRICE INDEX, ANNUAL AVERAGES:										
STD. DEV.*	0.9744	1.5312	1.2051	1.3608	0.9711	0.4107	0.6293	0.9411	0.8155	1.64985
NO. OF SERIES*	7.73	12.00	13.50	14.83	16.42	15.00	15.92	17.92	15.33	11.25

* See page 105.

Table C-62. Electric Batteries

(price indexes, 1964 = 100)

BLS

	1957	1958	1959	1960	1961	1962	1963	1964	1965	1966
JANUARY	0.00	0.00	0.00	0.00	96.03	96.03	96.03	96.03	100.93	100.93
FEBRUARY	0.00	0.00	0.00	0.00	96.03	96.03	96.03	99.30	100.93	100.93
MARCH	0.00	0.00	0.00	0.00	96.03	96.03	96.03	99.30	100.93	100.93
APRIL	0.00	0.00	0.00	0.00	96.03	96.03	96.03	100.26	100.93	100.93
MAY	0.00	0.00	0.00	96.03	96.03	96.03	96.03	100.26	100.93	102.56
JUNE	0.00	0.00	0.00	96.03	96.03	96.03	96.03	100.26	100.93	105.83
JULY	0.00	0.00	0.00	96.03	96.03	96.03	96.03	100.26	100.93	108.80
AUGUST	0.00	0.00	0.00	96.03	96.03	96.03	96.03	100.64	100.93	108.80
SEPTEMBER	0.00	0.00	0.00	96.03	96.03	96.03	96.03	100.93	100.93	108.80
OCTOBER	0.00	0.00	0.00	96.03	96.03	96.03	96.03	100.93	100.93	108.90
NOVEMBER	0.00	0.00	0.00	96.03	96.03	96.03	96.03	100.93	100.93	108.80
DECEMBER	0.00	0.00	0.00	96.03	96.03	96.03	96.03	100.93	100.93	108.80

NBER

	1957	1958	1959	1960	1961	1962	1963	1964	1965	1966
JANUARY	0.00	0.00	0.00	0.00	0.00	105.36	102.01	100.54	99.72	99.38
FEBRUARY	0.00	0.00	0.00	0.00	0.00	105.27	101.53	100.54	99.64	99.38
MARCH	0.00	0.00	0.00	0.00	0.00	105.18	101.07	100.54	99.55	99.38
APRIL	0.00	0.00	0.00	0.00	0.00	105.09	100.60	100.50	99.47	99.38
MAY	0.00	0.00	0.00	0.00	0.00	104.96	100.49	100.45	99.57	99.45
JUNE	0.00	0.00	0.00	0.00	0.00	104.83	100.38	100.40	99.68	99.53
JULY	0.00	0.00	0.00	0.00	0.00	104.71	100.27	99.86	99.78	99.60
AUGUST	0.00	0.00	0.00	0.00	0.00	104.75	100.20	99.32	99.69	99.36
SEPTEMBER	0.00	0.00	0.00	0.00	0.00	104.79	100.12	98.79	99.60	99.13
OCTOBER	0.00	0.00	0.00	0.00	0.00	104.83	100.05	99.10	99.52	98.89
NOVEMBER	0.00	0.00	0.00	0.00	0.00	103.88	100.21	99.41	99.47	98.89
DECEMBER	0.00	0.00	0.00	0.00	0.00	102.94	100.38	99.41	99.43	98.89

NBER PRICE INDEX, ANNUAL AVERAGES:

	1962	1963	1964	1965	1966
STD. DEV.*	0.8192	1.1645	0.5252	0.5850	0.3089
NO. OF SERIES*	17.00	17.00	17.00	17.00	16.33

NOTE: The NBER index is based exclusively on prices paid by the railroads.
* See page 105.

Table C-63. Plywood
(price indexes, 1964 = 100)

	1957	1958	1959	1960	1961	1962	1963	1964	1965	1966
BLS										
JANUARY	113.57	109.87	118.53	113.68	98.78	98.20	97.74	98.08	104.55	103.17
FEBRUARY	112.99	105.25	127.54	110.45	98.20	99.82	97.85	100.28	101.55	103.40
MARCH	112.41	103.51	128.70	106.63	100.63	104.55	99.12	104.32	99.93	110.68
APRIL	113.57	106.75	132.86	107.21	114.60	104.55	98.78	104.90	99.47	119.23
MAY	113.91	101.78	132.63	105.94	110.79	100.74	98.55	103.63	98.20	114.95
JUNE	116.22	108.02	129.28	105.48	110.79	102.01	101.90	100.51	96.70	100.16
JULY	114.26	115.88	123.27	105.48	110.79	100.97	118.07	99.93	97.74	97.74
AUGUST	110.10	120.38	119.92	103.63	107.21	100.51	124.31	99.01	104.67	94.85
SEPTEMBER	108.94	124.54	109.87	107.44	103.98	100.63	101.09	98.89	102.24	93.46
OCTOBER	112.99	126.04	109.87	108.94	98.43	100.05	100.63	97.74	98.78	91.15
NOVEMBER	111.72	120.15	105.25	107.10	99.59	98.78	100.28	96.70	99.01	88.96
DECEMBER	109.87	117.03	111.49	106.29	98.55	97.62	100.05	96.00	99.70	89.77
NBER										
JANUARY	106.32	106.00	108.21	109.05	102.26	98.78	98.03	100.34	98.06	99.21
FEBRUARY	105.99	104.78	110.61	107.97	102.63	99.81	98.33	100.93	98.84	100.58
MARCH	105.66	103.58	113.05	106.90	102.99	100.84	98.63	101.53	99.63	101.96
APRIL	105.33	102.38	115.55	105.84	103.36	101.88	98.93	102.13	100.43	103.36
MAY	104.71	102.10	115.68	105.18	103.23	101.52	101.75	101.47	100.23	103.57
JUNE	104.09	101.82	115.80	104.52	103.11	101.16	104.65	100.81	100.02	103.79
JULY	103.48	101.54	115.93	103.87	102.99	100.80	107.63	100.16	99.82	104.00
AUGUST	104.09	103.88	115.85	103.49	102.29	100.90	106.12	99.48	99.65	102.50
SEPTEMBER	104.70	106.27	111.81	103.10	101.60	101.00	104.63	98.81	99.48	101.02
OCTOBER	105.32	108.72	109.81	102.71	100.92	101.10	103.16	98.13	99.30	99.56
NOVEMBER	105.55	108.55	109.55	102.56	100.20	100.06	102.21	98.11	99.27	99.56
DECEMBER	105.78	108.38	109.30	102.41	99.49	99.04	101.27	98.09	99.24	99.56
NBER PRICE INDEX, ANNUAL AVERAGES:										
STD. DEV.*	1.4281	1.6490	1.6420	1.3530	1.3039	1.4667	2.2660	1.7153	1.6362	2.2173
NO. OF SERIES*	12.00	12.00	11.83	11.75	10.58	13.17	14.00	14.00	13.83	11.33

Note: The NBER index is based exclusively on prices paid by the railroads.
* See page 105.

Table C-64. Car Flooring

(price indexes, 1964 = 100)

BLS	1957	1958	1959	1960	1961	1962	1963	1964	1965	1966
JANUARY	112.98	106.70	101.61	103.35	100.32	98.91	99.23	100.32	100.32	105.73
FEBRUARY	110.49	106.70	101.51	103.24	100.10	98.91	99.02	100.10	100.32	107.57
MARCH	110.27	106.05	101.72	103.24	100.10	98.91	99.02	100.10	100.32	107.78
APRIL	109.84	104.75	102.05	103.24	99.99	99.13	99.13	100.10	100.75	113.19
MAY	108.76	104.32	102.37	102.91	100.42	99.02	99.67	100.10	100.75	113.19
JUNE	108.32	102.48	102.37	102.70	100.42	99.23	99.99	99.77	101.07	112.65
JULY	109.08	101.94	102.59	101.83	99.88	98.91	100.21	99.77	101.51	112.11
AUGUST	107.89	101.40	102.59	101.61	99.67	99.34	100.42	99.77	102.05	113.41
SEPTEMBER	107.89	101.40	103.02	101.29	99.88	99.45	100.75	99.67	103.02	113.95
OCTOBER	107.67	102.05	103.02	101.29	99.88	99.77	100.32	99.99	103.67	113.19
NOVEMBER	107.67	102.05	103.02	101.07	99.67	99.88	100.32	99.99	103.99	112.98
DECEMBER	107.02	101.40	103.35	101.07	99.67	99.56	100.32	100.32	104.97	112.44
NBER										
JANUARY	99.12	90.69	87.21	98.23	93.41	95.61	95.37	100.01	99.40	100.41
FEBRUARY	98.09	89.59	88.60	98.34	93.06	95.73	95.70	100.23	99.44	101.40
MARCH	97.07	88.51	90.01	98.46	92.72	95.84	96.04	100.45	99.48	102.41
APRIL	96.06	87.44	91.44	98.57	92.38	95.96	96.38	100.67	99.52	103.42
MAY	95.29	86.87	92.59	98.22	92.77	96.04	96.47	100.38	99.47	105.54
JUNE	94.53	86.30	93.77	97.87	93.16	96.12	96.55	100.09	99.42	107.71
JULY	93.77	85.73	94.96	97.52	93.55	96.21	96.64	99.80	99.37	109.92
AUGUST	92.77	85.50	95.04	96.49	93.12	96.31	97.06	99.78	99.46	110.15
SEPTEMBER	91.79	85.27	95.11	95.47	94.00	96.40	97.48	99.75	99.56	110.38
OCTOBER	90.81	85.05	95.19	94.46	94.23	96.50	97.90	99.73	99.65	110.61
NOVEMBER	90.77	85.76	96.20	94.11	94.69	96.12	98.66	99.62	99.90	110.61
DECEMBER	90.73	86.48	97.21	93.76	95.15	95.74	99.43	99.51	100.14	110.61
NBER PRICE INDEX, ANNUAL AVERAGES:										
STD. DEV.*	2.2091	1.2268	1.9434	1.4605	2.2716	0.9989	1.3590	0.8889	0.5072	1.5202
NO. OF SERIES*	17.00	17.00	17.00	17.00	16.17	16.58	17.00	17.00	16.83	13.67

NOTE: The NBER index is based exclusively on prices paid by the railroads.
* See page 105.

Appendix C

Table C-65. Metals and Products

(price indexes, 1964 = 100)

	1957	1958	1959	1960	1961	1962	1963	1964	1965	1966
BLS										
JANUARY	97.62	96.65	99.09	102.44	99.00	99.01	97.17	98.99	101.89	104.31
FEBRUARY	97.07	96.46	99.44	102.37	99.01	98.95	97.19	99.05	101.96	104.50
MARCH	96.85	96.17	99.63	101.93	98.85	98.80	97.17	99.38	101.96	104.79
APRIL	96.70	94.90	99.58	101.89	98.54	98.63	97.24	99.77	102.06	105.37
MAY	96.56	94.73	99.91	101.78	99.20	98.70	98.08	99.86	102.65	106.25
JUNE	96.21	95.08	100.01	101.25	99.33	98.62	97.83	99.50	103.11	106.52
JULY	97.61	95.01	99.58	100.67	99.37	98.55	97.98	99.58	103.27	106.52
AUGUST	98.12	97.07	99.44	100.67	99.57	98.50	98.07	99.93	103.38	107.18
SEPTEMBER	97.35	97.67	99.91	100.62	99.57	98.41	98.11	99.95	103.59	106.83
OCTOBER	96.75	98.00	100.38	100.35	99.05	97.57	98.83	100.75	103.72	106.99
NOVEMBER	97.07	99.05	101.48	99.77	98.95	97.61	98.82	101.49	104.33	107.14
DECEMBER	97.20	99.15	101.50	99.46	99.14	97.28	98.98	101.75	104.12	107.24
NBER										
JANUARY	101.14	98.69	100.98	104.34	100.94	99.86	97.87	99.00	101.78	106.06
FEBRUARY	101.43	98.22	101.48	104.36	100.66	99.72	97.84	98.98	101.82	106.39
MARCH	100.68	97.92	101.69	104.47	100.63	99.61	97.76	99.04	102.01	106.46
APRIL	100.43	97.66	102.07	104.48	100.63	99.48	97.77	99.34	102.28	107.26
MAY	100.08	97.53	102.09	104.31	100.73	99.48	98.17	99.41	102.88	107.74
JUNE	99.37	97.55	102.14	104.07	100.72	99.39	98.21	99.66	103.46	108.33
JULY	100.79	97.63	102.18	103.92	100.50	99.35	98.27	99.81	104.32	108.70
AUGUST	100.02	98.82	102.06	103.86	100.38	99.29	98.27	100.22	104.55	109.16
SEPTEMBER	100.00	99.33	102.46	103.65	100.12	98.76	98.18	100.43	104.66	109.10
OCTOBER	99.42	99.51	102.95	103.15	99.95	98.59	98.60	101.07	104.90	109.56
NOVEMBER	99.50	100.29	103.77	102.42	100.00	98.57	98.76	101.35	105.07	109.98
DECEMBER	99.16	100.81	103.99	101.85	99.94	98.58	99.04	101.69	104.94	109.76

Table C-68. Nonferrous Primary Refinery Shapes

(price indexes, 1964 = 100)

BLS	1957	1958	1959	1960	1961	1962	1963	1964	1965	1966
JANUARY	107.13	91.31	95.70	106.61	98.04	96.74	93.36	96.74	104.41	108.76
FEBRUARY	103.69	89.99	96.93	106.61	98.04	96.74	93.56	96.74	104.90	108.76
MARCH	101.63	89.88	98.75	106.22	98.04	96.74	93.56	98.69	104.90	108.76
APRIL	101.04	87.92	98.36	106.22	97.05	96.40	93.56	99.20	105.37	108.76
MAY	98.89	87.98	98.36	106.22	96.80	96.40	94.04	99.20	108.76	108.76
JUNE	97.98	89.35	99.24	105.26	99.51	96.40	94.11	99.84	108.76	108.76
JULY	95.38	89.25	98.96	105.26	99.51	96.33	94.74	99.84	108.76	108.76
AUGUST	96.37	91.30	98.34	105.16	99.51	96.33	95.21	99.84	108.76	108.76
SEPTEMBER	93.87	91.28	99.76	105.16	99.00	96.33	95.21	99.84	108.76	108.76
OCTOBER	93.26	93.35	100.58	103.78	96.82	94.82	96.33	102.29	108.76	108.76
NOVEMBER	93.37	95.80	103.40	100.50	96.82	95.13	96.33	103.59	109.98	108.76
DECEMBER	93.56	95.56	103.54	100.09	97.23	93.36	96.74	104.20	108.76	108.76
NBER										
JANUARY	105.66	91.30	93.87	107.67	97.56	95.80	93.50	97.02	105.14	110.13
FEBRUARY	106.36	89.03	96.64	108.71	96.59	95.53	93.85	97.07	104.90	111.27
MARCH	103.08	86.75	97.81	108.62	96.99	95.38	94.15	97.40	105.70	110.37
APRIL	101.52	86.31	99.30	107.42	97.32	95.12	94.53	98.88	106.54	110.83
MAY	99.88	86.17	99.21	107.12	97.72	95.03	94.64	99.07	108.21	111.29
JUNE	98.20	86.17	99.62	106.43	98.59	95.26	94.91	99.50	108.42	110.68
JULY	97.38	87.18	100.52	105.61	97.98	95.44	95.30	99.65	110.59	111.27
AUGUST	94.36	84.98	99.60	105.70	97.59	95.23	95.52	99.95	110.30	111.83
SEPTEMBER	94.84	88.35	100.81	105.08	97.21	95.12	95.67	100.07	110.80	109.85
OCTOBER	92.55	89.17	102.43	103.94	96.69	94.48	96.59	102.74	111.42	111.32
NOVEMBER	92.97	91.61	105.39	102.22	96.47	94.23	96.75	103.37	111.79	113.13
DECEMBER	91.14	94.16	105.79	101.11	96.08	94.18	96.99	105.27	110.70	111.74

Table C-69. Nonferrous Mill Shapes
(price indexes, 1964 = 100)

	1957	1958	1959	1960	1961	1962	1963	1964	1965	1966
BLS										
JANUARY	108.16	103.00	102.99	109.74	104.89	103.31	98.83	98.10	104.29	106.06
FEBRUARY	106.65	103.00	103.87	109.74	104.89	104.13	98.78	98.05	104.29	106.74
MARCH	105.06	102.97	104.87	109.74	103.88	104.12	98.59	99.00	104.29	107.82
APRIL	104.64	100.85	104.87	109.52	103.15	103.96	98.24	99.64	104.29	109.80
MAY	104.29	99.73	104.87	109.08	104.15	104.06	98.52	99.86	102.62	112.14
JUNE	104.27	99.70	104.87	108.79	104.15	103.46	97.27	97.66	103.76	112.47
JULY	102.03	99.16	103.09	108.79	105.23	102.88	97.99	98.22	103.76	112.47
AUGUST	104.05	100.16	102.78	108.91	105.69	102.57	98.12	100.01	104.02	113.44
SEPTEMBER	103.20	100.10	104.22	108.61	105.78	102.15	97.68	99.69	104.63	111.11
OCTOBER	102.93	100.62	104.61	107.41	106.33	98.67	97.34	101.42	104.33	112.08
NOVEMBER	104.51	101.91	106.87	107.53	105.10	99.20	97.41	104.05	106.49	112.60
DECEMBER	104.51	102.99	106.87	105.96	104.46	99.10	97.83	104.29	105.42	112.60
NBER										
JANUARY	119.81	112.53	113.01	117.37	103.65	108.81	100.86	98.04	103.67	116.68
FEBRUARY	118.09	112.08	113.42	118.19	111.54	108.39	100.70	97.73	104.15	117.24
MARCH	117.05	111.96	113.74	118.98	110.95	108.25	100.64	97.84	104.32	117.92
APRIL	116.82	109.50	113.93	119.73	110.65	107.99	99.54	98.20	104.27	121.24
MAY	115.70	109.37	114.11	119.93	110.68	107.86	99.76	98.35	106.39	123.09
JUNE	114.39	109.47	114.27	120.14	110.96	107.53	99.23	98.20	106.50	123.86
JULY	114.09	109.56	113.51	120.59	110.82	107.30	99.16	98.96	109.56	125.16
AUGUST	113.15	109.94	113.52	120.32	110.62	107.20	98.98	101.02	111.79	125.86
SEPTEMBER	113.48	109.87	114.58	119.50	110.41	103.94	98.12	101.98	112.17	125.78
OCTOBER	113.20	111.49	114.82	117.58	108.73	103.68	98.37	102.65	112.49	126.21
NOVEMBER	113.79	112.34	116.61	114.92	108.17	103.75	98.70	103.38	113.28	126.68
DECEMBER	113.67	113.40	116.60	112.69	108.58	104.04	99.40	103.66	113.09	126.42

Appendix C 177

Table C-70. Fuel and Related Products
(price indexes, 1964 = 100)

	1957	1958	1959	1960	1961	1962	1963	1964	1965	1966
BLS										
JANUARY	115.24	112.22	107.73	102.23	111.52	107.60	105.70	104.20	102.22	106.32
FEBRUARY	120.36	107.39	109.29	102.53	112.01	105.22	104.35	102.70	100.94	105.59
MARCH	120.11	105.40	109.89	103.68	111.56	102.43	105.79	99.97	101.01	104.82
APRIL	119.83	104.06	109.47	104.10	108.08	107.14	105.85	97.87	101.43	105.20
MAY	119.13	102.95	108.23	101.39	107.45	106.15	107.37	99.45	103.04	106.35
JUNE	117.78	103.82	104.50	104.43	107.69	106.38	108.48	99.65	103.79	108.73
JULY	115.66	106.57	104.28	106.80	108.04	106.21	107.21	99.97	103.82	108.36
AUGUST	115.01	109.11	106.27	109.29	107.24	105.29	103.89	98.70	104.13	109.40
SEPTEMBER	115.40	109.67	105.11	109.99	105.46	107.85	103.84	96.23	104.10	109.71
OCTOBER	114.29	107.09	103.91	110.25	103.51	107.30	103.34	99.22	104.35	109.97
NOVEMBER	112.70	106.17	102.97	109.84	105.22	106.85	100.95	100.70	106.20	110.07
DECEMBER	112.70	106.31	102.39	110.06	107.04	106.57	103.83	101.34	106.35	108.44
NBER										
JANUARY	111.16	110.90	104.14	104.13	106.27	104.04	102.96	101.63	98.88	99.04
FEBRUARY	112.98	109.54	104.23	104.26	106.43	103.73	102.85	101.47	98.74	99.09
MARCH	112.81	108.88	104.62	104.20	106.49	103.49	103.03	101.05	98.74	99.17
APRIL	112.69	107.88	104.99	104.02	106.19	104.09	103.06	100.54	98.76	99.01
MAY	113.21	106.24	104.75	104.37	105.92	104.03	103.50	100.44	98.77	99.23
JUNE	113.54	105.45	104.41	103.98	105.44	103.77	103.40	99.96	98.70	99.72
JULY	113.28	104.65	104.30	104.09	105.16	103.55	102.64	99.34	98.68	99.37
AUGUST	113.15	104.37	104.76	104.28	104.66	103.41	102.39	99.13	98.56	99.82
SEPTEMBER	112.80	104.50	104.69	104.52	104.54	103.64	102.30	99.14	98.54	99.94
OCTOBER	112.63	104.32	104.23	105.19	104.23	103.44	102.11	99.09	98.67	100.09
NOVEMBER	112.08	103.99	103.79	105.41	104.27	102.96	101.59	98.98	98.73	100.42
DECEMBER	111.73	104.30	102.42	105.97	104.40	103.10	102.06	99.23	98.91	100.81

Table C-71. Petroleum and Products
(price indexes, 1964 = 100)

BLS	1957	1958	1959	1960	1961	1962	1963	1964	1965	1966
JANUARY	115.44	112.33	107.69	102.10	111.59	107.65	105.73	104.23	102.24	106.46
FEBRUARY	120.66	107.40	109.29	102.41	112.10	105.22	104.36	102.70	100.93	105.71
MARCH	120.45	105.37	109.96	103.58	111.67	102.37	105.83	99.97	101.05	104.93
APRIL	120.23	104.13	109.61	104.15	108.25	107.30	105.95	97.89	101.54	105.39
MAY	119.52	102.99	108.33	101.37	105.56	106.31	107.54	99.49	103.17	106.50
JUNE	118.12	103.84	104.50	104.44	107.81	106.53	108.64	99.68	103.92	108.92
JULY	115.92	106.62	104.24	106.84	108.14	106.34	107.33	100.00	103.93	108.53
AUGUST	115.22	109.16	106.24	109.34	107.30	105.36	103.93	98.70	104.24	109.58
SEPTEMBER	115.60	109.72	105.05	110.04	105.47	107.97	103.87	96.14	104.19	109.89
OCTOBER	114.45	107.09	103.83	110.30	103.48	107.38	103.35	99.17	104.44	110.16
NOVEMBER	112.81	106.14	102.86	109.89	105.22	106.91	100.91	100.68	106.33	110.21
DECEMBER	112.81	106.28	102.27	110.11	107.08	106.63	103.85	101.34	106.49	108.55
NBER										
JANUARY	111.34	111.05	104.15	104.12	106.35	104.11	103.00	101.66	98.86	98.96
FEBRUARY	113.19	109.67	104.23	104.26	106.52	103.78	102.89	101.50	98.69	99.01
MARCH	113.00	109.00	104.63	104.20	106.58	103.54	103.09	101.08	98.67	99.09
APRIL	112.86	107.99	105.01	104.02	106.26	104.15	103.12	100.57	98.67	98.93
MAY	113.39	106.31	104.76	104.37	105.98	104.10	103.58	100.46	98.68	99.12
JUNE	113.72	105.50	104.41	103.97	105.50	103.84	103.49	99.96	98.62	99.60
JULY	113.46	104.68	104.30	104.07	105.22	103.62	102.72	99.32	98.60	99.73
AUGUST	113.33	104.41	104.77	104.29	104.69	103.47	102.45	99.11	98.47	99.67
SEPTEMBER	112.98	104.54	104.70	104.55	104.56	103.70	102.36	99.12	98.45	99.79
OCTOBER	112.81	104.36	104.24	105.24	104.23	103.49	102.15	99.06	98.58	99.95
NOVEMBER	112.25	104.02	103.78	105.47	104.30	103.00	101.62	98.96	98.64	100.28
DECEMBER	111.89	104.33	104.42	106.05	104.45	103.14	102.10	99.21	98.83	100.68

Table C-72. Rubber and Products
(price indexes, 1964 = 100)

	1957	1958	1959	1960	1961	1962	1963	1964	1965	1966
BLS										
JANUARY	112.06	114.03	113.59	100.11	103.13	99.99	100.25	102.31	99.80	102.77
FEBRUARY	112.16	114.03	113.59	103.13	103.13	98.65	100.25	102.31	99.80	102.83
MARCH	112.16	114.03	113.59	103.13	103.13	98.98	100.26	102.31	99.80	102.83
APRIL	112.16	114.03	113.59	103.13	103.89	98.27	100.27	100.27	99.79	105.27
MAY	112.16	114.03	113.59	103.13	103.89	98.63	100.27	99.00	100.62	105.27
JUNE	112.16	114.03	111.69	103.13	103.89	97.96	100.27	99.00	101.35	105.27
JULY	112.16	114.03	111.69	105.88	103.89	97.96	100.27	99.00	101.35	104.90
AUGUST	114.93	114.06	100.76	105.90	103.89	97.96	102.15	99.00	107.89	104.80
SEPTEMBER	114.93	114.06	100.78	105.90	103.82	97.96	102.58	99.01	107.89	104.26
OCTOBER	114.93	114.06	100.11	105.90	102.95	97.54	102.58	99.01	107.89	104.26
NOVEMBER	114.93	114.06	100.11	105.90	102.95	98.88	102.58	99.02	102.80	104.71
DECEMBER	114.93	114.06	100.11	103.13	100.50	100.25	102.31	99.80	102.80	104.71
NBER										
JANUARY	106.32	109.35	111.11	111.70	107.29	105.20	103.08	100.97	98.95	97.93
FEBRUARY	106.25	109.62	110.67	111.67	106.03	104.63	103.03	100.79	98.96	98.07
MARCH	106.37	109.73	110.19	111.91	106.16	104.65	102.61	100.38	98.99	98.16
APRIL	106.12	109.50	111.39	111.19	105.72	103.77	101.83	100.42	99.17	98.33
MAY	106.53	109.33	111.34	110.91	105.29	103.95	102.23	100.39	98.04	98.34
JUNE	106.30	109.09	111.26	109.84	105.05	104.16	102.21	100.19	98.34	98.36
JULY	105.95	109.03	111.40	108.87	105.52	104.05	102.07	100.22	98.26	98.80
AUGUST	106.25	109.40	111.52	108.44	105.89	103.43	101.99	99.66	98.35	98.80
SEPTEMBER	106.66	109.77	111.70	108.19	105.68	103.56	101.93	99.32	98.33	98.72
OCTOBER	106.72	110.28	111.90	107.87	105.51	102.55	101.06	99.19	98.24	98.65
NOVEMBER	107.15	110.56	111.61	107.95	105.62	103.48	101.08	99.18	98.07	98.55
DECEMBER	107.24	110.89	111.40	107.95	105.03	103.12	100.79	99.28	98.19	98.47

Table C-73. Tires
(price indexes, 1964 = 100)

	1957	1958	1959	1960	1961	1962	1963	1964	1965	1966
BLS										
JANUARY	114.47	116.97	116.40	99.19	103.02	99.70	100.36	102.95	99.72	103.50
FEBRUARY	114.60	116.97	116.40	103.04	103.02	98.16	100.36	102.95	99.72	103.55
MARCH	114.60	116.97	116.40	103.04	103.02	98.75	100.36	102.95	99.72	103.55
APRIL	114.60	116.97	116.40	103.04	103.98	97.84	100.36	100.35	99.72	106.66
MAY	114.60	116.97	116.40	103.04	103.98	98.29	100.36	98.73	100.76	106.66
JUNE	114.60	116.97	113.99	103.04	103.98	97.44	100.36	98.73	101.70	106.06
JULY	114.60	116.97	113.99	106.55	103.98	97.44	100.36	98.73	101.70	106.06
AUGUST	118.11	117.01	100.05	106.55	103.98	97.44	102.75	98.73	110.04	106.06
SEPTEMBER	118.11	117.01	100.05	106.55	103.98	97.44	103.29	98.73	110.04	105.38
OCTOBER	118.11	117.01	99.19	106.55	103.98	97.44	103.29	98.73	110.04	105.38
NOVEMBER	118.11	117.01	99.19	106.55	102.86	99.31	103.29	98.73	103.55	105.94
DECEMBER	118.11	117.01	99.19	103.02	100.36	100.36	102.95	99.72	103.55	105.94
NBER										
JANUARY	106.33	110.12	112.01	110.72	107.34	105.24	102.48	100.81	98.68	98.31
FEBRUARY	106.25	110.50	111.34	110.86	106.86	105.08	102.48	101.02	98.73	98.44
MARCH	106.20	110.64	110.64	111.01	106.46	104.97	102.48	100.49	98.79	98.58
APRIL	106.17	110.46	112.00	110.47	105.81	103.86	102.19	100.56	99.07	98.82
MAY	106.24	110.17	111.70	110.26	105.46	103.89	102.14	100.44	99.11	99.11
JUNE	106.31	109.87	111.40	109.07	105.21	103.93	102.08	100.31	99.09	99.23
JULY	106.08	109.71	111.31	108.15	105.86	103.62	101.98	100.16	98.91	99.70
AUGUST	106.26	110.29	111.28	107.93	105.82	102.67	102.01	99.65	98.88	99.71
SEPTEMBER	106.55	110.88	111.24	107.90	105.69	102.64	102.08	99.23	98.84	99.73
OCTOBER	106.79	111.28	111.21	107.75	105.63	102.52	101.24	99.16	98.64	99.75
NOVEMBER	107.17	111.54	110.82	107.96	105.44	102.97	101.15	99.07	98.70	99.75
DECEMBER	107.56	111.82	110.54	108.06	105.38	102.77	101.30	99.11	98.75	99.75

Table C-74. Synthetic Rubber
(price indexes, 1964 = 100)

BLS	1957	1958	1959	1960	1961	1962	1963	1964	1965	1966
JANUARY	103.87	103.87	103.87	103.87	103.87	101.30	100.00	100.00	100.00	100.00
FEBRUARY	103.87	103.87	103.87	103.87	103.87	100.65	100.00	100.00	100.00	100.00
MARCH	103.87	103.87	103.87	103.87	103.87	100.00	100.00	100.00	100.00	100.00
APRIL	103.87	103.87	103.87	103.87	103.87	100.00	100.00	100.00	100.00	100.00
MAY	103.87	103.87	103.87	103.87	103.87	100.00	100.00	100.00	100.00	100.00
JUNE	103.87	103.87	103.87	103.87	103.87	100.00	100.00	100.00	100.00	100.00
JULY	103.87	103.87	103.87	103.87	103.87	100.00	100.00	100.00	100.00	100.00
AUGUST	103.87	103.87	103.87	103.87	103.87	100.00	100.00	100.00	100.00	100.00
SEPTEMBER	103.87	103.87	103.87	103.87	103.87	98.00	100.00	100.00	100.00	100.00
OCTOBER	103.87	103.87	103.87	103.87	103.56	97.35	100.00	100.00	100.00	100.00
NOVEMBER	103.87	103.87	103.87	103.87	103.56	100.00	100.00	100.00	100.00	100.00
DECEMBER	103.87	103.87	103.87	103.87	101.27	100.00	100.00	100.00	100.00	100.00

NBER	1957	1958	1959	1960	1961	1962	1963	1964	1965	1966
JANUARY	106.59	106.57	107.83	116.22	107.27	105.13	105.62	101.66	100.08	96.34
FEBRUARY	106.56	106.41	108.35	115.45	106.19	102.87	105.33	99.84	99.94	96.51
MARCH	107.38	106.39	108.74	116.10	105.06	103.43	103.20	99.89	99.84	96.40
APRIL	106.23	105.92	109.35	114.57	105.47	103.48	100.35	99.85	99.59	96.31
MAY	108.03	106.25	110.30	113.97	104.70	104.28	102.63	100.18	93.56	95.16
JUNE	106.56	106.25	111.14	113.38	104.49	105.22	102.80	99.71	95.23	94.74
JULY	105.73	106.58	112.23	112.16	104.23	105.90	102.50	100.49	95.58	95.05
AUGUST	106.50	106.08	112.97	110.83	106.28	106.61	101.96	99.72	96.16	94.98
SEPTEMBER	107.42	105.58	114.08	109.62	105.78	107.43	101.33	99.70	96.21	94.50
OCTOBER	106.74	106.57	115.21	108.58	105.15	102.75	100.29	99.31	96.56	94.05
NOVEMBER	107.36	106.92	115.30	108.13	106.50	105.67	100.81	99.64	95.46	93.55
DECEMBER	106.27	107.53	115.39	107.70	103.68	104.64	98.66	100.03	95.88	93.11

Table C-75. Paper, Pulp and Allied Products
(price indexes, 1964 = 100)

	1957	1958	1959	1960	1961	1962	1963	1964	1965	1966
BLS										
JANUARY	98.39	100.15	100.48	102.60	102.56	100.13	99.77	100.94	99.77	102.16
FEBRUARY	98.39	100.15	100.48	102.61	102.31	100.33	99.85	101.06	99.90	102.40
MARCH	98.55	100.16	100.48	102.66	101.90	101.92	99.82	100.20	100.52	102.94
APRIL	98.60	100.16	100.88	102.74	101.36	102.68	99.86	100.24	100.62	103.22
MAY	99.17	100.47	100.88	103.04	96.03	101.93	100.05	99.42	100.73	103.54
JUNE	99.31	100.47	100.85	103.05	96.38	101.46	100.33	99.59	100.86	103.76
JULY	100.06	100.47	100.95	103.02	95.72	100.80	100.26	99.68	100.66	103.93
AUGUST	100.11	100.49	100.95	102.63	95.70	100.34	100.44	99.68	100.66	104.03
SEPTEMBER	100.11	100.49	100.96	102.63	99.56	100.21	100.44	99.68	100.76	104.06
OCTOBER	100.14	100.48	101.05	102.95	99.56	100.18	100.74	100.14	101.11	104.10
NOVEMBER	100.16	100.48	101.05	102.50	99.56	99.96	100.79	99.86	101.61	104.21
DECEMBER	100.16	100.48	101.05	102.50	100.39	99.85	100.79	99.77	101.75	104.21
NBER										
JANUARY	107.03	105.48	105.02	104.49	102.79	101.91	101.80	100.15	99.87	101.93
FEBRUARY	107.03	105.40	105.29	104.53	102.58	102.26	101.40	100.08	99.91	102.21
MARCH	107.03	105.51	105.38	104.60	102.56	102.39	101.29	100.03	100.00	102.44
APRIL	107.04	105.39	104.90	104.74	102.44	102.53	101.19	100.12	100.06	102.60
MAY	106.20	105.25	104.97	104.77	102.19	102.61	100.99	100.16	100.23	102.69
JUNE	106.21	105.03	104.97	104.74	101.96	102.59	100.89	100.18	100.23	102.89
JULY	107.41	104.86	105.00	104.54	101.87	102.64	100.84	100.10	100.28	103.42
AUGUST	107.18	105.36	105.00	104.04	101.68	102.47	100.56	100.03	100.43	104.17
SEPTEMBER	107.12	105.53	105.09	103.97	101.76	102.48	100.01	99.88	100.51	104.44
OCTOBER	107.02	105.48	105.11	103.98	102.18	102.30	100.23	99.82	100.70	104.66
NOVEMBER	107.15	105.37	105.01	103.89	102.26	102.26	100.25	99.75	100.91	105.08
DECEMBER	107.07	105.46	105.08	103.87	102.35	102.20	100.21	99.70	101.10	105.02

Table C-76. Paper, Converted Paper and Paper Products
(price indexes, 1964 = 100)

	1957	1958	1959	1960	1961	1962	1963	1964	1965	1966
BLS										
JANUARY	97.48	99.51	99.91	102.40	102.86	101.31	100.13	101.08	99.74	102.46
FEBRUARY	97.48	99.51	99.91	102.40	102.86	101.54	100.22	101.23	99.90	102.74
MARCH	97.66	99.53	99.91	102.47	102.41	102.86	100.19	100.23	100.63	103.33
APRIL	97.72	99.53	100.37	102.55	101.88	103.58	100.23	100.27	100.75	103.64
MAY	98.38	99.91	100.37	102.91	95.69	102.69	100.45	99.31	100.88	104.00
JUNE	98.55	99.91	100.34	102.92	96.10	102.12	100.79	99.31	101.03	104.26
JULY	99.41	99.91	100.47	102.89	96.10	101.34	100.70	99.52	100.80	104.46
AUGUST	99.48	99.91	100.48	102.43	96.10	100.79	100.91	99.64	100.80	104.57
SEPTEMBER	99.48	99.91	100.48	102.43	100.64	100.64	100.91	99.64	100.88	104.61
OCTOBER	99.48	99.91	100.59	102.81	100.64	100.60	100.84	100.18	101.28	104.65
NOVEMBER	99.51	99.91	100.59	102.78	100.64	100.36	100.91	99.85	101.87	104.78
DECEMBER	99.51	99.91	100.59	102.78	101.61	100.22	100.91	99.74	102.02	104.78
NBER										
JANUARY	107.57	105.64	105.10	104.85	102.89	101.95	101.75	100.15	100.05	102.52
FEBRUARY	107.57	105.54	105.42	104.88	102.69	102.26	101.40	100.06	100.14	102.93
MARCH	107.57	105.67	105.45	104.95	102.71	102.37	101.37	99.97	100.29	103.16
APRIL	107.57	105.69	105.31	105.07	102.68	102.51	101.34	100.07	100.41	103.34
MAY	106.58	105.54	105.46	105.08	102.50	102.57	101.20	100.11	100.64	103.42
JUNE	106.58	105.27	105.45	105.03	102.37	102.52	101.17	100.11	100.68	103.59
JULY	108.01	104.99	105.50	104.89	102.28	102.59	100.86	100.06	100.71	104.31
AUGUST	107.76	105.53	105.46	104.34	102.04	102.42	100.73	100.04	100.85	105.02
SEPTEMBER	107.70	105.63	105.59	104.29	102.09	102.44	100.06	99.90	100.91	105.34
OCTOBER	107.59	105.58	105.63	104.28	102.45	102.25	100.29	99.88	101.18	105.72
NOVEMBER	107.77	105.46	105.47	104.14	102.48	102.22	100.30	99.83	101.39	106.22
DECEMBER	107.67	105.58	105.54	104.16	102.54	102.17	100.23	99.83	101.59	106.15

Table C-77. Chemicals and Allied Products

(price indexes, 1964 = 100)

BLS	1957	1958	1959	1960	1961	1962	1963	1964	1965	1966
JANUARY	109.74	111.91	108.95	106.54	105.81	102.55	101.17	100.06	100.01	99.38
FEBRUARY	110.67	111.71	108.24	106.54	105.91	102.34	101.31	99.96	99.90	99.38
MARCH	110.54	111.52	107.03	106.54	105.65	102.31	101.28	100.28	99.57	99.38
APRIL	110.54	112.01	107.35	106.81	105.59	102.10	99.90	100.32	99.36	99.74
MAY	110.62	112.01	107.26	106.81	105.50	101.99	99.29	100.32	99.62	100.13
JUNE	110.61	111.44	107.26	106.81	105.50	101.73	99.29	100.06	99.31	100.23
JULY	110.55	110.95	107.26	107.09	104.11	101.43	98.73	100.01	99.38	100.56
AUGUST	111.43	110.06	107.16	107.09	103.85	101.04	98.71	99.66	99.18	100.34
SEPTEMBER	111.63	110.06	106.79	107.19	103.40	101.04	98.71	99.66	99.18	100.34
OCTOBER	111.90	109.45	106.91	107.19	103.31	101.15	99.54	100.05	99.89	100.56
NOVEMBER	111.28	109.38	106.91	106.94	102.75	101.15	99.76	99.82	99.70	100.66
DECEMBER	111.32	108.87	106.79	107.03	102.57	101.14	100.13	99.79	99.70	100.91
NBER										
JANUARY	117.02	116.30	113.20	112.01	110.27	105.90	103.90	100.98	98.93	96.78
FEBRUARY	117.49	116.45	113.03	112.04	110.48	105.85	103.68	100.95	98.74	96.58
MARCH	117.98	116.26	112.18	111.96	110.34	105.67	103.40	100.74	98.83	96.38
APRIL	117.91	116.31	112.12	112.20	110.43	105.57	102.66	100.54	98.28	97.39
MAY	118.07	116.14	112.14	112.22	110.04	105.52	102.67	100.31	97.54	97.58
JUNE	118.21	115.83	112.29	112.07	109.50	105.47	102.21	100.14	97.27	96.95
JULY	117.84	115.25	112.24	112.32	108.25	105.37	101.92	99.61	97.19	97.21
AUGUST	117.07	115.27	112.28	112.01	108.05	104.96	101.73	99.67	97.27	97.15
SEPTEMBER	117.48	114.90	112.70	111.86	107.41	104.83	101.53	99.57	97.26	98.04
OCTOBER	116.42	114.92	112.15	111.79	107.07	104.44	101.51	99.14	97.92	98.26
NOVEMBER	117.36	114.66	112.02	111.75	106.77	104.38	101.38	99.19	97.36	97.89
DECEMBER	116.43	114.86	112.31	110.75	106.72	104.35	101.16	99.15	97.36	97.79

Table C-78. Industrial Chemicals

(price indexes, 1964 = 100)

	1957	1958	1959	1960	1961	1962	1963	1964	1965	1966
BLS										
JANUARY	108.91	108.88	107.80	107.28	107.69	101.94	99.82	99.49	100.76	99.71
FEBRUARY	108.91	108.39	107.80	107.28	107.69	101.39	100.19	99.49	100.76	99.71
MARCH	108.57	108.39	107.53	107.28	107.06	101.32	100.19	100.33	100.53	99.71
APRIL	108.57	109.67	108.40	107.64	106.90	100.77	100.19	100.33	99.99	100.11
MAY	108.57	109.67	108.17	107.64	106.90	100.61	98.95	100.33	99.99	101.14
JUNE	108.57	108.27	108.17	107.64	106.90	100.02	98.95	100.33	99.68	101.14
JULY	107.40	107.62	108.17	107.37	103.28	99.82	98.95	100.12	99.81	101.45
AUGUST	107.40	107.10	107.91	107.37	102.63	99.31	98.44	100.12	99.30	100.93
SEPTEMBER	107.93	107.10	107.74	107.63	102.42	99.31	98.44	99.61	99.30	100.93
OCTOBER	108.63	107.68	107.92	107.63	102.42	99.82	98.95	100.12	100.55	100.93
NOVEMBER	108.63	107.52	107.92	107.31	102.42	99.82	98.95	100.12	100.55	100.93
DECEMBER	108.63	107.52	107.92	107.31	101.94	99.82	99.80	100.12	100.55	101.34
NBER										
JANUARY	114.31	114.26	112.90	112.54	110.70	104.48	101.48	100.56	99.47	98.43
FEBRUARY	114.32	114.32	113.07	112.51	110.61	104.36	101.42	100.52	99.46	98.17
MARCH	114.54	114.30	112.74	112.48	110.15	103.97	101.51	100.18	99.21	97.88
APRIL	114.01	114.18	113.18	112.67	109.95	103.89	101.42	100.31	99.21	98.39
MAY	114.05	114.17	113.28	112.60	109.66	104.11	101.34	100.28	99.27	98.57
JUNE	114.12	114.00	113.74	112.57	109.25	103.80	101.30	100.12	98.99	98.57
JULY	113.42	112.95	113.57	112.44	106.25	103.60	101.01	99.89	98.79	98.83
AUGUST	112.98	112.96	113.61	112.33	106.26	103.22	100.92	99.89	98.78	98.94
SEPTEMBER	113.83	112.84	113.60	112.18	105.56	103.15	100.82	99.76	98.71	99.12
OCTOBER	113.76	113.37	113.44	111.49	105.45	103.00	100.92	99.65	98.75	99.39
NOVEMBER	114.33	113.23	113.44	111.61	105.41	102.93	100.83	99.55	98.66	99.11
DECEMBER	114.39	113.30	113.35	111.34	105.52	102.91	100.82	99.28	98.46	99.08

Table C-79. Paint and Paint Materials

(price indexes, 1964 = 100)

BLS

	1957	1958	1959	1960	1961	1962	1963	1964	1965	1966
JANUARY	99.75	104.48	104.28	101.96	105.37	102.12	100.77	100.59	99.97	99.15
FEBRUARY	100.60	104.47	101.81	101.96	105.73	102.12	100.77	100.77	99.58	99.15
MARCH	100.60	104.47	101.81	101.96	105.73	102.12	100.67	100.23	98.75	99.15
APRIL	100.60	104.47	101.76	101.96	105.73	102.12	99.06	100.36	98.75	100.10
MAY	100.91	104.47	101.76	101.96	105.43	101.97	98.60	100.36	99.62	100.10
JUNE	101.32	104.37	101.76	101.96	105.43	101.84	98.60	99.73	98.98	100.50
JULY	102.65	104.37	101.76	103.29	105.43	101.71	96.67	99.83	99.04	101.24
AUGUST	102.65	104.37	101.76	103.29	105.41	101.07	97.29	99.33	99.04	101.24
SEPTEMBER	102.65	104.37	101.76	103.29	104.12	101.07	97.29	99.33	99.04	101.24
OCTOBER	102.65	104.37	101.96	103.29	104.02	100.77	99.48	99.97	99.79	101.54
NOVEMBER	102.65	104.37	101.96	103.29	102.07	100.77	100.24	100.07	99.15	101.91
DECEMBER	102.80	104.37	101.96	104.26	102.07	100.77	100.39	99.97	99.15	102.37

NBER

	1957	1958	1959	1960	1961	1962	1963	1964	1965	1966
JANUARY	105.65	107.63	104.96	106.85	109.36	107.49	106.01	100.69	99.31	98.41
FEBRUARY	105.86	107.53	104.79	106.80	110.04	107.63	105.47	100.66	99.05	98.49
MARCH	106.12	107.53	104.61	106.75	110.60	107.74	105.00	100.53	98.86	98.56
APRIL	106.36	107.44	104.44	107.24	111.19	107.73	103.66	100.50	98.50	98.59
MAY	106.88	107.12	104.40	107.29	110.99	107.65	103.41	100.46	98.38	99.61
JUNE	107.46	106.82	104.36	107.33	110.94	107.50	102.73	100.30	98.32	99.58
JULY	107.85	106.83	104.32	107.95	110.94	107.44	102.18	99.71	98.12	99.91
AUGUST	107.78	106.83	104.43	108.31	110.39	106.80	101.66	99.49	98.27	100.17
SEPTEMBER	107.72	106.83	104.56	108.67	110.02	106.47	101.30	99.30	98.38	100.56
OCTOBER	107.67	106.83	104.70	109.03	108.66	105.67	101.75	99.39	98.16	101.12
NOVEMBER	107.66	106.98	105.49	109.05	108.02	105.84	101.09	99.46	98.24	101.13
DECEMBER	107.66	107.15	106.32	109.16	108.08	106.00	100.43	99.53	98.34	101.13

Table C-80. Pharmaceutical Preparations, Ethical

(price indexes, 1964 = 100)

BLS

	1957	1958	1959	1960	1961	1962	1963	1964	1965	1966
JANUARY	171.51	210.41	152.01	121.73	115.30	114.14	103.25	102.93	96.33	96.75
FEBRUARY	210.41	210.41	152.01	121.73	115.30	114.14	103.25	102.93	96.33	96.75
MARCH	210.41	210.41	152.01	121.73	114.25	113.93	103.25	102.93	96.33	96.75
APRIL	210.41	210.41	152.01	130.44	114.25	113.93	103.25	102.93	96.33	92.71
MAY	210.41	210.41	152.01	130.44	114.25	113.93	103.25	102.93	96.33	92.71
JUNE	210.41	210.41	152.01	130.44	114.25	113.93	103.04	97.90	96.33	91.56
JULY	210.41	210.41	152.01	130.44	114.14	102.62	103.04	97.90	96.33	91.56
AUGUST	210.41	210.41	152.01	130.44	114.14	102.41	103.04	97.90	96.22	90.30
SEPTEMBER	210.41	210.41	130.44	130.44	114.14	102.41	103.04	97.90	96.22	90.30
OCTOBER	210.41	152.01	130.44	130.44	114.98	102.31	102.93	97.90	96.75	90.30
NOVEMBER	210.41	152.01	130.44	121.73	114.98	102.31	102.93	97.90	96.75	90.30
DECEMBER	210.41	152.01	121.73	121.73	114.98	101.26	102.93	97.90	96.75	88.00

NBER

	1957	1958	1959	1960	1961	1962	1963	1964	1965	1966
JANUARY	179.59	194.90	162.37	123.58	126.08	117.45	107.26	101.43	96.92	91.91
FEBRUARY	179.59	194.90	162.35	123.60	125.92	117.41	107.11	101.49	96.90	91.89
MARCH	221.70	194.90	162.33	127.79	125.74	115.03	107.18	101.39	96.71	91.70
APRIL	221.70	194.90	150.32	129.10	124.85	113.25	107.21	101.11	96.51	91.28
MAY	221.70	194.89	150.30	129.11	124.84	112.93	107.25	100.79	96.49	90.93
JUNE	221.70	194.89	150.32	129.12	124.24	112.67	107.39	100.67	96.42	90.91
JULY	214.95	194.88	150.35	129.10	124.14	111.95	106.10	99.46	94.53	90.37
AUGUST	208.43	194.88	141.44	129.09	123.67	112.00	105.71	99.38	94.24	89.80
SEPTEMBER	220.34	161.89	124.33	127.70	120.90	111.65	105.10	98.93	94.06	89.54
OCTOBER	213.64	161.88	124.33	127.34	118.76	109.63	104.40	98.63	93.37	89.73
NOVEMBER	207.18	161.88	124.36	127.00	118.77	109.65	104.30	98.56	93.31	89.74
DECEMBER	200.92	161.88	124.39	126.72	118.76	109.69	102.88	98.18	92.94	89.76

Table C-81. Nonmetallic Mineral Products
(price indexes, 1964 = 100)

BLS	1957	1958	1959	1960	1961	1962	1963	1964	1965	1966
JANUARY	96.87	98.66	99.08	100.27	99.41	98.38	98.35	99.36	100.15	99.22
FEBRUARY	96.87	98.66	99.08	100.31	99.41	98.41	98.38	99.36	99.55	99.34
MARCH	96.85	98.66	99.08	100.31	99.41	98.47	98.33	99.69	99.55	98.57
APRIL	97.35	98.81	99.08	100.31	99.41	99.17	98.31	100.17	99.46	98.60
MAY	97.35	98.81	99.08	98.84	99.41	99.19	98.26	100.02	99.61	98.93
JUNE	97.37	98.77	99.13	98.84	98.75	99.06	98.22	100.02	99.61	98.85
JULY	97.37	98.77	99.13	98.84	98.75	99.05	98.22	100.02	98.94	98.85
AUGUST	97.37	98.68	99.13	98.82	98.75	98.51	99.04	100.33	99.16	98.59
SEPTEMBER	97.37	98.58	99.11	99.36	98.75	98.51	99.44	100.33	99.03	99.19
OCTOBER	97.37	98.58	99.11	99.36	98.70	98.45	99.35	100.33	99.16	100.38
NOVEMBER	97.37	98.55	99.11	99.36	97.89	98.45	99.35	100.36	99.16	100.68
DECEMBER	97.37	98.60	99.11	99.36	97.27	98.36	99.35	100.02	99.16	100.68

NBER	1957	1958	1959	1960	1961	1962	1963	1964	1965	1966
JANUARY	97.94	98.90	99.97	101.27	100.73	101.46	100.13	99.24	100.03	100.86
FEBRUARY	98.29	98.79	99.95	101.25	100.74	101.46	100.15	99.28	100.14	100.74
MARCH	97.20	98.31	100.17	101.15	100.61	101.08	99.88	99.92	100.19	100.36
APRIL	97.50	98.41	100.17	101.22	100.76	101.18	99.82	99.90	100.41	100.33
MAY	97.54	98.32	100.17	101.26	100.88	100.13	99.07	100.35	100.87	100.20
JUNE	97.56	98.27	100.17	101.31	100.93	100.14	99.17	100.33	101.08	100.08
JULY	97.59	98.64	100.17	101.36	100.88	100.23	99.41	100.35	101.19	99.95
AUGUST	97.60	99.18	100.17	101.38	100.84	100.28	99.40	100.42	101.24	99.95
SEPTEMBER	97.52	99.61	100.09	101.47	100.79	100.14	99.35	99.98	101.28	99.95
OCTOBER	97.65	99.72	100.09	101.49	100.96	100.12	99.42	100.05	101.39	100.00
NOVEMBER	97.68	99.81	100.10	101.46	101.04	100.24	99.47	100.03	101.24	100.24
DECEMBER	97.72	99.91	100.10	101.43	101.09	100.30	99.48	100.15	100.96	100.28

Table C-82. Flat Glass

(price indexes, 1964 = 100)

BLS

	1957	1958	1959	1960	1961	1962	1963	1964	1965	1966
JANUARY	98.51	98.51	98.17	98.29	95.95	94.30	94.64	98.42	99.97	97.41
FEBRUARY	98.51	98.51	98.17	98.29	95.95	94.30	94.64	98.42	98.47	97.41
MARCH	98.51	98.51	98.17	98.29	95.95	94.30	94.64	99.24	98.47	95.47
APRIL	98.51	98.51	98.17	98.29	95.95	95.99	94.64	100.45	98.47	95.55
MAY	98.51	98.51	98.17	94.60	95.95	96.03	94.64	100.06	98.85	96.38
JUNE	98.51	98.51	98.29	94.60	94.30	96.03	94.64	100.06	98.85	96.21
JULY	98.51	98.51	98.29	94.60	94.30	96.03	94.64	100.06	97.16	96.21
AUGUST	98.51	98.29	98.29	94.60	94.30	94.64	97.20	100.83	97.72	95.56
SEPTEMBER	98.51	98.04	98.29	95.95	94.30	94.64	98.42	100.83	97.41	97.07
OCTOBER	98.51	98.04	98.29	95.95	94.30	94.64	98.42	100.83	97.41	100.05
NOVEMBER	98.51	98.04	98.29	95.95	94.30	94.64	98.42	100.83	97.41	100.80
DECEMBER	98.51	98.17	98.29	95.95	94.30	94.64	98.42	99.97	97.41	100.80

NBER

	1957	1958	1959	1960	1961	1962	1963	1964	1965	1966
JANUARY	110.22	106.53	106.51	105.37	102.84	102.79	99.02	97.54	100.41	100.37
FEBRUARY	110.22	105.85	106.44	105.05	102.84	102.67	99.02	97.71	100.41	100.02
MARCH	106.36	104.26	107.07	104.54	102.44	101.48	98.20	99.57	100.20	98.93
APRIL	106.36	104.26	107.07	104.54	102.78	101.59	98.20	99.57	100.20	98.93
MAY	106.36	104.26	107.07	104.54	103.12	98.66	95.95	100.80	100.22	98.93
JUNE	106.36	105.44	107.07	104.54	103.26	98.66	95.95	100.88	100.22	98.93
JULY	106.36	105.65	107.07	104.54	103.12	98.94	96.52	100.96	100.12	98.93
AUGUST	106.10	106.65	106.82	104.74	103.01	99.17	96.52	100.41	100.12	98.93
SEPTEMBER	106.10	107.54	106.82	104.74	102.87	98.81	96.38	100.50	100.12	99.05
OCTOBER	106.10	107.54	106.82	104.74	103.34	98.81	96.55	100.58	100.12	99.16
NOVEMBER	106.10	107.54	106.82	104.74	103.45	98.81	96.70	100.58	100.12	99.16
DECEMBER	106.10	107.54	106.82	104.74	103.56	98.81	96.87	100.66	100.12	99.28

Table C-83. Electrical Machinery and Equipment

(price indexes, 1964 = 100)

BLS	1957	1958	1959	1960	1961	1962	1963	1964	1965	1966
JANUARY	129.85	128.72	127.85	124.31	116.43	112.96	110.91	108.28	93.37	90.28
FEBRUARY	129.85	128.91	127.57	126.34	117.84	112.96	110.57	108.35	93.37	91.02
MARCH	130.30	128.91	127.57	126.34	118.14	112.96	109.60	108.07	93.37	91.60
APRIL	131.39	130.87	127.57	126.34	118.44	112.96	109.60	108.35	93.37	92.68
MAY	131.39	131.04	127.57	117.71	118.44	112.50	109.60	104.10	93.37	92.71
JUNE	130.73	131.26	125.49	118.13	118.44	112.61	110.25	95.66	92.26	93.11
JULY	129.14	131.26	125.49	116.43	117.18	112.61	110.63	95.66	91.11	93.18
AUGUST	129.14	131.18	124.03	116.43	112.96	112.61	110.79	95.67	91.11	93.18
SEPTEMBER	128.53	131.18	123.16	116.43	112.96	112.61	110.79	94.56	91.11	93.18
OCTOBER	127.95	130.93	123.16	116.43	112.96	112.50	110.79	94.56	90.57	93.79
NOVEMBER	127.83	129.41	123.16	116.43	112.96	112.50	110.33	93.37	90.57	96.72
DECEMBER	128.53	128.64	123.16	116.43	112.96	112.18	110.22	93.37	90.28	96.89
NBER										
JANUARY	122.49	129.17	123.47	117.84	108.44	106.76	103.85	100.59	98.05	95.87
FEBRUARY	122.16	121.99	123.58	117.49	108.64	106.54	103.89	100.69	98.04	95.88
MARCH	121.82	122.82	123.69	117.24	108.86	106.32	103.93	100.79	98.11	95.74
APRIL	123.42	123.91	123.28	114.82	108.71	106.10	103.97	100.79	98.26	95.91
MAY	123.16	124.38	121.71	114.53	108.56	105.89	104.02	100.09	98.21	96.12
JUNE	124.52	124.80	121.31	114.71	108.52	105.67	104.06	99.94	95.68	96.97
JULY	124.81	124.37	121.33	107.86	108.10	105.61	104.22	99.78	95.70	97.25
AUGUST	125.19	123.94	121.29	108.04	107.69	104.90	104.35	99.68	95.72	97.55
SEPTEMBER	125.57	123.81	123.35	108.21	107.34	104.85	102.11	99.54	95.10	97.90
OCTOBER	125.88	123.69	120.54	108.55	106.77	104.81	102.06	99.33	95.29	98.25
NOVEMBER	126.54	123.54	120.67	108.89	109.08	104.74	101.95	99.40	95.44	101.27
DECEMBER	127.38	123.39	120.35	109.24	108.50	104.70	101.86	99.39	95.60	101.64

Table C-84. Lumber and Wood Products
(price indexes, 1964 = 100)

BLS

	1957	1958	1959	1960	1961	1962	1963	1964	1965	1966
JANUARY	113.55	109.78	118.05	113.39	98.82	98.22	97.78	98.14	104.43	103.24
FEBRUARY	112.92	105.29	126.80	110.25	98.25	99.79	97.88	100.28	101.52	103.52
MARCH	112.35	103.58	127.93	106.53	100.62	104.39	99.12	104.20	99.94	110.60
APRIL	113.46	106.69	131.98	107.10	114.18	104.40	98.79	104.76	99.51	119.06
MAY	113.76	101.85	131.77	105.85	110.50	100.69	98.58	103.53	98.27	114.90
JUNE	116.00	107.86	128.51	105.40	110.50	101.93	101.85	100.49	96.83	100.52
JULY	114.11	115.48	122.68	105.38	110.48	100.91	117.56	99.93	97.85	98.15
AUGUST	110.04	119.84	119.43	103.57	107.00	100.48	123.63	99.03	104.60	95.38
SEPTEMBER	108.91	123.88	119.68	107.27	103.86	100.60	101.08	98.91	102.26	94.04
OCTOBER	112.84	125.36	109.68	108.72	98.47	100.04	100.62	97.80	98.92	91.78
NOVEMBER	111.61	119.64	105.19	106.93	99.59	98.81	100.28	96.79	99.15	89.64
DECEMBER	109.79	116.59	111.26	106.14	98.58	97.68	100.06	96.12	99.85	90.42

NBER

	1957	1958	1959	1960	1961	1962	1963	1964	1965	1966
JANUARY	106.10	105.54	107.57	108.72	101.99	98.68	97.95	100.33	98.10	99.25
FEBRUARY	105.75	104.32	109.94	107.68	102.34	99.69	98.25	100.91	98.86	100.61
MARCH	105.40	103.12	112.35	106.64	102.68	100.69	98.55	102.09	99.63	101.97
APRIL	105.05	101.93	114.82	105.62	103.03	101.70	98.85	102.09	100.40	103.36
MAY	104.43	101.64	114.98	104.97	102.91	101.35	101.59	101.44	100.21	103.63
JUNE	103.80	101.35	115.13	104.32	102.81	101.01	104.41	100.79	100.00	103.91
JULY	103.19	101.06	115.29	103.68	102.70	100.66	107.30	100.15	99.81	104.18
AUGUST	103.75	103.32	113.28	103.28	102.01	100.76	105.85	99.49	99.64	102.73
SEPTEMBER	104.31	105.63	111.30	102.87	101.37	100.86	104.41	98.84	99.48	101.30
OCTOBER	104.88	108.00	109.37	102.46	100.72	100.96	103.00	98.18	99.31	99.90
NOVEMBER	105.10	107.86	109.15	102.30	100.03	99.94	102.10	98.16	99.29	99.90
DECEMBER	105.32	107.72	108.93	102.15	99.36	98.94	101.21	98.13	99.27	99.90

Table C-85. All Industrial Commodities

(price indexes, 1964 = 100)

	1957	1958	1959	1960	1961	1962	1963	1964	1965	1966
BLS										
JANUARY	105.00	104.81	104.28	103.43	104.19	102.03	100.78	101.16	100.89	102.99
FEBRUARY	106.14	103.55	104.79	103.61	104.28	101.45	100.51	100.89	100.56	102.96
MARCH	106.05	102.96	104.85	103.71	104.05	101.23	100.82	100.26	100.65	103.09
APRIL	106.02	102.47	104.94	103.85	103.29	102.43	100.68	99.84	100.76	103.73
MAY	105.97	102.16	104.73	102.97	101.53	101.97	101.23	99.85	101.38	104.30
JUNE	105.62	102.49	103.70	103.54	102.13	101.85	101.55	99.51	101.66	104.76
JULY	105.62	103.18	103.46	104.03	101.86	101.58	101.49	99.63	101.62	104.70
AUGUST	105.78	104.29	103.28	104.48	101.54	101.16	101.01	99.41	102.12	105.06
SEPTEMBER	105.65	104.65	102.92	104.73	101.94	101.70	100.68	98.82	102.15	105.02
OCTOBER	105.32	104.08	102.78	104.82	101.24	101.31	100.92	99.87	102.35	105.19
NOVEMBER	104.95	104.02	102.79	104.40	101.48	101.21	100.39	100.28	102.82	105.37
DECEMBER	104.98	103.95	102.75	104.23	101.97	101.06	101.12	100.48	102.83	105.06
NBER										
JANUARY	107.53	106.72	105.25	105.87	104.27	102.55	101.23	100.31	99.92	101.29
FEBRUARY	108.11	106.06	105.47	105.88	104.20	102.49	101.08	100.25	99.90	101.45
MARCH	107.86	105.80	105.58	105.89	104.16	102.41	101.02	100.15	100.00	101.53
APRIL	107.79	105.47	105.75	105.79	104.06	102.51	100.89	100.12	100.07	101.90
MAY	107.66	104.97	105.67	105.81	103.90	102.46	101.09	100.08	100.15	102.13
JUNE	107.58	104.69	105.61	105.57	103.65	102.36	101.06	99.99	100.21	102.40
JULY	108.10	104.41	105.60	105.31	103.36	102.28	100.86	99.79	100.44	102.71
AUGUST	107.76	104.85	105.66	105.16	103.13	102.10	100.73	99.80	100.52	102.97
SEPTEMBER	107.74	105.09	105.84	105.12	102.94	102.00	100.45	99.76	100.54	103.13
OCTOBER	107.42	105.16	105.70	105.13	102.85	101.77	100.50	99.84	100.76	103.35
NOVEMBER	107.49	105.25	105.76	104.97	102.91	101.66	100.39	99.88	100.79	103.68
DECEMBER	107.21	105.52	106.01	104.84	102.89	101.65	100.51	100.03	100.84	103.70

Prices in

Specific Cycles

The specific cycles are identified in the outputs of industries or products as part of the National Bureau cyclical analysis. Such cycles must be at least fifteen months, and preferably two years, in length, in order to eliminate seasonal and short-lived fluctuations. Our interest is somewhat different. It is in those sharp changes in output which presumably reveal substantial, unpredicted changes in demand that would normally lead to price changes in the same direction. To this end we define a specific cycle as a change in seasonally corrected monthly output data having the following characteristics:

1. The expansion (contraction) of output must last at least eight months. A ten month change was used in the calculations.
2. The level of output rises (falls) by at least 20 per cent.
3. The expansion succeeds a period of contraction or at most stability of output, and similarly for contractions.

These criteria are intended to identify periods in which one would expect a substantial force to have been exerted on the market price by changing demand. Of course if the output changes are brought about by supply (curve) changes, we would expect the opposite price behavior to that resulting from demand (curve) changes; in this latter case, price would fall when output rose, and vice versa. But since none of our commodities is agricultural, we expect sharp short-run fluctuations in output of these durations to be dominated by demand changes.

Specific cycles were sought in forty-six commodities for which we have output data. Few specific contractions were found, and the latter half of our period was too continuous in its expansion. A tabulation of price movements against output movements in specific cycles leads to unprepossessing results (see Table D-1); in general, neither price index conforms to output changes.

One possible explanation for these results is that we employ a much too simple model of behavior. It is possible that short-run demand fluctuations are usually less than the eight months in duration that is our minimum specific cycle, and are met chiefly from inventory. The period of eight months is sufficient to allow a very large change in the rate of output in most industries. An alternative hypothesis is that the output changes may be cost-induced and then our cases of "non-conformity" are actually conforming to the law of demand. If output (production) rises but inventory is stable, there is less probability of a rise in demand

TABLE D-1

Movements of BLS and NB Prices in Specific Cycles
(conformity = movement of price and output in same direction) [a]

Commodity Class	Number of Commodity Cycles			
	BLS Conforms, NB Does Not Conform	NB Conforms, BLS Does Not Conform	Neither Index Conforms	Both Indexes Conform
1. Expansions after Trough				
Metal products	1		6	2
Rubber products		1	7	
Paper products			3	1
Chemical products	3	1	22	2
Other products	1	1	4	1
2. Contractions after Peak				
Rubber products	1	1	2	
Chemical products			5	
Other products			1	

[a] Price changes of less than 2 per cent are considered nonconforming. Percentage changes are between three-month average at turning point and three-month average centered ten months later.

TABLE D-2

Illustrative Specific Cycles in Commodity Groups

Commodity	Beginning of Specific Cycle		Percentage Change [a]		
	Trough	Peak	NB Price Index	FRB Output Index	FRB Inventory Index
Steel products		2/57	4.4	−28.9	13.3
	4/58		1.9	55.2	3.6
		11/59	−0.8	−33.3	17.5
	11/60		−0.4	41.9	3.0
Nonferrous metals		7/57	−9.1	−19.3	−4.0
	6/58		8.7	24.7	3.8
	4/61		−1.7	14.2	−18.4
Petroleum and coal	3/58		−4.2	10.0	−7.3
Rubber tires		3/57	5.4	−16.5	10.1
	4/58		0.8	39.9	0.9
		6/60	−3.0	−17.0	1.7
	2/61		−1.4	24.4	−7.2
	8/63		−1.7	21.4	−2.8
Paper and paperboard	4/58		−0.3	10.5	1.0
	11/60		−1.9	9.8	2.6

[a] Percentage change over ten months: beginning and ending date based on three-month averages.

than if inventory falls (but more than if inventory rises). Conversely, if output falls and inventory rises, there is a higher probability of downward pressure of demand upon price. When inventories exist, in principle much more precise investigations of the impact of short-run demand changes should be possible.

Unfortunately, seasonally adjusted inventory data are not available for any appreciable number of individual products. Indeed such data are not plentiful for commodity groups—and the price indexes of groups are an inappropriate place in which to look for large short-run demand changes because the demand for a group of commodities is more stable than the demand for one commodity. A few specific cycles for such groups are available, however, and are presented in Table D-2. This particular collection of price indexes shows a moderately better conformity to expectations than the individual commodity price indexes of Table D-1: six of fifteen cases are "conforming". It is apparent that a useful study of price flexibility cannot be undertaken with only price data.

Antitrust Cases

The antitrust cases involving products for which we had usable price series are listed below with citations:

Product	Case
Carbon steel sheet	United States vs. United States Steel Corp. Indictment April 7, 1964 in New York City, Cr. No. 64 CR 344, Case No. 1796
Aluminum conductor cable	United States vs. Aluminum Co. of America Filed October 31, 1962 in Philadelphia, Cr. 21243, Case No. 1715
Gasoline (mid-Atlantic)	United States vs. American Oil Co. Filed April 8, 1965 in Newark, N.J., Cr. No. 153-65 and Civil No. 370-65, Case No. 1849 (criminal) and No. 1850 (companion civil case)
Rubber belting	United States vs. Rubber Manufacturers Assn., Inc. Filed March 4, 1959 in New York City, Cr. No. 158-159, Case No. 1433
Caustic soda Chlorine	United States vs. Pennsalt Chemical Corp. Filed December 24, 1964 in Philadelphia, Civil No. 37123, Case No. 1840
Tetracycline Terramycin	United States vs. Charles Pfizer & Co., Inc. Filed August 17, 1961 in New York City, Cr. No. 61 Cr. 772, Case No. 1622
Meprobamate	United States vs. Carter Products, Inc. Filed January 27, 1960 in New York City, Civil No. 60-375, Case No. 1494

Index